D0975376

A "must read" book setting forth the thesis that much of contemporary televangelism is grossly deficient in its doctrinal foundations, a matter more significant than the moral and ethical problems plaguing the phenomenon. *The Agony of Deceit* affirms that the immorality characterizing some televangelists is a *result* of the root cause of heresy. The authors represent several denominations, including Reformed Episcopal, Lutheran, Assemblies of God, and Presbyterian. They are united in their charge that some televangelists are preaching

- that private intuitive insights are God-revealed and carry divine authority; and
- that the believer is divine, or a "little god."

The authors charge that many TV pulpits are occupied by those who are preaching "another Word, another God, another Christ, and another gospel." This book is strong medicine, but the affliction it decries is grievous and threatens to engulf the church and sweep many professed believers into dangerous currents of false and destructive doctrine.

—Donald K. Campbell

No book could be more timely than this one. In a day when quantity rather than quality is the measure of effectiveness for Christ, when numbers or size is the criterion for success, when the area to be reached by a TV ministry is referred to as a "market," when computer mail fills mailboxes (and wastebaskets), this book is consummately relevant. It is a strong antidote for the secularism that has infected the evangelical community.

—Richard C. Halverson

The Bakker-Swaggart debacles signaled to the evangelical world that a number of televangelists are parading under false colors. Historic orthodoxy is being diminished by heretical departures from the true faith over the airwaves. Along with some biblical truths a poisonous stream of error is to be found in the bloodstream of the telecasts scrutinized by the authors of this book. A solid case is made for the charges leveled, and God's people should pray fervently for the errant broadcasters either to repudiate their false views and teach the full truth of God's Word or get off the air.

—*Harold Lindsell*

Few books in recent years have pinpointed problems in the church more precisely than this one. It should be read by every Christian. The array of writers is impressive and the topics important. There is adequate documentation for anyone interested to glean an understanding of the erroneous teachings propounded by a number of televangelists who, for too long, have been spreading falsehood unchallenged.

—*Jay Adams*

The Agony of Deceit is a book whose time has come. For more than fifteen years Christians have listened with dismay and watched with astonishment as their faith and their Lord Jesus Christ have been caricatured on modern religious television. They have sensed that something is profoundly wrong. They have been embarrassed and disquieted—but charitable—giving the speaking, singing electronic images the reluctant benefit of the doubt.

But beyond the observed emotional excesses, listeners have been disquieted at the suspicion that something is amiss *theologically.* "Is this the same Christ, the same gospel, the same faith as mine?" they have asked. They suspected it was not, but no one seemed to perceive or to articulate the difference.

Now the difference has been articulated. In *The Agony of Deceit,* twelve scholars have shown that much on television that passes for Christianity is a new Gnosticism, a revived pantheism. The authors of the book have recoiled from and deplored the media message, and they have analyzed it. They have told us why and wherein it is heretical.

This book is must reading for thinking Christians. Discerning viewers and listeners need not relax into tranquil gullibility before media hype. They will "prove all things," which is our constant responsibility.

—*Dave Breese*

The
Agony
of
Deceit

The Agony of Deceit

Edited by

Michael Horton

MOODY PRESS
CHICAGO

To brother Walter Martin,
defender of the faith,
who passed away just after completing
his chapter for this volume.
He will be sorely missed.

Contents

Part Two: Facing the Future

Preface

"Heresy always does affect morality, if it's heretical enough." So said G. K. Chesterton.[1] And we have seen plenty over the last few years to confirm the general state of affairs in Christian thinking. The goal of this volume is not to call into question the character or motives of those we critique. Since God has shown pity on us, we can hardly fail to identify with fallen brothers and sisters. But this book is not about falling—in the way we usually think about it. It is not about moral scandals. Being sinners ourselves, we are hardly qualified to point fingers of condemnation. Rather, it is about the rotted foundation under so many of the popular ministries: errant beliefs, distorted doctrine, and unsound convictions with regard to the heart and soul of biblical faith.

Of the modern mentality, Chesterton added, "The word 'heresy' not only means no longer being wrong; it practically means being clear-headed and courageous. The word 'orthodoxy' not only no longer means being right; it practically means being wrong." "It means," he concluded, that "people care less for whether they are philosophically right. For obviously a man ought to confess himself crazy before he confesses himself heretical."[2] Indeed, many audiences of today's televangelism are commended by their leaders for having the

1. G. K. Chesterton, *The Father Brown Omnibus* (New York: Dodd, Mead, 1927), p. 919.
2. Chesterton, *Heretics* (New York: Devin Adair, 1950), p. 4.

11

courage to be at odds with mainstream (including evangelical) Christianity. Standing alone, these souls are convinced that they have discovered (through their prophet) that secret everybody else has missed for nearly two thousand years. It is a powerful feeling—but terribly misleading.

First, let me tell you what this book is *not* about. It is *not* about success. Nearly 500 million viewers worldwide take in TV preachers every week. In spite of the "Pearlygate" scandals, many of the unaffected ministries have actually grown. Among the fastest growing are the most aberrant (indeed, in some cases, heretical). If numbers prove anything, we should all join Islam, the fastest-growing religious movement today. But numbers don't prove anything. In fact, Jesus was always cautious about crowds. Whenever they grew too large, He sifted the disciples from the spectators by announcing an unpopular truth.

Second, this book is not about helping people. No doubt, even the TV ministers who are irresponsible have helped people feel better about themselves, have given down-and-outers new hope, and have inspired new enthusiasm in the hearts of many. In fact, it is undeniable that God has even used the truth in their message (every heresy is concealed in some truth) to convert and restore sinners. No, we do not deny that God, in His sovereign grace, can display His power in our own weakness. Nor do we suggest that no temporal benefit is derived from such ministries.

Third, this book is not concerned to promote a sectarian doctrinal viewpoint. It is not about the charismatic gifts. The authors are not agreed among themselves on that point. Nor is it an indictment of the whole charismatic movement or all of the Pentecostals. Doubtless, our most enthusiastic supporters will be among the Assemblies of God and other Pentecostal and charismatic groups. They, after all, were the first to confront and then to sound the alarm against their unorthodox fellows.

No, this book is concerned with one thing only: truth—and not negotiables, about which discerning Christians can and do graciously disagree, but with that sum of doctrine that has always defined a Christian in contrast to cults, the occult, or non-Christian religions. Heresy inspires: it makes people feel good and can make people feel better about themselves and their future. It can attract large followings and provide vast benefits for its faithful. It can provide meaning, fulfillment, and a sense of love and acceptance. None of this should come as a surprise for those who know that Satan can disguise himself as an angel of light.

And motives? Motives are relative. The apostle Paul speaks of people who preach the truth, but with wrong motives. That is better than people who preach heresy with sound motives. We do not doubt for one moment that some of those we are including in our criticism are sincere, compassionate, and genuinely concerned to build up their followers. But judging their motives is beyond our competence. Judging glaring distortions of biblical teaching is not.

We hope the reader will not judge *our* motives too harshly. We are not detached, "ivory tower" scholars, but fellow- pilgrims, seeking no shortcuts on the road to the Celestial City. When our leaders fall, we pick them up. When wolves invade the pen, we warn our fellow sheep. Such an unhappy task can only be taken up when the issues are clear and the stakes are high.

We have sought out those in question. We have asked them, "Did we get this right? Do you really believe, this?" We have asked them to reconsider their positions in the light of Scripture and have repeatedly attempted to settle the confusion behind closed doors. All attempts have failed, so we have placed this book in your hands. You must judge the content in the light of clear biblical teaching. Truth *does* have consequences—eternal ones—and our prayers join yours for the struggle before us.

Special thanks should be offered to the following: to the Christian Research Institute, particularly their researchers, who guided us through the mountain of material; to Judith Matta, whose own study on the born-again Jesus was helpful in rubbing the sleep out of our eyes; to St. Luke's church in

Anaheim, California, for providing much needed moral support; and, finally, to Christians United for Reformation (CURE) for organizing and coordinating the project. Names to be mentioned are Larry Johnson, Shane Rosenthal, Virgil Johnson, and Alan and Laura Mayben.

MICHAEL HORTON

Contributors

DR. R. C. SPROUL, popular author and lecturer, is founder and president of Ligonier Ministries, in Orlando, Florida. Among his published works are *Stronger Than Steel, The Holiness of God,* and *In Search of Dignity.* Dr. Sproul can be heard daily on his radio program "Ask R. C."

DR. ART LINDSLEY is theologian in residence at the C. S. Lewis Institute, a think-tank for Christian scholars in Washington, D.C. He has served on the board of directors for the Spiritual Counterfeits Project, in Berkeley, California, and has contributed extensively to a careful and balanced critique of the New Age movement.

DR. HENRY KRABBENDAM is a distinguished professor of New Testament at Covenant College in Lookout Mountain, Tennessee. He has also contributed a vast amount of material for books and academic journals on the methods of interpreting and applying Scripture.

DR. WALTER MARTIN was the founder and president of the Christian Research Institute in southern California. Considered one of America's most important apologists by such varied representatives as Archbishop Fulton Sheen and Billy Graham, Dr. Martin was the author of such books as the best-selling *Kingdom of the Cults* and *The Mormon Maze.* Dr. Martin's daily audience for his radio call-in program numbered in the millions. He had just completed this chapter when he passed away.

DR. ROD ROSENBLADT, Lutheran scholar and popular lecturer, is professor of theology at Christ College in Irvine, California. He also leads training seminars for Campus Crusade for Christ staff leaders and for InterVarsity Christian Fellowship.

DR. W. ROBERT GODFREY is professor of church history at Westminster Theological Seminary in California, at Escondido. He has served as chairman of the Consultation on Conversion in Hong Kong, for the Lausanne Committee on World Evangelization, and as a senior editor for *Eternity* magazine.

DR. C. EVERETT KOOP is the recently retired Surgeon General of the United States. Active (as well as controversial) in his post, Dr. Koop is regarded by many as the most effective Surgeon General ever to have held that office. Dr. Koop was president of Evangelical Ministries and has been for many years an elder at Tenth Presbyterian Church in Philadelphia, Pennsylvania.

DR. QUENTIN SCHULTZE, Calvin College communications professor, has been widely quoted by *Time, Newsweek,* and *U.S. News and World Report* and has appeared on numerous local and national broadcasts, speaking particularly on the phenomenon of TV evangelism. In addition, he was the author of a *Christianity Today* cover story on gospel broadcasting. Before coming to Calvin, Dr. Schultze was director of graduate studies in communications at the University of Illinois.

MR. JOHN DART is an award-winning religion writer for the *Los Angeles Times* and president of the Religion Newswriters' Association. Highly regarded for his coverage of the evangelical movement (and televangelism in particular), Mr. Dart offers a penetrating analysis from the perspective of a nonevangelical.

MR. KEN CURTIS, president of Gateway Films, has earned two British Academy Awards and an American international Emmy. He produced *Shadowlands* for the British Broadcasting Corporation (BBC) and has been involved in a number of successful programming innovations. His chapter offers creative and positive alternatives to the sort of media involvement televangelism represents.

DR. JOEL NEDERHOOD is the host of the popular radio program "The Back to God Hour" and television's "Faith 20." The goal of both those denominational ministries is to present the gospel to as many non-Christians as possible by syndication on secular stations. Dr. Nederhood's daily broadcasts are heard around the world in several languages.

MR. MICHAEL HORTON, the editor of this volume, is the founder and president of Christians United for Reformation, in Anaheim, California. He is also a minister at St. Luke's Reformed Episcopal Church in Anaheim. The author of *Mission Accomplished*, his work has appeared in *Religious Broadcasting, The Journal of Pastoral Practice,* and *Christianity Today.*

Part One
Facing the Facts

1

The Agony of Deceit

Michael Horton

Nobody likes a wise guy.

Critics often fall into that category. Artists—whether they be painters, writers, actors, directors, sculptors, or architects —depend on satisfactory critical reviews for their bread and butter. Unflattering reviews can end an artist's career. So nobody likes a critic who is just a wise guy. But a critic who protects the public from spending its money on "flops"— that's another story. He provides an essential, and appreciated, function. The same goes for consumer advocates such as Ralph Nader and David Horowitz, and for the various sports commissions. The former help the public negotiate the promises and pitfalls of the marketplace; the latter serve as a check on the personal ambitions of celebrity athletes.

In short, we have critics to help us identify false (or, at least, substandard) art, consumer advocates to help us recognize false advertising, and sports commissions to maintain the integrity of the game. But where are the "laity advocates" who help folks spot false prophets? Are we suggesting by our silence that our arts, products, and sports are worth more than our eternal souls?

As I said, nobody wants to sit next to the obnoxious fellow who finds his niche in the world by blowing the whistle on his brothers and sisters. After all, none of us has all the answers. But isn't there another extreme? One in which charlatans and outright heretics are allowed to pass for orthodox, evangelical spokesmen?

This book argues that there is, indeed.

Trinity Broadcasting Network's president, Paul Crouch, has repeatedly mocked those who would confront false teachers. During a "Praise-A-Thon," Crouch stated:

> There are those who spend a lifetime—we call them apologists—they spend their whole lives apologizing for the Scripture. They spend their whole lifetime defending the orthodoxy of the doctrines of the church and, as I said a while ago, what is orthodox to *them* is what is in agreement with their *opinion* of what the Bible says. . . . You can spend a lifetime gazing at the orthodoxy of the church and let a world go straight to hell and never hear the message of Jesus Christ.[1]

This book argues that the struggle for orthodoxy *is* the struggle for the authentic "message of Jesus Christ" that *will*, in fact, save those who place their confidence in it. It argues that by ignoring the orthodoxy of the message being preached by those who call themselves Christians, we are, in fact, assisting in a delusion that results in the very loss about which Crouch and the "faith teachers" say they are concerned.

"But," says Earl Paulk, defending himself, "a prophet is not to be judged."[2] And elsewhere one hears the warning, "Touch not the Lord's anointed!"

Is that really what God commands? Consider the words of the book of Deuteronomy: "If a prophet . . . appears among you and announces to you a miraculous sign or wonder" and through it leads the people astray, "you must not listen to the words of that prophet or dreamer. The Lord your God is testing you to find out whether you love him with all your heart and with all your soul." As for the prophet? "That

---

1. Paul Crouch, "Praise-A-Thon," Trinity Broadcasting Network, November 10, 1987.
2. Earl Paulk, *Satan Unmasked* (Atlanta: K Dimension, 1984), p. 125.

prophet or dreamer must be put to death" (Deuteronomy 13:1-5).

True, you might say, but we live in the New Covenant era and do not put people to death for heresy. Indeed we do not, but nevertheless the biblical evidence suggests that only an insecure prophet would try to claim that the prophets are beyond the judgment of the people of God. Throughout the Old Testament, and not just in the book of Deuteronomy, believers are called upon to test the prophets. And in the New Testament Jesus warns, "Watch out for false prophets" (Matthew 7:15). Elsewhere He cautions, "False Christs and false prophets will appear" (Matthew 24:24). John commands, "Dear friends, do not believe every spirit, but test the spirits to see whether they are from God, because many false prophets have gone out into the world" (1 John 4:1). Whenever someone claiming to be a prophet announces, "A prophet cannot be judged," warning lights should flash!

The contributors to this volume are concerned ultimately not with air-conditioned dog houses or sexual dalliances but with the *real* scandal: heresy. Ralph Waldo Emerson once said, "Tell me what a person believes and I'll tell you what he'll do." Theology and ethics are inextricably bound together. Yet under the supposed banner of unity, we have harbored enemy ships—as long as they flew our flag. That policy must change. Tolerating enemies of the historic Christian faith as though they were our brethren is not love, but adultery. The *substance* of the faith is the only basis for unity.

Those who embrace the apostolic substance of Christianity (summarized in the Apostles', Nicene, and other ecumenical creeds) have a basis for unity. Similarly, the fundamentals of Marxist-Leninist dogma hold factions within the Communist Party together. Communists might disagree over minor points, but they stick together because of the fundamentals. Essentials serve as the common denominators for a group. When those foundational affirmations are eroded, the group loses its essential identity. And when a group loses its identity, it ceases to offer a common core of commitment that inspires unity and brotherhood. Give up the defense of the fundamentals and you give up any hope of real unity.

How ironic it is, then, that only five decades after the "Modernist-Fundamentalist" controversy evangelical and fundamentalist churches find themselves in the position of harboring—or tolerating—outright denial of orthodoxy. They are doing that because they have mistaken outward tokens for essential unity. So long as the preacher waves his Bible under the bright lights, or has an altar call, they do not object to what he says, even if he preaches doctrines as dangerous to the soul as those propagated by the "liberals" he so cheerfully mocks.

One consequence of this tolerance is to leave the way open for an inaccurate understanding of Christianity to be spread abroad. The world sees televangelists as the spokesmen for the evangelical movement. It does not distinguish between those who preach the gospel "once for all given to the saints" and those who preach a fraudulent gospel. So when the world examines televangelism—its programming, its triumphs, its failures—and concludes from looking at some, but not all, televangelists and concludes that televangelism is materialistic, exploitative, power-hungry, and success-and-numbers oriented—in short, is just as worldly as the world itself—it condemns the whole evangelical movement—and Christianity—not just fraudulent televangelists.

Does the world realize that televangelism does not necessarily represent the evangelical movement? Does it know that the evangelical movement is concerned with truth? Do those who occasionally view televangelistic programming know that evangelical Christianity offers an intelligent interpretation of and hope for human existence? Does the average unbeliever come away from an ordinary telecast with a better grasp of the *substance* of the Christian faith?

Unless the ordinary evangelical is willing to stand up and be counted, the answer will be no. And if the answer is no, that may well mean that evangelical commentators, reflecting the movement generally, have not been as interested in truth as in success. After all, the incarnation is not as interesting as "Body-Builders for Jesus." Or is it? The celebrated mystery-novelist Dorothy Sayers once asserted, "Doctrine is not boring! Dogma *is* the drama!" She was right. The drama lies not in the crying and the shouting, but in the great truth of the gospel.

The apostle Peter understood the responsibility an orthodox Christian has and addressed the subject of doctrine directly. He was well aware that his Master had given him the charge, "Feed my sheep"—and had emphasized it (John 21:15-18). That command weighed heavily on Peter's conscience as he reminded the members of the ancient church that though they had once been "like sheep going astray," they were now "returned to the Shepherd and Overseer of your souls" (1 Peter 2:25). They needed, Peter said, to "make every effort to be found spotless, blameless, and at peace with [Christ]" (2 Peter 3:14)—and to pay attention to doctrine. Not to do so was to bring condemnation upon themselves. The letters of "our dear brother Paul," Peter said, "contain some things that are hard to understand," but the "ignorant and unstable" who distort them, "as they do the other Scriptures," do so "to their own destruction" (2 Peter 3:15-16).

Notice the elements of Peter's warning. There is the recognition that the Bible contains a number of truths that *are easily reshaped by the subtlest distortion.* And there is the assertion that such distortions are caused by those who are "ignorant and unstable." That is an important clue as to the sort of person we must suspect. *Ignorance* among many associated with televangelism is no less prized than it was among the ranters who eschewed thought in favor of objectless fascination with feeling during the frontier revivals of the last century. It was in that setting that many of the cults were born. "No creed but Christ," the evangelist cheered. And *instability* has been characteristic of many religious celebrities in the past and in the present.

Again, some today would say, "Well, sure, truth is important. But what's really essential is that we know the Person, not the propositions." Not so, the apostle James would say: "My brothers, if one of you should wander from the truth and someone should bring him back, remember this: Whoever turns a sinner away from his error will save him from death and cover over a multitude of sins" (James 5:19-20). There is no such thing as a personal relationship with Christ apart from an understanding and acceptance of the nature, character, and mission of Christ. Turning people from error is not a trivial concern. It is bound up with the severest of consequences: saving a soul from death.

Maybe we have the attitude we do because we no longer believe eternal questions are important. And perhaps that means that we—who should have been the last to do so—have become so preoccupied with this world (success, power, fame, and fortune) that we have tolerated a creeping cynicism about the importance of the next.

The apostle Paul understood that souls are saved and lost in the struggle over truth and heresy. Paul said he was "innocent of the blood of all men" because he had "not hesitated to proclaim to [the people] the whole will of God." Therefore, he issued his own warning to the leaders of the church at Ephesus: "Guard yourselves and all the flock of which the Holy Spirit has made you overseers. Be shepherds of the church of God, which he bought with his own blood." And then the apostle anticipated apostasy: "I know that after I leave, savage wolves will come in among you and will not spare the flock. *Even from your own number* men will arise and distort the truth in order to draw away disciples after them. So be on your guard! Remember that for three years I never stopped warning each of you night and day with tears" (Acts 20:26-31, italics added).

With as many as 500 million viewers worldwide, the televangelists under critical examination in this book have until recently been protected from censure. After all, were they not successful evangelists? But eventually there came an end to their privileged status. What brought about their downfall? Not that they were preaching "another gospel," though that was in fact what they were doing. No, they were brought down when news of lavish expense accounts and sexual deviance reached the public and shocked the church—shocked it more, apparently, than the televangelists' unabashed disregard for biblical truth. Only when some televangelists were found to be frauds in general were Christians brave enough to confront them on theological grounds.

More uncomfortably, the rise and fall of televangelism in our country points up a more general state of affairs in the evangelical movement. For, as Quentin Schultze points out, scandals rocked religious radio before television. And many of us have had experiences with local churches or parachurch ministries that gave evidence of giving method priority over message, quantity over quality, volume over clarity, comfort over confrontation. "But they're winning souls!" we are always told. "Isn't that enough?" Not really. If success and growth be always a sign of God's favor, we should be elated with the spread of Mormonism, Islam, and Oriental mysticism. But, of course, we are not. We know that numerical growth can be caused by spectacular distortions of Scripture. It is not necessarily the outcome of the preaching of a theologically sound message. Put another way, an arena filled with persons shouting, "Praise the Lord!" is not necessarily a sign of God's blessing.

"In the last days," Paul warned, "people will be lovers of themselves [so we tailor a self-esteem gospel] . . . lovers of pleasure rather than lovers of God [so we put together a gospel of health, wealth, and happiness]." Such people have "a form of godliness but [deny] its power," and Paul's command concerning them is urgent: "Have nothing to do with them" (2 Timothy 3:1-5). But they are our brothers! "Have nothing to do with them!" But they love Jesus! "Have nothing to do with them!"

Not only have we had a great deal to do with them, we have often *been* "them." Though the Westminster Catechism asserted that man's chief end was "to glorify God and enjoy Him forever," the modern creed insists that we use God to glorify ourselves and enjoy ourselves forever. Christianity must be fun, never demanding. It must sweep the believer from one experience of "victory" to another. Talk of discipleship's rewards far outweighs talk of its cost. In short, the modern gospel is marketed to consumers, not proclaimed to sinners.

In spite of all the present dangers, Jesus promised, "I will build *my* church, and the gates of Hades will not overcome it" (Matthew 16:18, italics added). Similarly, although Paul warns Timothy (and all believers) that "the time will come when men will not put up with sound doctrine," he still challenges him to "keep [his] head." For though men will "gather around them a great number of teachers to say what their itching ears want to hear" and will "turn aside to myths," there *is* hope for those who pursue an accurate proclamation of the faith (2 Timothy 4:3-5).

The intention of this volume is to strike at the root, which we are convinced is heresy. That is not to say that immorality is unimportant but to say that it is consequential—an effect rather than a cause. Yes, sometimes we know the truth but act contrary to it. But taken on the whole, our lifestyle is patterned after our belief system. Martin Luther said it best:

> But nowadays people generally say: What shall I do? I am only a layman and no theologian. I do not understand matters of theology. How do I know who is right or wrong? I go to church, hear what my minister says, and him I believe.[3]

But, says Luther, ignorance is *not* bliss and the layperson can—indeed, *must*—learn the essentials of biblical theology:

> I am not permitted to let my love be so merciful as to tolerate and endure false doctrine. When faith and doctrine are concerned and endangered, neither love nor patience are in order. . . . For a defective life does not destroy Christendom, but exercises it. However, defective doctrine and

3. In Ewald M. Plass, *What Luther Says* (St. Louis: Concordia, 1959), p. 637.

false faith ruin everything. Therefore, when these are concerned, neither toleration nor mercy are in order, but only
anger, dispute, and destruction—to be sure, only with the
Word of God as our weapon.[4]

The German Reformer characterized the heretics of his
day as "strutting peacocks" who "seek self-made, individualistic doctrine and manner of faith and life, apart from the
commonly accepted ones." Thus, a heretic is "one who is
self-willed in matters pertaining to God, a queer fellow who
knows of something better and chooses his own way to heav-
en, a way the ordinary Christian does not travel." As for the
"miraculous signs" that often accompany heretics, Luther
made this chilling prediction:

> If seduction and darkness were again to begin
> through the wrath and decree of God (as will happen after
> our days, it is to be feared), and the devil were to begin to
> perform signs through some false prophet and perhaps
> cure a sick person, you would no doubt see the mob press
> to espouse the cause in such a way that no preaching or
> warning would be of any avail. . . . For in those who have
> no love for the truth, the devil will be powerful and strong
> . . . . If, then, these teachings [of a false prophet] contra-
> dict the chief doctrine and article of Christ, we should ac-
> cord them neither attention nor acceptance though it were
> to snow miracles daily.[5]

The scenario Luther describes is not far from Christ's
own description of the coming Judgment Day. As many faith
healers make their way to Jesus, surprised that they have
been excluded from the very kingdom they insisted they were
building, they plead, "Did we not prophesy *in your name,*
and *in your name* drive out demons and perform many miracles?" And Jesus says, "I will tell them plainly, 'I never knew
you. Away from me, you evildoers!'" (Matthew 7:22-23, italics
added).

4. Ibid.
5. Ibid, p. 632.

Clearly, we are in perilous times. We have paid the price of ignorance and shallowness, and our fall has been great. Heretics have been tolerated as divinely-appointed messengers; prophets have been stoned. Nevertheless, God has proved Himself faithful in the trials of our own unfaithfulness. Though we do not despair, we do call upon the Body of Christ to repair its own system of beliefs and to bring its faith and life into line with sound biblical teaching without delay. That reformation, as we see it, must take two forms: first, it must be defensive. Those who propagate heresy among us and refuse correction must be excommunicated by their local, regional, and national bodies. Denial of the Trinity is, after all, more damnable than pornography. Second, it must be offensive. We must put ourselves to the arduous—but exciting—task of feeding the sheep on the great themes of biblical faith. The laity are begging for substance. They are often more anxious to deepen their faith than their pastors are to help them deepen it.

Paul makes holding to "the deep truths of the faith" a prerequisite for holding the office of deacon or elder (1 Timothy 3:9). Those who lead our churches—whether ordained or laypersons—are required to be educated in biblical and systematic theology. They must not just assent to a series of simple fundamentals but must be trained in the "deep truths of the faith." After all, said Paul, the church is "the pillar and foundation of the truth" (v. 15).

We must heed a final caution from Peter: "False prophets also arose among the people, just as there will also be false teachers among you, who will secretly introduce destructive heresies." "In their greed," Peter said, "they will exploit you with false words" (2 Peter 2:1-3, NASB*). So, too, today, the "Word of Faith" movement in particular is a destructive heresy of "false words." And it is a growing movement. To date, Kenneth Copeland is climbing from a weekend spot to a daily telecast—and other "Word" ministries are also increasing in popularity.

* *New American Standard Bible.*

These heretics, Peter continues, "indulge the flesh in its corrupt desires and despise authority. Daring, self-willed, they do not tremble when they revile angelic majesties, whereas angels who are greater in might and power do not bring a reviling judgment against them before the Lord" (vv. 10-11, NASB). So, too, today, many of the leading televangelists rave about their power over Satan and make sport of taunting and teasing the devil concerning their alleged authority over him. "But these," said Peter, "like *unreasoning* animals, born as creatures of instinct to be captured and killed, *reviling where they have no knowledge*, will in the destruction of those creatures also be destroyed" (v. 12, NASB).

This book, then, consists of a general theological critique. With contributions from leading evangelical theologians, it will analyze the errant teachings of some televangelists and then, on that basis, attempt to gain greater insight into the phenomenon of televangelism as a movement and its long-term effect on evangelicalism and society. Leaders in our public life—all of them evangelicals, with the exception of John Dart—these contributors are amply qualified to analyze the electronic pulpit's social ramifications.

Throughout church history, periods of heresy, apathy, and ignorance have been both times of danger and of opportunity—opportunity to set the record straight, to confront a new age with an old message. Such a time is upon us. Only through a renewing of our minds, a rededication of our hearts, and a reformation of our church can such a chapter of history have a happy ending, like so many other chapters before it. May God use this book in some modest measure to that end.

Is the Lord not in Zion?
Is her King no longer there?

—Jeremiah 8:19

They make ready their tongue
like a bow, to shoot lies;
it is not by truth
that they triumph in the land.
They go from one sin to another;
they do not acknowledge me. . . .

—Jeremiah 9:3

Then the Lord said to me, "The prophets are
prophesying lies in my name. I have not sent them
or appointed them or spoken to them. They are
prophesying to you false visions, divinations, idol-
atries and the delusions of their own minds.

—Jeremiah 14:14

2

A Serious Charge

R. C. Sproul

Heresy.

The word has a chilling ring to it, evoking images of ecclesiastical torture chambers and zealous witch-hunts. It smacks of intolerance and rigid, unyielding dogmatism. Indeed, in our relativistic age, the word itself has outlived its function. Heresy trials are virtually nonexistent in the contemporary church.

Historically, the church has distinguished between "heresies" and "errors," indicating a difference in degree rather than in kind. That is, though all heresies are errors, not all errors are elevated to heresy. That heinous word *heresy* is reserved for an error of a most severe sort. All errors of truth matter, but not all errors threaten the very substance of the truth.

Error invades the thinking of every Christian. None of us is infallible. None of us is omniscient—not only because we are sinners, but because we are *creatures*—inherently limited and finite. *Finitum non capax infinitum*—the finite cannot comprehend the infinite. Omniscience is a divine attribute. God does not impart it to us. We concur with the adage "To err is human."

Our error, however, is not limited to our human boundaries of finite limitations as human beings. Errors are also a real and often deadly result of our sin. We wonder, for example, why there are so many diverse views as to what the Bible teaches. God is neither the author of confusion nor of error. The fault does not lie with Him or with the Bible, but with us. We are the ones who are guilty of distorting what the Bible teaches. To distort the Word of God is no small matter. It does violence to the very Author and Spirit of truth.

PRIVATE INTERPRETATION

Since Dr. Krabbendam's fine chapter on the way we interpret the Bible awaits us, I will only touch on the subject briefly.

An essential element of the Protestant Reformation was the principle of *private interpretation* of the Bible. That is not to say that the view was never articulated before Martin Luther, but the Reformation did emphasize the position. The concept of private interpretation is subject to much confusion. It suggests to some a license for subjective and relativistic interpretations: "What is God telling *me* in this passage?" or, "Well, there are a number of ways to read the text." How often we have heard the phrase "That's *your* interpretation," with the unspoken assumption that *your* interpretation and *my* interpretation can be equally valid—even though they contradict each other. Here the Bible becomes a wax nose, capable of being formed and twisted to suit anyone's prejudice.

That is hardly the intention of the historic doctrine of private interpretation. Against the relativistic view of subjective interpretation stands the classical principle of the *objective truth* of Scripture. The Scriptures do not contradict themselves. When we disagree, your view may not be correct; mine may not be—both can be wrong, but both cannot be right at the same time in the same place. There may be thousands of *applications* of a given text, but there is only one correct *meaning.*

The idea of private interpretation arose as a protest against limiting the translation the Bible into the vernacular (i.e., the common language of the people). Translating the

Bible into French, German, and English, for example, was motivated largely by the desire of the Reformers to allow the laity to read the Bible for themselves. But the right of private interpretation always carries with it the responsibility of inter- preting the Bible accurately. God grants no one the "right" to distort the meaning of Scripture. "Private interpretation" does not mean that the individual Christian is free to find in Scrip- ture something that is not there. That is why we look to the interpretations of those who have gone before us. Although tradition does not rule our interpretation, it does guide it. If, upon reading a particular passage, you have come up with an interpretation that has escaped the notice of every other Christian for two thousand years, or that has been cham- pioned by universally recognized heretics, chances are pretty good that you had better abandon your interpretation. Private interpretation is not only a right; it is a grave responsibility.

Our distortions or misinterpretations of Scripture are not caused so much by the lack of biblical clarity as by our own weaknesses in handling the text. Here private interpretation touches another cardinal maxim of Protestant theology: the *perspicuity of Scripture*.

THE PERSPICUITY OF SCRIPTURE

Perspicuity is a fancy word for "clarity." The Reformers insisted that, in most cases, the clearest interpretation of a text is the correct one. The Bible isn't a puzzle. It is not de- signed to lead the "initiate" into a maze of obscure or ambig- uous passages. One does not need a Ph.D. in theology to understand that the Bible teaches we are sinners in need of the atoning work of Christ.

Though we believe in the basic clarity of Scripture, we do not mean by this that all parts of the Bible are equally clear. The Bible teaches some very complex and difficult things. Though its essential message is clear, there is enough complexity in the Bible to keep the sharpest minds busily en- gaged for a lifetime. The message of the Bible may be simple in its essence, but the Bible as a whole is anything but simplistic. To be able to handle the whole of Scripture, with all of this complexity, is a difficult task. It requires diligent study and, for the vast majority of serious students, years and years of disciplined training. Hence, James's warning, "Not many of you should presume to be teachers, my brothers, because you know that we who teach will be judged more strictly" (James 3:1).

God requires us to love Him with all of our minds. To apply our minds diligently to His Word is hard work. There is no magical (or superstitious) substitute for that work. "Words of knowledge" do not suffice when we have the final "Word of Knowledge" (the Bible) to teach us. Thinking is not "carnal" or "unspiritual." But it *is* hard work. That is one reason people find it so easy to turn their minds over to a high-powered evangelist who convinces them that he is "plugged in" to the Divine intelligence. Pious appeals to direct supernatural insights are often, if not always, spiritual masks for our own indolence. It requires far less effort to listen to private subjective hunches than to pay the price of mastering Greek, Hebrew, historical backgrounds, and the science of hermeneutics.

A Personal Confession

I am sure that many of the errors I make in theology are due to my own slothfulness. I have not studied all parts of the Bible with equal diligence. I doubt if I have ever applied myself totally and completely to the careful mastery of the Bible. No, it is not a question that allows for doubt. Let me say it honestly: *I have never applied myself totally to the careful mastery of the Bible.*

I am aware that the confession I have just made is a confession of sin. I wish I could believe that this type of sin is mine alone. But just as Isaiah recognized that his was not the only dirty mouth in Israel, so I recognize that I am not alone in this deficiency. Indeed, I am convinced that it is universal. None of us is blameless in his or her diligence of study. Some are far more diligent than others, but none has done his or her homework perfectly.

Not only sloth but also pride affects our biblical interpretations. Pride breeds prejudice and prejudice a kind of blindness to the teaching of the Scripture. It is not any accident that God has sent His Holy Spirit to illumine the text and to assist in applying it to our lives. We need this divine and supernatural help precisely because we bring our baggage of sin to the reading of the Bible. Pride and prejudice enter precisely because there are certain messages in the Bible we simply do not want to hear. The Bible is critical of us. It exposes those areas of our lives that are in conflict with God's law.

So we err.

Sometimes the errors are grievous and represent immediate dangers to the people we teach when the errors reach the level of compromising the very essence of Christianity; then they certainly reach the rank of heresy.

Reform or Revolt?

The Protestant movement was a reformation, not a revolution. That is, the motive was to restore the church to biblical and historic orthodoxy, not to create a new religion. It is for this reason that Protestant churches did not reject all that was catholic. Indeed, one cannot be considered a genuine Protestant—indeed, a genuine Christian, unless he or she is "catholic." The term *catholic* means "universal" and refers to that core of Christian doctrine accepted by Lutherans, Reformed, Baptists, Anglicans—by all Protestant bodies, as well as by the Eastern Orthodox and the Roman Catholics.

All of the Protestant creeds retained catholic allegiance to the doctrine of the Trinity, the two natures of Christ, the atonement, and the like. Though Lutherans differ from Presbyterians and Baptists differ from Methodists at certain points of doctrine, those groups do not consider the other groups to be non-Christian (i.e., "heretical"). Though they disagree—

often on important matters—there is an essential catholic unity among them that involves a historic commitment to the so-called *ecumenical councils.*

What alarms those of us contributing to this volume is not that there has emerged disagreement over denominational or sectarian doctrines, but that there has been a growing rejection of those essential teachings that define a group as genuinely "catholic," hence, genuinely "Christian." The authors of this book represent about seven denominations, ranging from Lutheran to Presbyterian to Independent Charismatic. Although we could have some lively debates, we can come together when *catholic* faith is at stake. You will read shocking statements from so-called evangelical preachers challenging the classical doctrine of the Trinity, the biblical view of man, Christ, and personal redemption.

THE GNOSTIC HERESY

One of the earliest and most potent threats to early Christianity came from the heretical group known as the Gnostics. Blending elements of Christianity, Greek philosophy, and oriental mysticism, the Gnostics denied the orthodox view of God, man, the world, and Christ. The apostle John included them in the camp of the Antichrist.

The Gnostics were so called because of their view of revelation. The word *gnosis* is the Greek word for "knowledge." In many cases the Gnostic heretics did not make a frontal assault against the apostles or against the apostolic teaching of Scripture. In fact, many of them insisted that they were genuine, Bible-believing Christians. It wasn't that they rejected the Bible; they just claimed an *additional* source of knowledge or insight that was superior to or at least beyond the knowledge of Scripture. The "gnostikoi" were "those in the know." Their knowledge was not derived from intellectual comprehension of Scripture or by empirical research, but was mystical, direct, and immediate. God "revealed" private, intuitive insights to them that carried nothing less than divine authority.

Here is a typical Gnostic statement:

> We cannot communicate with God mentally, for He is a Spirit. But we can reach Him with our Spirit, and it is through our Spirit that we come to know God. . . . This is one reason God put teachers (those who are really called to teach) in the church—to renew our minds. Many times those who teach do so with only a natural knowledge that they have gained from the Bible and other sources. But I am referring here to one of the ministry gifts. Those who are called and anointed by the Spirit to teach.
>
> God has given us His Word, and we can feed upon that Word. This will renew our minds. But He also puts teachers in the church to renew our minds and to bring us the revelation of the knowledge of God's Word.[1]

Notice that this quotation does not include a direct assault on the Bible. The Bible is recognized as God's Word. But in order to understand the Bible we need something beyond our natural mental ability. We need the Spirit-anointed teachers to "bring us the revelation of the knowledge of God's Word." This is a typically Gnostic statement, but the quote is not from Valentinus or any of the other early Gnostics. It is from the pen of a modern missionary of Gnosticism, Kenneth E. Hagin. It is from Hagin's *Man on Three Dimensions.* Hagin's theology echoes the tripartite epistemology of early Gnosticism (man as having three separate entities: body, soul, and spirit).

Robert Tilton also claims a direct pipeline to divine revelation:

> God showed me a vision that almost took my breath away. I was sucked into the Spirit . . . , caught away . . . and I found myself standing in the very presence of Almighty God. It just echoed into my being. And he said these words to me . . . exactly these words. . . .
>
> "Many of my ministers pray *for* my people, but I want you to pray the Prayer of Agreement *with* them." . . . I have

1. Kenneth E. Hagin, *Man on Three Dimensions* (Tulsa, Okla.: Faith Library, 1985), 1:8, 13.

never seen the presence of God so powerful. This same anointing flooded my Spirit-man. . . . It's inside of me now, and I have supernatural faith to agree with you.

From that day forth, as I have been faithful to that heavenly vision, I've seen every kind of miracle imaginable happen when I pray the Prayer of Agreement with God's people.[2]

It seems that in Robert Tilton the church is blessed with a twentieth-century apostle whose visions of revelation exceed that of the apostle John and whose miracle powers surpass that of the apostle Paul. If we are to believe Tilton's astonishing claims, there is no reason we should not include his writings in the next edition of the New Testament.

Paul Crouch of the Trinity Broadcasting Network (TBN), has revelatory dreams and has warmly embraced the neo-Gnostic dogma. His network has become a prime distribution center for the growing movement. Kenneth Copeland also receives phrases from God in "his spirit."

CHRISTOLOGICAL HERESIES

The fourth and fifth centuries proved to be critical for the development of the Christian church. Central to theological debate was the issue of the Person of Christ: Who is this Person whom we worship as God? The Council of Nicea (4th century) and the Council of Chalcedon (5th century) were pivotal for all future generations of Christian orthodoxy.

The Council of Chalcedon (A.D. 451) defined Christ for all time as *vere homo, vere deus,* "truly man, truly God." In other words, the Person of Christ was seen as involving one person with two natures, a divine and human. The unity of those two natures was protected by the boundaries of the so-called "Four Negatives" of Chalcedon. The two natures are united in such a way as to be (1) without mixture, (2) without confusion, (3) without separation, and (4) without division. *Each nature* (divine and human) *possesses its own attributes.*

2. Robert Tilton, newsletter from Robert Tilton Ministries, Word of Faith World Outreach Center, Box 819000, Dallas, TX 75381.

Chalcedon established boundaries for Christological reflection in order to stave off various ancient heresies. Every affirmation and denial was carefully worded to exclude competing cultic positions.

On the one hand, the church had to combat the Monophysite heresy, and on the other hand, the Nestorian. The Monophysites believed that Jesus was one person with one nature. Hence, the term *monophusis* (*mono*, "one"; *phusis*, "nature"). This single nature was neither divine nor human. It was a blend or mixture of the two. It consisted of a single "theanthropic nature," which could be conceived of as either a humanized divine nature or a deified human nature. The confusion of the two natures into one involved a transfer of divine attributes to the human or human attributes to the divine. Hence the crucial clause of Chalcedon, in contrast to the Monophysite heresy, "Each nature *retaining* its own attributes."

The Nestorian heresy, on the other hand, wanted two natures with two distinct personalities. Here the unity of Christ was *separated* or divided.

The church rejected both Monophysism and Nestorianism as heresies, just as it had rejected the Arian heresy in the fourth century at the Council of Nicea. The Arian heresy denied the eternal deity of Christ. In 1965, professor G. C. Berkouwer lectured on "The History of Heresy" at the Free University of Amsterdam in the Netherlands. In that lecture series Berkouwer pointed out the tendency in church history of reactionism to breed heresy; that is, when one heresy emerges, the zeal to combat that heresy often produces another heresy in the other direction.

For example, when the church was faced with heresies that denied the true humanity of Jesus, as the Docetic heresy did, the tendency was to so emphasize the humanity of Christ that the deity of Christ was threatened, as in the Arian heresy. When the deity of Christ was threatened, the reaction was to so emphasize the deity that the humanity of Christ was threatened, as in the Monophysite heresy. Reaction tends to breed more reaction.

We see this problem clearly in the Arian controversy of the fourth century. During the second half of the third century the church was faced with the Sabellian heresy. Sabellius had a gnostic view of Christ. He taught that Christ was of the same *substance or essence* as God (*homoousios*) but was *less* than God. The analogy was like that of the sun and its rays. The rays that emanate from the sun are of the same essence as the sun but may be distinguished from the sun. The further the sunbeam extends away from the sun the more dissipated it becomes.

To combat the Sabellian heresy the church declared in A.D. 268 that Jesus was *homoiousios*, that he had a *like*-substance with the Father. The church rejected the term *homoousios* because it was loaded with Sabellian baggage.

With the rise of the Arian crisis in the fourth century the situation changed dramatically. Now the Sabellian threat had faded and the church was faced with a different heresy. Arius taught that Jesus was not divine but instead was adopted by God and was merely of *like* essence with the Father. The unity between the Father and the Son was restricted to a unity of aim, desire, and purpose. The Father and the Son were one in purpose but not one in essence.

To combat the Arian heresy the Council of Nicea insisted that Jesus and the Father were *homoousios,* one in essence, sharing a divine nature. That view was sustained later at Constantinople and Chalcedon and became the classical, orthodox formulation of the Trinity. Orthodox Christianity affirms that the Father, Son, and Holy Spirit are distinct persons but with *one* essence—they are all *homoousios.*

This view of the Trinity has been the orthodox view of all Christian bodies since the fourth century. It is denied by Mormons and Jehovah's Witnesses and also by individuals from time to time. It is the view attacked, for example, by Jimmy Swaggart. Swaggart clearly rejects the *homoousios* view of orthodox Christianity in favor of restricting the unity of the Godhead to a unity of purpose and design:

Many people conclude that the Father, the Son, and the Holy Spirit are all one and the same. Actually, they are not. These people take 1 John 5:7 to mean one in number, when this is not what is meant at all. They evidently have not studied this in the original Greek language to get its actual meaning. The word "one" in this passage means one in unity. . . .

You can think of God the Father, God the Son, and God the Holy spirit as three different persons exactly as you would think of any three other people—their "oneness" pertaining strictly to their being one in purpose, design, and desire.

When Genesis says that God made man in His own image, I am convinced that it meant not only in the spiritual image, but also in the physical image. I realize many Bible scholars would chuckle at this statement, but this is the way I see it. I believe that God has a spirit body. . . . I believe His body is in one place at one time, wherever that may be.[3]

Another crucial point of orthodoxy has to do with uniqueness of Christ's incarnation (conception and birth). Christ alone is the God-Man. His person and work effect marvelous benefits for us. They secure our redemption. They are the basis for our receiving the indwelling Holy Spirit. Christ *redeems* our humanity but in no way *deifies* it. Christ shares His humanity with us, but not His deity. He does not impart deity to His people. The Spirit dwells in us and works in us, but that indwelling does not make us gods-incarnate.

The crass view that salvation imparts some measure of deity to us is a popular conception with many television teachers. Since Walter Martin will be concentrating specifically on this grave heresy, I will only introduce the topic here. Known historically as the heresy of *Apotheosis* ("becoming God"), many modern Gnostics appear to think they have found something everybody else has failed to notice. Evidently, they either do not know or do not care that these flashes of

3. Jimmy Swaggart, *Questions and Answers* (Baton Rouge, La.: Jimmy Swaggart Ministries, 1985), p. 199.

insight have been articulated by heretics from time to time for two thousand years.

Copeland writes: "Every man who has been born again is an incarnation and Christianity is a miracle. *The believer is as much an incarnation as was Jesus of Nazareth*."[4]

And again: "God has been reproduced on the inside of you."[5]

This view of Apotheosis is echoed by both Kenneth Hagin and Paul Crouch. Hagin writes in *Zoe: The God-Kind of Life*: "This eternal life He came to give us is the nature of God."[6]

Again: "It is, in reality, God imparting His very nature, substance, and being to one human spirit. . . . Zoe, then, means eternal life, or God's life. This new kind of life is God's nature."[7]

The most clear expression of Hagin's view may be seen in the following:

> Even many in the great body of Full Gospel people do not know that the new birth is a real incarnation, they do not know that they are as much sons and daughters of God as Jesus. They only have a hazy concept of what God has done, of what He is to them, and of what they are to God. Jesus was first divine, and then He was human. So He was in the flesh a divine-human being. I was first human, and so were you, but I was born of God, and so I became a human-divine being![8]

Hence Hagin views himself as a God-Man in the same sense as the only eternally begotten Son of the Father. In a

4. Kenneth Copeland, *Word of Faith* (Fort Worth, Tex.: Kenneth Copeland, 1980), p. 14.
5. Kenneth Copeland, *The Force of Righteousness* (Fort Worth, Tex.: Kenneth Copeland, 1984), p. 12.
6. Kenneth E. Hagin, *Zoe: The God-Kind of Life* (Tulsa, Okla.: Faith Library, 1981), p. 1.
7. Ibid., p. 9.
8. Ibid., p. 40.

televised interview with Kenneth Copeland, Trinity Broadcasting Network's Paul Crouch made the following comment:

> Do you know what else has settled in tonight? This hue and cry and controversy that has been spawned by the devil to try to bring dissension within the body of Christ that we are gods. I am a little god. I have His name. I am one with Him. I'm in covenant relation. I am a little god. Critics be gone![9]

I am a critic who refuses to be gone. The heresy of Apotheosis threatens the very essence of Christianity. Crouch apparently sees orthodox criticisms against this ghastly heresy as being stirred up by Satan. What seems to be happening here is not a willful, informed attack on orthodox Christianity. The heresies of TV preachers like Crouch seem to follow more from ignorance than from malice. Very little evidence of any significant knowledge of either church history or theology is displayed by Copeland, Hagin, Tilton, Crouch, and others. These men are not scholars. There is nothing wrong with that. Not all Christian ministers are called to be technical theologians. There are other godly vocations to be pursued than scholarly ones. What *is* alarming, however, is the attitude with which these "teachers" assert their novelties, claiming divine authority for charting a new course. Some of them (Paul Crouch, for example) have been approached charitably and privately by theologians warning of these heresies, but to no avail.

Though neither scholars nor theologians, these men have assumed the role of teachers. Their "classroom" attendance numbers in the millions. They have become the populist teachers of this generation, perceived by the secular media as the spokespersons of evangelical Christianity. Yet, though these TV preachers are *evangelistic,* they are not *evangelical.* Evangelical Christianity affirms the Trinity and

9. Paul Crouch, "Praise the Lord," Trinity Broadcasting Network, July 7, 1986.

Chalcedonian Christology and eschews all forms of Apotheosis. Those teachers who deny these classical evangelical and catholic doctrines misrepresent themselves when they call themselves evangelicals.

There is such a thing as heresy. The tragedy is that it pervades the electronic church.

Hear the word of the Lord, you Israelites,
    because the Lord has a charge to bring
    against you who live in the land:
"There is no faithfulness, no love,
    no acknowledgment of God in the land.
There is only cursing, lying and murder,
    stealing and adultery;
    they break all bounds. . . ."

—Hosea 4:1-2

You stumble day and night,
    and the prophets stumble with you.
So I will destroy your mother—
    my people are destroyed from lack of knowledge.
Because you have rejected knowledge,
    I also will reject you as my priests; . . .
    a people without understanding will come to ruin!

—Hosea 4:5-6, 14

3

Settling for Mud Pies

Art Lindsley

What's missing?

Many of the televangelists discussed in this book make appeals that focus on fulfilling human desires—especially health, wealth, and happiness. But other things, too, like peace of mind, joy, satisfaction, self-esteem, power, and victory. It's not that these things are always wrong in themselves. Indeed, they are often gifts of God. However, it is difficult to resist the impression that there are televangelists who have set their sights too low.

C. S. Lewis gave us the following insight:

> Our Lord finds our desires not too strong, but too weak. We are half-hearted creatures, fooling about with drink and sex and ambition, when infinite joy is offered us, like an ignorant child who wants to go on making mud pies in a slum because he cannot imagine what is meant by the offer of a holiday at the sea. We are far too easily pleased.[1]

Many TV preachers, reflecting a common emphasis in modern evangelicalism generally, are settling for "mud pies" because they "cannot imagine what is meant by the offer of a holiday at the sea." These preachers appeal to our selfish in-

1. C. S. Lewis, *The Weight of Glory and Other Addresses*, rev. ed. (New York: Macmillan, 1988).

stincts, which may be momentarily satisfied by promises of success, unfailing happiness, and good times, when all the while our deepest needs, our truest needs—for eternal love and acceptance in a world where performance is usually a prerequisite for acceptance, for certainty in the midst of doubt, and for purpose in a period of despair—go untouched.

Our desires are too weak if we are simply making our own comfort and success our focus, while ignoring the larger issues. Our desires should be broader, transcending our self-centeredness. We are far too easily pleased!

Something is missing. This chapter is concerned to discover the identity of that missing element. The particular type of message many media preachers communicate has come to be known as the "Health and Wealth" gospel. Prosperity teaching abounds on their television programs as well as in their written material. One statement summarizes the technique used: "God's got it, I can have it, and by faith I'm going to get it."[2]

We see additional examples in titles such as Kenneth E. Hagin's pamphlet "How to Write Your Own Ticket with God" and Robert Tilton's magazine, *Signs, Wonders and Miracles of Faith*, in which testimonials of financial and physical success abound. Or in Kenneth Copeland's brochures "God's Will Is Health" and "God's Will Is Prosperity." Oral Roberts promises people on his mailing list, "Prosperity miracles that are within fingertip reach of your faith," and his most recent book to date is titled *How I Learned Jesus Was Not Poor*. Peter Popoff invites his followers to wash with an "anointed" sponge and then to send a monetary gift to his ministry. This "will unlock heaven's storehouse of blessings for you."

We have seen responses to such teachings in Bruce Barron's *The Health and Wealth Gospel* and Gordon Fee's *The Disease of the Health and Wealth Gospel*. Yet whether or not the Health and Wealth teachings are true, this chapter maintains that they reduce life to a tragically narrow and trivial

2. Quoted in James S. Tinney, "The Prosperity Doctrine," *Spirit*, April 1978.

focus, meeting only surface needs. They ignore a larger vision of reality. Christians must know truth about all areas of life and must develop a character that is able to make commitments to people, the community, and the nation outside themselves. These teachings promise a satisfaction of our desires. But we need to ask, "Are these desires too weak; are they too trivial?" Are we far too easily pleased?

KNOWING TRUTH

Neglecting the serious questions for cheap thrills, one way some televangelists have settled for less is by depreciating the mind, centering almost entirely on feelings.[3] Sometimes the impression is given that faith and intellect are in a state of war. "The mind," says Hagin, "is something that might trip you and cause you to fall."[4] Yet, in truth, though our minds are fallen, they are the door to our heart, our conscience, our feelings, and our actions. What we believe determines how we feel and act.

The call Jesus gave to love God "with all of your heart, soul, strength, and *mind*" is not at all foreign to Christianity. Some of the greatest intellects of all time have found no contradiction between faith and reason. We have only to recall Augustine, Aquinas, Leibnitz, Edwards, and C. S. Lewis as examples of a few believers who thought long and hard about the compatibility of faith and reason. Since God is the author of both, faith and reason can (indeed should) be as compatible as a left and a right hand.

Augustine maintained that "all truth is God's truth." Thus, we ought to learn everything we can about anything we can. Every truth will lead us back to the God of truth. B. B. Warfield, a Christian scholar, echoed Augustine when earlier this century he wrote:

3. Kenneth E. Hagin, *Man on Three Dimensions* (Tulsa, Okla.: Faith Library, 1985), 1:18-21, 31.
4. Kenneth E. Hagin, videotape 1, on file with Christians United for Reformation (CURE).

We must not, then, as Christians, assume an attitude of antagonism toward the truths of reason or the truths of philosophy, or the truths of science, or the truths of history, or the truths of criticism. As the children of light, we must be careful to keep ourselves open to every ray of light. Let us, then, cultivate an attitude of courage as over against the investigations of the day. . . . It is for us, as Christians, to push investigation to the utmost, to be leaders in every science, to stand in the van of criticism, to be the first to catch in every field the voice of the Revealer of truth who is also our Redeemer.

The curse of the church has been her apathy to truth, in which she has too often left to her enemies that study of nature and of history and philosophy. . . . She has nothing to fear from truth, but she has everything to fear and she has already suffered nearly everything from ignorance.[5]

If God is the Creator, if He did indeed send His Son, Jesus Christ, if He has revealed Scripture to all believers, Christians have nothing to fear from thoughtful investigation.

Yet, many object, arguing that it is more spiritual and faithful to believe without any intellectual reasons. "Just love Jesus," they say, apart from any serious knowledge of who this Jesus is or what He accomplished. Their argument, of course, is wrong. Paul wrote, "We are destroying speculations and every lofty thing raised up against the knowledge of God, and we are taking every thought captive to the obedience of Christ" (2 Corinthians 10:5, NASB). In other words, it is a profoundly spiritual task to critique the philosophies that hold us back from knowing God and His Son, Jesus Christ. It is actually a sign of a *lack* of spirituality that makes one fail to provide a well-argued alternative to secularism in our universities and in our culture.

Christians often object to studying philosophy (and even theology!) on the basis that in Colossians 2:8 Paul warns us to beware that no one takes us captive to such deceptive principles of the world. Although Paul did issue such a warning, the only way for one to beware of the negative influence

5. B. B. Warfield, *Shorter Writings*, 2: 463-65.

of some philosophy is to study and understand it thoroughly. In order to *beware* of philosophy we need to be *aware* of it. If we understand the competing ideologies well, we will know when they are affecting us. For instance, because the televangelists under criticism in this book apparently do not know church history, they are unaware that they are repeating the errors of past ages. Because they do not understand Greek philosophy or Oriental mysticism or nineteenth-century theosophy, they do not know how seriously they have been affected by such thinking. To take thoughts captive, we have to think.

FEELING

There is often much enthusiasm surrounding a TV ministry. Some of the TV ministries make great appeals to the emotions and stir up rousing sentiments but deny the importance of the mind. Now feelings are not wrong. Feelings of love, joy, peace, and many other responses are all gifts from God. He created our capacity to feel, and above all He created us with a capacity to enjoy Him. One important Christian catechism asks, "What is man's chief end?" and answers, "To glorify God and enjoy Him forever." So we see that enjoyment of God is one of the central purposes of our creation. God also created us to enjoy relationships with other creatures and to enjoy the natural world. The problem with the message of many televangelists is not their appeal to desires or feelings; the problem is that they settle for "mud pies in the slum" rather than "a holiday at the sea." They, along with their followers, are far too easily pleased.

Even if we do gain perfect health and perfect wealth and achieve the power to accomplish many miracles, we can still lack the key to ultimate satisfaction: knowing God. Augustine once said, "Our hearts are restless until we find our rest in Thee," not, "until we find our rest in miracles," or, "in prosperity," or "in great feelings," but in God Himself. All humans have a spiritual hunger that only God Himself can satisfy.

Even an atheist, Franz Kafka, recognized the importance of satisfying his own spiritual hunger. In one short story, *The Hunger Artist*, he summed up his thoughts. He wanted his other works burned but insisted that this one story be saved.

In a typically bizarre fashion, Kafka has the hunger artist making his living by professional fasting. He is the practitioner of a once venerated profession. Seated on straw in his small barred cage, he is marveled at by throngs of people. After forty days, his fasts were terminated in triumph. His manager would make a speech, the band would play, and one of the ladies would lead him staggering in his weakened state out of the cage.

However, the day arrived when fasting was no longer understood or appreciated by the people. He lost his manager and had to join a circus. His cage was placed next to the animals. He became depressed by the smell, the restlessness of the animals at night, the raw flesh carried past him, and the roaring at feeding time. The people barely glanced at him in their hurry to see the animals. Even the circus attendants failed to limit his fast by counting the days. Finally, he was discovered lying in the straw, and in his dying breaths he told his secret: "I have to fast," he whispered. "I can't help it. I couldn't find the food I liked. If I had found it, believe me, I should have made no fuss and stuffed myself like you or anyone else."

Kafka was a writer of parables. The parable of the hunger artist is not about physical hunger but about spiritual hunger. Kafka was the hunger artist, and he realized he was starving to death spiritually, but he couldn't find any food he liked.

There is a hunger within us all that only God can satisfy. That's what C. S. Lewis meant when he said, "We are half-hearted creatures fooling about with drink and sex and ambition, when infinite joy is offered us." The meeting of those material desires is not wrong in its proper context. Yet we can be far too easily pleased. The followers of these televangelists are gorging themselves on junk food. It is attractive. It is sweet. It tastes good. But it does not satisfy, and it ends up destroying its host.

Many TV preachers appeal to our desires for well-being but fail to emphasize (or perhaps fail even to *see*) the *real* need. Christians need the knowledge of a just, holy, and merciful God. We need to know God's character, His attributes. It is not that we desire too much. We are not asking for too *much* when we demand health, wealth, and happiness, but too *little*! Some televangelists are passionate about things that can only bring partial satisfaction. They appeal to half-heartedness when infinite joy is offered. They call us to settle for "mud pies in a slum" because they cannot imagine what is meant by "a holiday at the sea."

KNOWING *AND* FEELING

Feelings, as we've just seen, are indispensable. But how are feelings generated? The psalmist cried, "My heart is stirred by a noble *theme*" (Psalm 45:1, italics added). Again and again, we see that it is a *truth*, a *thought*, that inspires devotion, sacrifice, love, anger, or any other emotional response. Knowing *produced* feeling, not the other way around.

Certain TV preachers are seen in their emotional tirades, telling heart-wrenching stories and making pleas for money while dancing across the stage, all in an attempt to arouse our feelings. They know, as we do, that emotions can be easily manipulated.

Film and television producers are also masters at knowing how to touch our emotions. We understand how chanting slogans at a football pep rally or at a political rally can make people excited. These tactics are appropriate for those particular functions but *not* when the gospel is at stake! The motive used to move people in the church must be truth, not emotional appeals. But does this mean we should be cold and rationalistic? Jonathan Edwards, a man described in the *Encyclopaedia Britannica* as the most brilliant scholar ever produced in America, wrote a book titled *Religious Affections*. In that book he wrote:

> I should think myself in the way of my duty, to raise the affections of my hearers as high as I possibly can, provided they are affected by nothing but the *truth* and with affections that are not disagreeable to what they are affected *with*.[6]

While pointing out the importance of our affections, or emotions, Edwards nevertheless cautioned,

> If a minister be driven with a fierce and intemperate zeal and vehement heat, without light, he will likely kindle the like unhallowed flame in his people and to fire their corrupt passions and affections, but will make them never the better, nor lead them a step towards heaven, but drive them apace the other way.[7]

Many ministers have no light and all heat. I believe that is too often the case with many televangelists. But that does not mean it is better to have light (knowledge) and no heat (firey emotions). Are the feelings of those who follow TV preachers affected by nothing but the truth, or are they characterized by heat without light? Christians must be known by both their heat *and* light.

In any case, there is nothing that produces emotion like the truth. In Luke 24 two disciples are on the road to Emmaus, and they have just had what may be the greatest Bible study ever taught. While they were walking with Jesus, He spoke to them from the Law, the Prophets, and the Writings (those prophecies pertaining to Himself throughout the Old Testament). Later, the two disciples told the others, "Were not our hearts *burning* within us . . . while He was explaining the Scriptures to us?" (Luke 24:32, NASB, italics added).

---

6. Jonathan Edwards, *Religious Affections*, quoted in John Piper, *Desiring God: Meditations of a Christian Hedonist* (Portland.: Multnomah, 1987).
7. Ibid.

There is nothing that produces that "burning" in our hearts like truth.

John Stott, a contemporary British evangelical theologian, says that preaching should be "logic on fire." We need fire (heat/emotions), but in relation to logic (light/truth). It is not enough to be pleased with the things that touch our feelings. We need to further ask, "What *kind* of feelings are produced?" and, "Do our feelings correspond to what is really true?"

KNOWING, FEELING, AND *DOING*

One of the things characterizing the message of the "Health and Wealth" evangelists is quick, easy solutions to complex problems. They tend to reduce the Christian life to knowing the right technique or formula, or following the prescribed steps to achieve prosperity. Thus, the Christian life is reduced to methods of success rather than to the gradual, life-long, and painful task of forming character.

Although many Christians do prosper and achieve good health, often strong character is developed through times of difficulty, struggle, and pain. There is no quick and easy way to develop character. Character is a quality of life produced by consistent actions and thousands of little decisions during times of testing. In Romans 5:3-5, Paul says, "We also exult in our tribulations, knowing that tribulation brings about perseverance; and perseverance, proven character; and proven character, hope; and hope does not disappoint, because the love of God has been poured out within our hearts through the Holy Spirit who was given to us" (NASB).

In their desire to be positive and provide quick, easy, victorious solutions, many televangelists say nothing about the character acquired through sufferings (see also James 1:12; Philippians 2:22). The desire for quick and easy solutions to problems also short-circuits the scriptural process of gaining wisdom and discernment. Those qualities of character are gained not by reciting a formula, having a positive attitude, or knowing the prescribed steps. The way to discernment involves deep thought and consistent practice.

Hebrews 5:14 reads, "Solid food is for the mature, who because of *practice* have their senses *trained* to discern good and evil" (NASB, italics added). Notice the connection between solid food and maturity. Not only do the mature digest solid food, but they also *practice* what they have learned. They have *thought* hard about what they believe, and then have *felt* whatever emotion that thought produces, and then have *acted* on it. One cannot act on something without being *moved* to do so (emotions). But one cannot be moved to do something unless one is inspired by a particular thought, concept, doctrine, or idea.

Those who press on to know more about God, and then experience and live out that knowledge, become men and women of character: "Get wisdom, discipline and understanding," Scripture commands (Proverbs 23:23). "The fear of the Lord is the beginning of wisdom" (Psalm 111:10). Although we may, in our sinfulness, be tempted to take a shortcut to character, we must remember that such neglect is not in accord with Scripture (see Galatians 5:16-25; Philippians 4:8-9; Colossians 3:9-17; Romans 12:2; Philippians 2:12-13).

Essential to the development of character is the solid food discussed above. One important step in developing character involves educating the conscience. Recently, many writers have described the moral decay in our culture. One author in particular has discussed the "death of ethics in America" and locates the solution in moral education: an education of the conscience. The televangelists could help here, but I am afraid they do not.

Again, a few simple answers are not adequate to prepare us for the complexities of life, and the fruit of their own shortcut mentality has been amply demonstrated. The absence of an emphasis on conscience from the preaching of televangelists indicates a lack of connection between knowing and doing. Conscience is where doctrine and practice meet and is where general principles are brought to bear in concrete cases.

Conscience is viewed in Scripture as one of the central goals of instruction. Paul says, "The goal of our instruction is love from a pure heart and a good conscience and a sincere faith" (1 Timothy 1:5, NASB). Do you see "a good conscience" as one of the central goals in the teaching of the televangelists? If you were asked to give two phrases to describe what it means to "fight the good fight," how would you respond? Paul says, "Fight the good fight, *holding on to faith and a good conscience*" (1 Timothy 1:18-19, italics added). Most of the leading televangelists are doing neither.

I believe that how well we are going to be able to conduct ourselves in this life will be determined by whether we are able to get and keep a clear conscience. Getting a clear conscience, of course, is essential to maintaining one (see Paul's goal in Acts 23:1; 24:16; 1 Timothy 3:9; 2 Timothy 1:3). Getting a clear conscience depends on how convinced we are that God's grace and not our own spirituality or obedience is our sole salvation. Without assurance of our acceptance before God, based entirely on Christ's performance and sacrifice, not our own, we can never have a clear conscience. We will always be wondering if there is one thing we've left undone.

Keeping a clear conscience means that we are regularly examining our lives and confessing our sins to God and others if we have offended them. Also involved is refusing to compromise our conscience. The recent moral lapses on the part of some televangelists raises the question of conscience and character. It could be that the message of easy solutions is too superficial to deal with the deep struggles in our lives. We must recapture a wholeness in our lives, which may be summed up in the word *integrity*. In order to do that, we must recapture the profound relationship between knowing, feeling, and doing.

Our Lord tells us, "If you *know* these things, *happy* are you if you *do* them" (John 13:17, NKJV,* italics added). Christ first addressed the importance of knowing, then on

* *New King James Version.*

feeling (happy), and finally on doing. The apostle Paul thanked God that "you *obeyed* [doing] from the *heart* [feeling] that form of *doctrine* [knowing] to which you were delivered" (Romans 6:17, NKJV, italics added). Integrity is the heart-felt response to sound doctrine. It is the "amen" cheered by the whole person in response to God's truth.

This is the way to wholeness and integrity: truth (light), experienced (heat) and lived in such a way that the world is once again stirred to ask concerning our Lord, "Who is this Man from Nazareth?"

If a prophet or a priest or anyone else claims, "This is the oracle of the Lord," I will punish that man and his household. This is what each of you keeps saying to his friend or relative: "What is the Lord's answer?' or "What has the Lord spoken?" But you must not mention "the oracle of the Lord" again, because every man's own word becomes his oracle and so you distort the words of the living God, the Lord Almighty, our God.

—Jeremiah 23:34-36

4

Scripture Twisting

Henry Krabbendam

There is a solemn obligation for the minister of the gospel to preach the Scriptures of the Old and New Testament (2 Timothy 4:2), to preach *all* of the Scriptures (Acts 20:27), and to preach *only* the Scriptures (Galatians 1:8). This should be a non-negotiable starting point for any type of ministry. After all, these Scriptures and these Scriptures only compose the inspired Word of God (2 Timothy 3:16). Every word is needed to produce and sustain life (Deuteronomy 8:3), and no other "word" is on a par with it or can claim to be without error in whatever it asserts. Neither, therefore, can any other such "word" have unquestionable authority in what it addresses. That is the prerogative of the word of Scripture only (John 10:35).

The minister of the gospel is under the equally solemn obligation to handle the Scriptures *accurately* (2 Timothy 2:15; 2 Peter 3:16), and to proclaim its message *clearly* (Hebrews 4:12). In order to achieve this, the Christian church has insisted on developing a system or "science" of interpreting the Bible. This science is called "hermeneutics." It sets forth principles, virtually agreed upon by orthodox Christians everywhere, that form the necessary guidelines for all biblical interpretation, whether in personal devotions or in public speaking.

It is unrealistic to expect all Christians to be in agreement on the precise *interpretation* of every passage of Scripture. But they should agree on the fundamental *approach* to biblical interpretation. As R. C. Sproul, in emphasizing the fundamental significance of the historic positions of the church, distinguishes between errors and heresy, so I wish to make a distinction between occasional *misinterpretations* and unacceptable *methods* of biblical interpretation. All have fallen victim to the former, but no one should be guilty of blatantly disregarding a responsible methodology.

This applies to every minister of the gospel, whether his setting is rural or urban, whether his focus is edification or evangelism, whether he labors in relative obscurity or in the limelight. After all, no minister runs a free-lance operation. The person who proclaims the Scriptures is under strict orders from God and is fully accountable to him. He is God's ambassador and, therefore, his Master's voice. Televangelists are no exception. The often-reported immediate "conversations" with God seem to give the impression not only that they possess a source of truth beyond the Bible, but also that they are exempt from following acceptable methods of biblical interpretation. This should evoke a protest. Not only is the Bible sufficient. But also the proper principles of interpretation are universal and, therefore, binding upon all.

The electronic preacher stands in need of a special reminder in this regard, since possibly more than anyone else he has the potential of being a force for tremendous good or a source of incalculable harm. The man and his message may earn the respect of his audience and have a life changing impact upon it. But by who he is and what he says, he may also leave cynicism and public ridicule in his wake, dealing a severe setback to the cause of Christ.

Also the televangelist must face up to the necessity of a biblical hermeneutics that heralds the Scriptures as its only starting point and champions a responsible method of interpretation. In a word, he must honor Scripture as the only inerrant and binding Word of God, and present its meaning accurately and clearly. Only so can he set forth God's truth properly and bring out its significance appropriately.

This chapter elaborates upon both concerns under two headings: (1) The Televangelist and the Word of God, and (2) The Televangelist and the Interpretation of the Word of God.

THE TELEVANGELIST AND THE WORD OF GOD

It is not common for a message to be beamed into our living room that brazenly contradicts Scripture. But it does happen. So we are told on one television program that Paul made a grave mistake when he called "the love of money the root of all evil" (1 Timothy 6:10). No, we are informed, the "lack of money is the root of all evil." Neither is it common to hear the inerrancy of Scripture questioned. But that has happened as well. Writes Pat Robertson, "I can hardly think that the Bible, which was transmitted through human beings, is totally perfect. I believe it to be the Word of God and a fully inspired book, but not perfection."[1]

Most reputable televangelists will decry such approaches to the Bible. This of course, is gratifying. Yet, even the *formal* insistence upon biblical inerrancy in no way guarantees that its message will be faithfully proclaimed. Traditional Roman Catholicism and traditional Protestantism both hold to biblical inerrancy. But their messages are poles apart. Can any steps be taken to help ensure that God's message comes through? Most definitely. There are at least two steps, essential for a properly functioning hermeneutics, that should be taken to secure an interpretive procedure that will do justice to the biblical text so that it will speak for itself.

Just as a doctor dares not practice surgery until he has studied the several branches of medicine, so a minister, including a media minister, should not presume that he broadcasts the biblical faith until he has a grasp of systematic and

1. Pat Robertson, *Answers,* Christian Broadcasting Network (CBN) Partner's Edition (Virginia Beach: Christian Broadcasting Network, 1984), p. 71.

biblical theology. It exhibits a glaring deficiency in both to claim, as does Charles Capps, that Job "was sure not under the anointing" when he said, "The Lord gives and the Lord takes away." Capps calls this statement a "lie."[2] Similar quotations can be multiplied.

SYSTEMATIC THEOLOGY

The call for a systematic theology may seem elitist, as if every televangelist should have a Ph.D. But this is not the case. Such a call does not need to sound threatening. Systematic theology aims at nothing more than an orderly presentation of the teachings of Scripture. It seeks to "round up" all biblical data on a particular subject and form a conclusion as to what the Bible teaches on that subject. Eventually a systematic order of beliefs is in place, not a grid that we press upon the Bible, but an order that we construct from the Bible. Scripture repeatedly argues for the need to develop a sound doctrinal position (Titus 1:9).

Frankly, it *cannot* be threatening. No student of Scripture engages himself in the interpretive process without a "systematic theology" already in place, whether consciously or unconsciously, partially or fully, whether it is profound or shallow, straight or twisted, right or wrong. This applies to Jesus (Matthew 7:28), the Pharisees (Matthew 16:2), the apostles (Acts 5:28), and to everyone else. From one's own doctrinal perspective, anything that is espoused must appear "good" (Proverbs 4:2, NKJV), "true" (1 Timothy 4:6), "sound" (Titus 1:9; or "wholesome"), the "opposite" of all this (see 1 Timothy 1:10), or simply "new" (Mark 1:27).

That is not to say that systematic theology should dominate the interpretive process. It may never dictate the meaning of the biblical text or in any way be its final determinant. The text should always speak for itself. What it does not *say*, it cannot *mean*. Neither is this to propagate the intellectualizing of the biblical message. The ultimate aim is not the in-

2. Charles Capps, *Can Your Faith Fail?* (Tulsa, Okla.: Harrison House), pp. 27-28.

tellectual grasp of the truth, but the submission in heart and the conformity in life to God in response to that truth.

But it is to ask for the recognition of the fact that everyone enters into the hermeneutical process with some kind of systematic theology, good or bad, the influence of which must not be underestimated. In view of this it would be irresponsible not to develop the best systematic theology possible. Too much depends upon it. Although it may not impose or determine meaning, systematic theology can ensure that no interpretation of a particular text clashes with any part of God's revealed truth. It provides the parameters for possible and acceptable meaning. Systematic theology is a watchdog, then, specifically equipped to challenge our interpretation of any passage when our interpretation conflicts with the overall biblical view of God, man, Christ, the Spirit, salvation, the church and the consummation. One can fail or neglect to build a systematic theology only at one's own peril.

In short, the parts can never be interpreted apart from the whole. The individual pieces, in other words, have to fit the total system. Of course, it is also true that the whole cannot be grasped apart from the parts. In fact, the individual pieces must be allowed to perfect, or change, the system whenever and wherever that is necessary. Ideally speaking, a "spiral" should be in evidence in which one's doctrinal position "checks" one's interpretation of a text and one's interpretation of a text "balances" one's doctrinal position. But the run-of-the mill electronic message has such a glaring need for a properly developed systematic theology that in this context the emphasis is upon one side of the spiral! The deficiency in the systematic understanding of many modern day televangelists will be substantiated in further detail below.

BIBLICAL THEOLOGY

The second step is a properly constructed biblical theology. Whereas systematic theology aims at the orderly comprehension and methodical presentation of the whole range of the biblical data on a particular subject, biblical theology looks at these same data from the historical perspective. It can be summed up under three main points.

The first point is that God revealed himself in time and space. His self-disclosure in word and deed is truly historical. The Flood, the call of Abraham, the legislation on Mt. Sinai, the promise to David, Jonah in the fish, the birth of Christ, the resurrection of Christ, the outpouring of the Spirit, and so forth, are space-time events that really took place. At the same time, history is also revelational. It discloses who God is, in His trinitarian being and work, who man is as creature and sinner, how God lovingly extends His covenant to man, and how man is taken up into it. The biblical narrative specifically focuses upon God's covenant dealings with man and the response that is expected from him. Any preacher who fails to categorize these covenant dealings and the necessary response to them is bound to misread God's revelation and misinform his audience.

The second point is that God's self-revelation is an unfolding process that is both organic and progressive. Its earlier stages are foundational for the later ones and give rise to them. Its later stages are natural "sequels" atop the earlier ones and add substantially to them. History is the progressive unfolding of God's covenantal dealings with man. Those dealings culminate in the New Covenant that merges against the backdrop of the radical and total bankruptcy of man. That New Covenant has a trinitarian foundation and is triadic in its scope. It is trinitarian in that it is promised by the Father (Jeremiah 31:31), personified in the Son (Isaiah 42:6), and personalized by the Spirit (Isaiah 59:21). It is triadic in that it aims at a new heart (in regeneration: Ezekiel 36:26; John 3:5; Romans 6:6), a new record (in justification: Ezekiel 36:25; 2 Corinthians 5:21; Ephesians 1:13-14), and a new life (in sanctification: Ezekiel 36:27; John 15:5; Romans 15:15). Of these three New Covenant benefits, the new life in sanctification is its crowning piece. Not a man-centered happiness, but a God-centered holiness is the grand theme and aim of the New Covenant. But once again, unless this is recognized,

God's self-disclosure to man is bound to be misread, and the preaching based upon such misreading is bound to mislead.

The third point is that God's self-revelation was committed to writing, which resulted in the Scriptures of the Old and New Testaments. As they rehearse the past, interact with the present, and open up vistas upon the future, the Scriptures are not simply reflections upon God's self-revelation, presenting the thoughts or opinions of lone individuals such as Moses and Paul or of communities such as Israel and the early church, nor are they simply the record of God's revelation in word and deed put into writing by the human authors. No, the Scriptures are in and of themselves the self-disclosure of God. That is, they are God's authoritative and complete canon, the final and sufficient Word for all mankind. They are such because they present both the universal principles and patterns of God's covenant dealings and the universal principles and patterns of man's response. As such, they are meant for all people at all times and in all situations. These universal principles and patterns come either ready-made, such as the Ten Commandments, or they are embedded in the text. It is the preacher's task to lift them or harvest them from the text. Unless he succeeds in doing so, the horizons of the exposition and application of the text will not merge and the message will have no basis in truth. The Scriptures as the record of God's revelation will not be fundamental for the preaching of God's revelation to man. "Wood, hay, [and] stubble" (1 Corinthians 3:12, KJV*) will be the inevitable result.

A biblical theology that takes these three points into account is well poised to make a lasting contribution. It will set forth the process and progress of God's self-disclosure and His Kingdom program as presented in Scripture. First, it will seek to determine the theme, structure, and objective of Scripture as a whole, in its component parts, in the relationship of the whole and the parts, and in the relationship of the parts to each other. Then it will seek to trace any particular

* King James Version.

theme, concept, or motif in its origin and development throughout the Scripture as presenting covenantal history, taking both the text and the context into account. Finally, it will couch its findings in terms of universal principles and patterns.

This puts biblical theology in perspective. In general, the recognition of the covenantal nature of Scripture guarantees that biblical interpretation will be undertaken in a God-centered rather than a man-centered fashion and with a holiness-centered rather than a happiness-centered focus. In particular, the recognition of the historical unfolding process ensures that the meaning of any biblical text will be established in the light of previous Scripture and that every biblical text will be assigned continued validity except when it is abrogated or superseded by later Scripture. Ultimately, this procedure will produce a Kingdom message in which the truth of God in a full-orbed fashion is brought to bear upon every and all audiences.

A PRELIMINARY ASSESSMENT OF TELEVANGELISM

In the light of all this, a preliminary assessment of televangelism can now be made. We will confine ourselves to the two types that are most prominent today. The first type is that of positive or possibility thinkers such as Norman Vincent Peale and Robert Schuller. The second type is that of the positive confessionists, such as Kenneth Copeland, Kenneth Hagin, Oral Roberts, and Robert Tilton.

The positive/possibility thinker believes in the power of the mind, the power of visualizing, the power of imagination, the power of faith. What one thinks, visualizes, imagines, or believes strongly enough will be realized. One's inner potential is so enormous and one's inner energy so powerful that one can literally think, visualize, imagine, or believe into being what one desires.

To the possibility thinker, the greatest threat to the possibilities that can be brought into being are a bad self-image and an absence of self-love. Those negative elements are produced by negative thinking, it is said, including the type of thinking that entertains man's lostness before God, not to mention his total depravity. In fact, the emphasis upon human sinfulness is itself the cardinal sin, for such emphasis would quickly turn a beckoning success story into a string of failures. Instead, all the God talk, Christ talk, Spirit talk, and Bible talk in general should be designed to bolster or produce self-esteem so that one can begin to tap one's vast inner resources and realize one's incredible potential.

The positive confessionists have much in common with this approach. But there is a difference. Whereas the positive/possibility thinker is more "natural" in his orientation, the positive confessionist is more "supernatural." The former emphasizes success as the natural outflow of the enormous human spirit. In a sense, it is one-upmanship—what the secularist can accomplish, the Christian can achieve more effectively . . . with Jesus. The latter holds out the prospect of prosperity and success as the supernatural realization of the even more enormous possibilities that are presented to him in the framework of salvation.

In short, according to the positive/possibility thinker, man succeeds by mobilizing what he already is and regards success as no surprise. Overcoming a bad self-image, of course, is part of the total package. According to the positive confessionist, man prospers by claiming what God promises and calls this a miracle. Part of the package is that he wrests from Satan what is already his.

However these types may differ, they are at one in that they place man in the center rather than God. And in spite of their different shades, they are only too eager to cooperate with one another. For instance, the leading proponent of possibility thinking, Robert Schuller, frequently participates in the conferences of the positive confessionists and has even contributed the foreword to *The Fourth Dimension*, a book written by one of their foremost spokesman, Paul Yong Cho. The objective of both groups is to secure success and happiness for man rather than to present the biblical message of sin and grace. Forget "glorifying God and enjoying Him forever"! The goal of the Christian life is to "name it and claim it."

It appears that biblical theology as defined earlier in this chapter and a systematic theology carefully built upon that theology and, on the other hand, the two types of televangelism described thus far are worlds in collision, for a properly constructed systematic theology reverts our attention upon the sin-holiness polarity with all that that entails. Biblical theology does not allow a single issue—and a man-centered issue at that—isolated from the thrust of Scripture to dominate the preaching enterprise.

It should further be underscored that both types of televangelism are quite pretentious and aware of the different direction they take. The first type of televangelism holds that the perspective of self-esteem puts its own imprint upon, and therefore requires a radical change in, the way one does (systematic) theology and in one's philosophical outlook upon life.[3] The second type of televangelism is of the opinion that it has finally unearthed the "full gospel," well beyond any gospel that (biblical) theology has been able to formulate.

The apostle Paul informs the Romans that he desires to come in the "fulness of the blessing of the gospel of Christ" (Romans 15:29, KJV). In the light of the context of the epistle, in which he describes the "full gospel," it is questionable whether the theology of self-esteem squares with that "gospel," or whether the theology of prosperity squares with that gospel in its "fulness." In a nutshell, the full gospel according to Paul is that sinners are accepted in the presence of God as members of the Kingdom only through the righteousness of Christ and subsequently as saints enjoy that presence and serve in that Kingdom only by surrendering everything to Christ. Prerequisite for entrance into the Kingdom is a loss of self rather than an esteem of self, although characteristic of service in that Kingdom is self-sacrifice rather than health and wealth.

There is a more traditional type of televangelism that seeks to avoid these tragic departures from the "full Gospel."

3. Robert Schuller, *Self-Esteem: The New Reformation* (Waco, Tex.: Word, 1982), pp. 150-55.

Rather than analyzing it, however, it seems preferable in this context to suggest the standards that all televangelism should meet in order to build with "gold, silver, [and] precious stones" (1 Corinthians 3:12, KJV).

A televangelist, just like any other evangelist, must preach the Word. He must do so properly, informed by a properly construed biblical theology, one that springs from a covenantal perspective. He must do so fully, informed by a carefully constructed systematic theology, which is to say that he does not confine himself to some popular themes, let alone fund-raising schemes.

His preaching must be evangelistic and edificational. In his evangelistic preaching, he must invite the sinner to come to Christ with his rebellious heart for it to be killed (Romans 6:6), with his guilty record for it to be cleansed (Romans 3:25), and with his unholy life for it to be transformed (John 15:5). In short, he must invite the sinner to come to Christ for regeneration, justification, and sanctification, the sum and substance of the New Covenant, promised by the Father, personified by the Son, and personalized by the Spirit.

In his edificational preaching, he must bring the Word of God, including promise and law, to bear upon the believer. He must seek to bring him into an ever-closer conformity to the image of Christ (Romans 8:29) and be intent upon mobilizing the church as the light of the world and the salt of the earth (Matthew 5:13-14) in the areas of evangelism and edification, so as to make an impact upon all of society (Acts 17:6).

This, then, sets the stage for the focus upon the second major hermeneutical concern, that of the interpretation of Scripture.

The Televangelist and the Interpretation of the Word of God

The field of interpretation is vast. But the basic issue is rather straightforward. Before a text can be understood, its meaning must be established. That requires acquaintance with a number of principles so that the task can be done properly. We cannot expect to accomplish much without the right tools! Two of the most essential principles will now be enumerated. Then, in the light of those principles, the several types of televangelism will be assessed.

THE GRAMMATICO-HISTORICAL METHOD

The expression *grammatico-historical* is simply a term intended to remind us that the Bible should be read like any other book. Because it is God's book, some Christians are afraid to read it as they would Dickens's *Tale of Two Cities.* But God intends that the poetry of the Bible be read like any other poetry. Similarly, the Bible's narrative portions are not allegorical. Neither is its allegory narrative. In short, we should not expect the Bible to violate the commonly accepted rules of interpreting any other piece of literature.

The grammatico-historical method of interpretation did not really come into its own until the Reformation. It was chosen as a conscious alternative to the allegorizing method that had reigned for centuries. That allegorical method sought to interpret the text in terms of something else, whether that "something else" was a philosophical system (the Alexandrians) or a doctrinal position (the Scholastics). The Reformation wanted the text to speak for itself. That required that the words and sentences that made up the text were to be explained according to the dictionary meaning, the grammatical structure, the normal rules of syntax (hence the "grammatico" part of the equation), and also in their historical setting, in their own cultural context, and in their specific situation (the "historical" part of the equation).

Hand in hand with the rejection of the allegorical method goes the opposition of the multiplicity of meaning. From the Alexandrians in the early church to the Schoolmen of the Middle Ages, the conviction prevailed that one biblical text could simultaneously harbor four meanings: the literal, the allegorical, the moral, and the eschatological meaning. The Reformation decried this approach as "biblical alchemy" and effectively brought its dominance to an end. It was replaced by an emphasis upon the unity of meaning. It should, indeed, seem preposterous to treat the language of Scripture as essentially different from any other language.

The Reformation also insisted that the meaning of the biblical text is determined by that text as addressed to and understood by its original audience—in its own historical situation and cultural setting. The sense of Paul's letter written to the Corinthians, for instance, never does nor ever can transcend the sense it did or could make to those same Corinthians. Scripture is not a jack-in-the-box. Its language does not function as a secret code that requires a special key, whether of revelatory insight, of ecclesiastical interpretation, or of private illumination, to decipher its hidden message intended for a later audience. Only by full compliance with this principle in the interpretation of a text can one secure a solid basis for its application. Since Scripture has already applied truth for its original audience, its legitimate applicatory force for a later audience emerges only when a demonstrably identical or analogous setting or situation prevails.

In a word, the use of the grammatico-historical method, with its insistence upon the unity of the original meaning of a Bible text, is a necessary condition for arriving at its message.

THE PURPOSE OF THE TEXT

The issue at stake under this heading is this: *Never isolate a passage, text, sentence, or word from its literary context.* The purpose of the larger unit (a chapter, a section or a whole book) must be recognized before the meaning of the parts can be established. Specifically, it is wrong to ask a text questions that it does not seek to answer in the first place, to draw lessons from it that it is not designed to yield, to settle issues by it that it does not address, or to glean information from it that it is not prepared to give.

For instance, it is a serious hermeneutical error to inquire of John 3:16 about the extent of the atonement, to build a case for man as trichotomous on 1 Thessalonians 5:23, or to use Luke 1:56 as a blueprint for hospitality. Yet all of this, and more, is done regularly. People frequently squeeze a message out of a biblical passage without any consideration for its focus or intention.

Concretely, the aim of John 3:16 is to bring out the astounding character of the love of God. That, then, should also be the aim of the exposition of the passage. Further, to determine the constituent elements of the nature of man, one should turn to Genesis 2, which explicitly deals with this subject, and not to 1 Thessalonians 5. An ingenious student of Scripture, as has been aptly observed, could combine 1 Thessalonians 5:23 and Matthew 22:37, and conclude that man is made of five component elements: body, soul, and spirit, as well as heart and mind. Yet that is clearly preposterous.

At times, the purpose of a book or passage is explicitly stated, as in John 20:31 and Luke 18:1. More often, however, the purpose will have to be determined from the aggregate of available clues to be found in the biblical text itself. That, of course, is not always easily accomplished. But a careful and detailed outline of both the larger context (preferably a whole book), and the more immediate context (a specific section or chapter) will go a long way toward recognizing the purpose.

A Concluding Assessment of Televangelism

In the light of the hermeneutical principles outlined in the first two sections we can now come to a more detailed and concluding assessment of televangelism. Because this chapter cannot become too lengthy, the assessment will focus more specifically, although not exclusively, upon what has been designated as the second type of televangelism, that of positive confessionism. The discussion will be given in two parts.

The first part will deal with doctrinal positions that have resulted from a failure to employ proper hermeneutical procedures. The second part will be concerned with the interpretive process itself and will spotlight unacceptable hermeneutical procedures. The doctrinal positions will often prove to be confused, confusing, errant, and at times even heretical;

the interpretive procedures arbitrary, ill-advised, deficient, and at times even damaging. A cross section of examples should suffice to document the disarray prevailing in much of present-day televangelism. The doctrines of man and of justification will serve as samples to indicate deficiencies caused by improper hermeneutical procedures.

MAN

In a recent publication, the trichotomous nature of man (i.e., the view that man consists of three parts: body, soul, and spirit) was defended on the basis of Hebrews 4:12 and 1 Thessalonians 5:23.[4] But neither passage, properly interpreted, supports the weight of this position, which, as R. C. Sproul has pointed out, is essentially Gnostic and has been rejected by orthodox Christianity.

Hebrews 4:12 does not inform us that the Word of God is so sharp that it *divides* the soul *from* the spirit, as if they are two separate entities, but rather that it pierces so deeply that it *splits* even *the soul,* the nonbodily part of man, or the spirit, that same part but now designated as nonmaterial, *down to its very root.*[5] The focus of the verse is the piercing capability of the Word of God and not the nature of man.

Similarly, in 1 Thessalonians 5:23—which is somewhat of a "sign-off"—the nature of man is not the issue either, but rather the sanctifying process. Paul emphasizes that it is all-encompassing. It easily could have read, "May God . . . sanctify you through and though. May your whole spirit, soul, body, mind, heart, emotions, and so forth, be kept blameless." That language would hardly have justified the conclusion that man consists of seven constituent elements. No, the two passages under consideration do not even come close to teaching that man is trichotomous.

4. Kenneth E. Hagin, *Man on Three Dimensions* (Tulsa, Okla.: Rhema Bible Church, 1985).
5. Jay Adams, *More Than Redemption* (Phillipsburg, N.J.: Presb. and Ref., 1979), p. 112.

It is important to recognize this point especially in the light of the constructs the positive confessionists build on their misinterpretation of these verses. They treat the body, soul, and spirit, as well as the corresponding physical, mental, and spiritual dimensions of man, as unrelated entities. They further hold that God has no immediate contact with either the mind or the body. He communicates with man only through the spirit. This concept is dangerously akin to the Gnostic view of the spirit as the "divine" aspect of man. Incidentally, the communication the positive confessionists speak of is not just a matter of illumination of Scripture, but rather of substantive revelation. In their view, Scripture merely addresses the mind with a view to moral renewal, whereas spiritual realities are seen as being conveyed immediately by God to the spirit. Such a misunderstanding on the part of the positive confessionists puts both the necessity and the sufficiency of Scripture in serious jeopardy.

Quite in line with their view that the body, soul, and spirit are unrelated elements and their misunderstanding of the nature of God's communication to man, the positive confessionists do not acknowledge the body as the temple of the Spirit. The designation appearing in 1 Corinthians 6:19 is only conceded to be true in a derived sense, inasmuch as the Spirit indwells the human spirit, which in turn is connected with the body. Further, the positive confessionists hold that when the Spirit-filled spirit controls the body, the result is a committed Christian, whereas when the body dominates the spirit, a "carnal" Christian emerges.[6] This misinterpretation has Gnostic overtones as well and is as much a misreading of Scripture today as it was in the second century.

The trichomomous view also has serious consequences for the doctrine of Christ. In the incarnation, God, who is a spirit, is portrayed as adopting the body of a man. This interpretation represents a type of Appollinarianism (another an-

6. Kenneth E. Hagin, *Man on Three Dimensions*, pp. 6-8, 15-16, 18-20, 22-26; and *Zoe: The God-Kind of Life* (Tulsa, Okla.: Rhema Bible Church, 1981), pp. 3-4, 6-8.

cient heresy) that was condemned centuries ago. In that same incarnation, furthermore, Christ is said to come into the possession of an actual sinful nature. As a result, He was severed from God and became a man who was spiritually dead and physically mortal. That condition required, before anything else, the transformation of his nature. That took place in the resurrection, which constituted his rebirth and paved the way for the rebirth of others (apparently no one was ever born again in the Old Testament).[7] This interpretation, of course, is totally unacceptable to orthodox Christians anywhere.

Clearly, the insistence upon the trichotomous nature of man in the televangelism of the positive confessionists produces a staggering amount of damage. It paves the way to continuing revelation that qualitatively transcends Scripture, and it saddles the church with a heretical view of the Person and work of Christ.

JUSTIFICATION

The doctrine of justification is no less twisted. Confusing regeneration and justification, one positive confessionist defines "righteousness" simultaneously as having the "nature of God" and as possessing "the right standing with God."

It is argued as well that once the believer possesses "the nature of God" and "the right standing with God," all sin consciousness ought to be driven out and every sin tag removed. The apostle Paul serves as an example. He claims that he has never defrauded anyone (2 Corinthians 7:2). In view of his persecution of the Christians in the early part of his career, that seems an astonishing claim that may raise more than a few eyebrows. But it really should not. The "old" Paul, we are told, who did the persecuting, "died" on the way to Damascus and is gone, effectively replaced by the "new" Paul. This

7. Kenneth Copeland, "What Happened from the Cross to the Throne?" tape, side 2, on file with Christians United for Reformation (CURE); Kenneth Copeland, *Believer's Voice of Victory,* April 1982, p. 3; and Kenneth E. Hagin, *Word of Faith*, April 1982, p. 3.

Paul is perfectly justified in refusing to own any sin-consciousness or sin tag. It can, indeed, be said of the new Paul,
according to the positive confessionists, that he never defrauded anyone.[8]

The picture is grim. Justification is confused with regeneration. The necessity of repentance is ignored. Now also
progressive sanctification vanishes from sight. There is apparently no need to remind the believer that he is locked in a
battle with sin that too often still clings to him. In fact, such a
reminder is said to be counterproductive. It would emphasize
the negative unduly.

All this fits in with the avowed aim of the positive confessionist. Only what serves the twin ends of health and
wealth goes. Never mind what right standing with God is,
how it comes about, and what it implies, as long as the
speaker gets across the message that the gospel produces a
son of the King, who reigns with the King and has all the
privileges and rights of the King! Such a person may expect, if
not demand, health and wealth. For anyone who is sin-con-
scious, the doors of prosperity will close. But for a righteous-
ness-minded person, they will open wide. After all, unlike the
former, who will feel fettered and flustered, the latter will be
in a perfect position freely and boldly to exercise his royal
right to "name it and claim it." The message of the Bible,
which is God-centered and holiness-centered, is thus
eclipsed by a man-centered and happiness-centered
ideology.

In this regard the theology of the positive confessionist
is akin to that of possibility thinking. The latter would regard
the verdict rendered just above as a badge of honor. Its major
proponent holds that classical theology, which had its inception in the Reformation in 1517, is in error precisely because
it is God-centered. Its definition of sin as a rebellion against
God, for instance, is seen as being typical of the whole of
classical theology and as a reactionary definition, because it

8. Kenneth Copeland, *The Force of Righteousness* (Fort Worth, Tex.: Kenneth Copeland Publications, 1984), pp. 2-4, 7-13, 15-17, 21.

is insulting and bound to produce an inferiority complex in people. A New Reformation, the proponent insists, is desperately needed. Theology ought to be man-centered and take the value of the individual as its starting point. Then sin can be properly defined as a lack of self-esteem, and the cross can be presented as the means to prop up that self-esteem. After all, the infinite price paid on the cross indicates the infinite worth of man.[9]

What is proposed without blushing is a gospel that is different from the one preached by the Reformers, a gospel that is man-centered. It is to be feared that it also constitutes a "different gospel" in Paul's eyes, different, that is, from the gospel he preached (Galatians 1:8), the gospel of the justification of the ungodly through faith in the blood sacrifice of Christ that pacifies the wrath of God against the sinner (Romans 3:25).

All in all, the picture that emerges with regard to the doctrinal position of much of modern televangelism is not encouraging. It simply does not square with a properly constructed systematic theology or with the covenantal themes of a properly constructed biblical theology. The hermeneutical procedures of much of modern televangelism are no less discouraging. Space does not allow us to give more than three examples, but one hopes that they will prove to be telling and persuasive. The examples pertain to such terms as *everything*, *anything*, and *whatever* found in many passages of Scripture, to the phrase *greater works* mentioned in John 14:12, and to the text of Isaiah 53:4, quoted in Matthew 8:17.

Everything, Anything, Whatever. Does *everything* always mean "everything" ("whatever," "anything")? The positive confessionist answers this question emphatically in the affirmative. When the expressed scope of a biblical promise, such as in John 14:13-14, is "everything," *whatever*, *anything* can be named, claimed, and even demanded, whether it is good weather, a new car, financial success, the recovery of

9. Schuller, *Self-Esteem*, pp. 38, 64-65, 98, 101, 175.

lost property, or the salvation of a loved one.[10] Herewith the prosperity "gospel" is born.

Such use of Scripture is hermeneutically irresponsible. *Everything* does not always mean "everything." A simple illustration will make that evident. Upon paying his bill in a restaurant, the customer will invariably be asked by the cashier, "Is everything all right?" Clearly, "everything" here is not "everything-in-general," but "everything-in-context," the restaurant context of the food, the service, the seating, and possibly even the restrooms. In a word, the context supplies terms such as *everything* with natural limits, usually not explicitly stated, but by the same token routinely recognized.

This hermeneutical principle may now be applied to John 14:13-14. The passage holds out the promise that Christ will supply "whatever" ("anything") that is asked in His name. In the context His name stands for the crucified Savior as the only avenue to the Father (14:6) and for the ascended Lord as the enthroned King (14:12*b*). Herewith the parameters (and boundaries) of the promise emerge. It seems no more than natural to understand from this passage that Christ will act only upon requests that are made by believers who embrace him as Savior and acknowledge him as King, and only upon petitions that are made through His continuing mediation and serve the purposes of His Kingdom. Otherwise, someone might come to the preposterous conclusion that Christ would be bound to honor requests that are made by adherents of the Enemy and aim to promote the realm of darkness.

It ought to be noted that the purposes of the King, according to 1 John 5:14, are spelled out in the Word of the King. Therefore, for a request to be honored by the King, it must be based upon His Word, whether it is a promise, an injunction, a prohibition, or a universal principle. Of such requests that are sanctioned by the Word, John says categorically that they will be granted (1 John 5:15). By the same

10. Robert Tilton, *God's Miracle Plan for Man* (Dallas: Robert Tilton Ministries, 1987), pp. 9-62.

token, when a request is not authorized by the King's Word, it is illegitimate, and neither may, nor should be, made.

This point has powerful implications for the "name it and claim it" doctrine. The Bible never assures anyone of health, wealth, recovery of lost property, a promotion, salvation of loved ones, and so on. So they should not be "demanded" or expected. Legitimate requests always stick scrupulously to the boundaries of the Word.

In short, "everything" does not always mean "everything" indiscriminately. By the same token, "everything" for the King and based upon His Word invariably means "everything." Such an interpretation precludes an approach that is man-centered and happiness-centered and promotes an approach that is God-centered and holiness-centered.

Greater works. It is difficult to envision anyone able to produce miracles that are more numerous or impressive than those of Jesus. Surely, the miracles that accompanied His presence on earth are unsurpassed in quantity and quality. Still, the claim is made that according to John 14:12 in the realm of the spectacular (in the production of health and wealth), the accomplishments of the disciples of Jesus (should) outstrip those of the Master. The context, however, suggests a better explanation.

It connects the "greater works" with Christ's ascension and the outpouring of the Spirit. That brings Acts 1 and 2 into view. The King is on the march. After he left the Twelve to occupy His throne and baptized them with the Spirit from that throne, they were instrumental in one day in the salvation of a throng that exceeded the total number of converts their Master assembled in three years. Then they proceeded with a massive discipling program that dwarfed anything that had ever gone on before. These are the only kinds of works, attested to in Scripture and history, that can be characterized as truly "greater" than those of Jesus. This not only makes any accomplishment in the area of the spectacular pale by comparison. It also provides a focus to ministry that no emphasis upon health and wealth could ever transcend. In fact, the differences in focus between a ministry of greater works that Jesus holds out according to Scripture and the type of activity that fascinates the positive confessionists is as vast as the difference between heaven and earth.

Isaiah 53:4. Isaiah 53:4 is the *locus classicus* and cornerstone for the view that it is the Christian's prerogative to claim healing in any type of sickness. In fact, the only roadblock for healing "name it and claim it" proponents see is lack of faith on the part of the potential recipient. Basic to this view is the interpretation that has both the removal of sin and the deliverance from sickness bound up with Christ's substitutionary atonement.

Now in the light of Matthew 8:17 it seems, indeed, irrefutable that the cross of Christ constitutes a conquest over both sin and sickness and, of course, constitutes a conquest over Satan as well (Colossians 2:15). But to recognize the parallels properly is to recognize them across the board. The conquest over Satan does not bring the spiritual warfare and the suffering that spiritual warfare entails to an end (1 Peter 5:8-9). Similarly, the conquest over sin does not spell sinless perfection. The heartache that this produces is only too genuine (1 John 3:20). So the conquest over sickness does not imply perfect health (Philippians 2:26-27). The "thorns and thistles" with which this world is cursed after the Fall do not leave any area of life untouched and will not be removed until the consummation.

Of course, this is not a plea for defeatism. The battle against Satan, sin, and sickness is wholesome and necessary. But if there is a break in the parallelism, it emerges at this juncture. Whereas there is no excuse not to be victorious over Satan (James 4:7) or sin (James 3:9-12) in the ongoing battle, the same can not be said about sickness. The persistence or recurrence of sickness does not point to a deficiency in the one who intercedes against it, or a lack of faith in the one who is afflicted with it.

First, the apostle Paul acknowledges routinely the presence of sickness in a way that is sharply different from his attitude toward Satan and sin. Paul does not lay a guilt trip on Timothy when he hears about his condition, but recommends a little wine for his stomach and his frequent ailments (1 Timothy 5:23). If he had been confronted with a situation in which Satan and sin had made inroads, he would have reacted much more strongly (1 Corinthians 5:1-8).

Furthermore, the prayer of a righteous man, according to James 5:14-16, accomplishes much—but apparently not *everything*! James would never have said anything remotely like that if the battle against Satan (James 4:7) or sin (James 4:4) had been the context. Why the difference? To begin with, the claim that perfect health is obtainable through faith runs counter to the Scripture's witness of man's mortality. Then it completely overlooks a well-attested purpose of sickness. Just as in the case of judgments (1 Corinthians 11:30), chastisements (Hebrews 12:5-11), and trials (James 1:2-3), there are times when sickness is designed to elicit repentance, to produce endurance, and to result in holiness.

There is a connection between cross and cure. But it is wide of the biblical mark to claim that indiscriminate healing is simply waiting to be appropriated by the faith of the Christian. Isaiah 53:4, the so-called cornerstone of the "name it and claim it" teaching in the area of sickness, cannot support the weight that is placed upon it.

CONCLUSION

The portrait of today's televangelism is not encouraging. In general, we have little choice but to recommend that much, if not most, of televangelism return to the drawing board to develop a hermeneutics that honors the Word of God. The situation is extremely serious.

Televangelists at times emphasize the necessity "to stay with the Word," "to stay with all of the Word," and "to stay with the Word only."[11] That advice is excellent. But the practice usually lags far behind the theory.

11. Kenneth E. Hagin, *The Believer's Authority* (Tulsa, Okla.: Rhema Bible Church, 1984), p. 49.

To preach the prosperity gospel is *not* to "*stay* with the Word." It has correctly been called "a modern heresy . . . to say that those who have genuine faith will unfailingly experience health, wealth, success and freedom from trouble."[12] It is simply unbiblical to advocate that God is the author of health and wealth, Satan the source of sickness and poverty, and that the believer has the right to demand health and wealth. It is biblically unconscionable to insist that upon paying the tithes (Malachi 3:10), or any kind of "seed" money (2 Corinthians 9:6-10), the Christian may decree physical vigor, financial success, a comfortable home, a new car, or even the salvation of a loved one as part of his reign over anything satanic and evil. The "name it and claim it" position cannot be reconciled with biblical truths such as found in Genesis 15:13; 50:20; Job 1 and 2; Psalm 119:67, 71, 75; Amos 3:6; John 15:18-20; 16:2; Romans 8:18-23; Hebrews 11:35-38; 12:4-11; Revelation 2:8-11, and so on.

Further, to make success and the "name it, claim it" message the main focus of one's ministry is *not* to "stay with *all* of the Word." At worst it is heresy and at best majoring in minors. The whole counsel of God vanishes from view (Acts 20:27), and so does the truly "full gospel" of Christ (Romans 15:29). Modern televangelism is advised to return to the solid themes that in the past brought on the genuine and mighty revivals, such as total depravity, original sin, sovereign grace, the substitutionary atonement, regeneration, repentance, saving faith, justification, holiness, the judgment, and the twofold eternal state.

Finally, the all-too-frequent references to private communications from God or the Spirit do *not* square with the emphasis "to stay with the Word *only*." Since the canon is closed, there is every reason to hold that such communications have ceased. New and authoritative revelation is a thing of the past. Reliance upon extrabiblical revelation, therefore, brings the sufficiency of Scripture into serious question.

12. Robert McQuilkin, "Where We All Have Failed . . . " *World* 2, no. 21 (Oct. 26, 1987), p. 7.

The only standard of faith and practice is, indeed, the Word, all of the Word and the Word only. But a formal commitment to this is insufficient. It takes a properly constructed and detailed systematic and biblical theology to flesh this out and to ensure substantive adherence to it. Regrettably such theology is not in evidence.

Under the present circumstances no respite can be expected from the interpretive process either.

The possibility thinker makes self-esteem the material principle of the interpretation of Scripture and therefore the ultimate determinant of its meaning and of the theology built upon it.[13] The net effect is "another gospel." The contention that Jesus came into the world to save from the shame of a low self-image and to instill self-esteem[14] hardly warrants any other conclusion.

The positive confessionist has a similar problem. For him health and wealth is the material principle of the interpretation of Scripture. The upshot is that he believes that every Scripture passage and every Scripture doctrine affirms that the believer may anticipate, indeed decree, success. This is "another gospel" as well.

On balance, it is appropriate to recommend that much, if not all, of televangelism take a second look at its hermeneutics so as to ensure that the voice of God, the full voice of God and only the voice of God comes through to the audience. Otherwise, the viewer should be advised frequently to make his first look his last.

13. Schuller, *Self-Esteem*. pp. 44-45.
14. Ibid., pp. 31ff., 39.

"You will not surely die," the serpent said to the woman. "For God knows that when you eat of it, your eyes will be opened, and you will be like God."

—Genesis 3:4-5

You have abandoned your people, the house of Jacob. They are full of superstitions from the East; they practice divination like the Philistines and clasp hands with pagans.... The eyes of the arrogant man will be humbled and the pride of men brought low; the Lord alone will be exalted in that day.

—Isaiah 2:6, 11

In the pride of your heart you say, "I am a god; I sit on the throne of a god in the heart of the seas." But you are a man and not a god, though you think you are as wise as a god.

—Ezekiel 28:2

5

Ye Shall Be As Gods

Walter Martin

Throughout almost two thousand years of her turbulent history, the Christian church has been set upon by many adversaries. The apostle Paul, in his great charge to the Ephesian elders in Acts chapter 20, anticipated the threat of heresy and schism in his own lifetime:

> I declare to you today that I am innocent of the blood of all men. For I have not hesitated to proclaim to you the whole will of God. Keep watch over yourselves and all the flock of which the Holy Spirit has made you overseers. Be shepherds of the church of God, which he bought with his own blood. I know that after I leave, savage wolves will come in among you and will not spare the flock. Even from your own number men will arise and distort the truth in order to draw away disciples after them. So be on your guard! Remember that for three years I never stopped warning each of you night and day with tears. (Acts 20:26-31)

It should be observed that Paul mentions two specific categories for the attacks being made upon the church. The first category includes overt enemies of the faith: atheists, agnostics, skeptics, secularists, and scoffers. It also includes non-Christian religions, the cults, and the occult. But the "savage wolves" are even more dangerous when they are part of the second category: "Even from your own number," says Paul, "men will arise and distort the truth in order to draw away disciples after them." Today, the words of Paul are fulfilled in plain sight as the church is divided by schismatic sheep who mix cultic and occultic doctrine with biblical truth, perverting the gospel of Christ.

Some, for example, teach that Christians are actually gods. The Mormons teach that men may *become* gods by accepting their revelations and by submitting to their authority. However, this is something that takes place in the future and is designated as exaltation. Since the Mormons are genuine polytheists (i.e., believing in "many gods") as opposed to monotheists (accepting only one God), they maintain that faithful Mormons can eventually become gods in the same manner and of the same nature as Jesus Christ and His Father. Mormonism has never been recognized by the Christian church as a bona fide Christian faith since its inception in 1830 through the work of Joseph Smith, Jr.

We should not fail to note that Mormons affirm that the divinity of man is to be accomplished *after* the death of the body, a bad enough departure from the Christian faith. But, sadly, there are those who function *within* the Christian church who do not hesitate to make the claim *now*!

The "Little Gods" Doctrine

Earl Paulk, Charles Capps, Robert Tilton, Kenneth Copeland, and Kenneth E. Hagin are among the leading televangelists who espouse the "little gods" teaching.

Earl Paulk writes, "Adam and Eve were placed in the world as the seed and expression of God. Just as dogs have puppies and cats have kittens, so God has little gods." But, he says, "we have trouble comprehending this truth." He adds, "Until we comprehend that we are little gods and we begin to act like little gods, we cannot manifest the Kingdom of God."[1]

Robert Tilton asserts, "You are . . . a God kind of creature. Originally you were designed to be as a god in this

1. Earl Paulk, *Satan Unmasked* (Atlanta: K Dimension, 1984), p. 97.

world. Man was designed or created by God to be the god of this world. . . . Of course, man forfeited his dominion to Satan who became the god of this world."[2]

Kenneth Copeland insists that "man had total authority to rule as a god over every living creature on earth, and he was to rule by speaking words. His words would carry the power and anointing of God that was in him from the time he was first created."[3]

Casey Treat, pastor of Seattle's Christian Faith Center, tells us in his tape series "Believing in Yourself" to come to the point where we feel comfortable claiming our godhood:

> The Father, the Son and the Holy Ghost had a conference and they said, 'Let us make man an exact duplicate of us.' Oh, I don't know about you, but that does turn my crank! An exact duplicate of God! Say it out loud—"I'm an exact duplicate of God!' [The audience repeats it a bit tentatively and uncertainly.]
>
> Come on, say it! [He leads them in unison.] 'I'm an exact duplicate of God!' Say it again, 'I'm an exact duplicate of God!' [The congregation is getting into it, louder and bolder, with more enthusiasm each time.] Say it like you mean it! [He's yelling now.] 'I'm an exact duplicate of God!' Yell it out loud! Shout it! [They follow as he leads.] 'I'm an exact duplicate of God!' 'I'm an exact duplicate of God!' [Repeatedly]. . . .
>
> When God looks in the mirror, He sees me! When I look in the mirror, I see God! Oh, hallelujah!. . . .
>
> You know, sometimes people say to me, when they're mad and want to put me down. . . . 'You just think you're a little god!' Thank you! Hallelujah! You got that right! 'Who d'you think you are, Jesus?' Yep!
>
> Are you listening to me? Are you kids running around here acting like gods? Why not? God told me to! . . . Since I'm an exact duplicate of God, I'm going to act like God!"[4]

2. Robert Tilton, *God's Laws of Success* (Dallas: Word of Faith, 1983), pp. 170-71.
3. Kenneth Copeland, *The Power of the Tongue* (Fort Worth, Tex.: Kenneth Copeland), p.6.
4. Casey Treat, "Believing in Yourself," tape 2 (Seattle Christian Center).

Kenneth Copeland informs us, "You don't have a god *in* you. *You are one!*"[5] Others in the world of the cults teach variations on the above themes of human divinity. Herbert W. Armstrong's Worldwide Church of God, for instance, teaches that there is a "god family" in which all Armstrongists will eventually share. They will become just as much deity as the Father and Son. (Armstrong denies the personality of the Holy Spirit, as do Jehovah's Witnesses.)

Christian Science, the Unity School of Christianity, the Science of Mind or Religious Science, New Thought Metaphysics, and so on, believe that all humans have within themselves the "Christ consciousness," or "Christ idea," which is allegedly the true divinity of *all* men. They maintain that Jesus Christ had possessed this divinity to a greater degree than others, which is what sets Him apart, but none of those groups confess the eternal deity of Jesus Christ, the Word of God made flesh, and His unique relationship to the Father as the "*only* begotten Son" (see John 1:18; 3:16).

In the mind science cults, man is already divine—in the Hindu-New Age sense of shared deity, or, as Mary Baker Eddy once wrote, "Man as God's idea is already saved with an everlasting salvation."[6] "God, Spirit, being all, nothing is matter," said the founder of Christian Science.[7] The Unity School of Christianity confirms that thesis: "God is not a person . . . but very real, something we call life."[8] "The Christ, or perfect man . . . is the true spiritual higher self of every individual."[9]

As we have previously noted, these cultic views are expressed by organizations that are recognized as outside the pale of the Christian church. Nevertheless, the "little gods" doc-

5. Kenneth Copeland, "The Force of Love," tape BCC-56 (Fort Worth, Tex.: Kenneth Copeland), on file with Christian Research Institute (CRI).
6. Mary Baker Eddy, *Miscellaneous Writings* (Boston, Mass.: First Church of Christ, Scientist), p. 261.
7. Mary Baker Eddy, *Science and Health, with a Key to the Scriptures* (Boston, Mass.: First Church of Christ, Scientist), p. 113, verse 18.
8. Emilie H. Cady, *Lessons in Truth* (Unity Village, Mo.: Unity School of Christianity), p. 6.
9. *The Metaphysical Bible Dictionary*, ed. Unity School of Christianity staff (Unity Village, Mo.: Unity School of Christianity), p. 150.

trine taught by the leaders of the "faith movement" is firmly situated within groups generally—but falsely—regarded as evangelical. It is circulated in Christian bookstores all over the United States and is widely disseminated via Christian radio and television. The president of Trinity Broadcasting Network, Paul Crouch, has taught this doctrine openly and once spent almost two hours attempting to convince me and three other ministers that we were "little gods." Many evangelical organizations, consciously or not, are helping "savage wolves" spread such diabolical errors.

A Spurious Appeal

In a thorough article in *Christian Research Journal,* Robert Bowman made a penetrating observation. Some faith teachers appeal to the fact that the church Fathers and, indeed, some of the writings of the Eastern Orthodox church itself, mention the concept of "Christian deification." This, the faith teachers believe, legitimizes their claim to being "little gods." However, as Bowman clearly points out, nothing could be further from the truth.

"In keeping with monotheism," says Bowman, "the Eastern Orthodox do *not* teach that men will literally become 'gods,' which would be polytheism. Rather, as many of the church fathers, they teach that *men are deified in the sense that the Holy Spirit dwells within Christian believers and transforms them into the image of God in Christ*, eventually endowing them in the resurrection with immortality and God's perfect moral character."[10] The faith teachers do not speak of the believer's "deification" in the sense merely of the Holy Spirit's *indwelling* presence, since, as Copeland says, "You don't have a god *in* you. *You are one.*"[11] Of course, the Orthodox church and the Fathers judged this very same teaching (Gnosticism) as heresy.

10. Robert Bowman, *Christian Research Journal,* Winter/Spring, 1987, p. 19.
11. Kenneth Copeland, "The Force of Love," tape.

The biblical concept of monotheism—"Hear, O Israel: The Lord our God, the Lord is one" (Deuteronomy 6:4) directly contradicts Mr. Copeland's belief that "dogs beget dogs, and cats beget cats, and God begets gods. You are all little gods."[12]

The late Paul Billheimer did not hesitate, in his popular book *Destined for the Throne*, to discuss man as an extension of the Godhead. Virtually paraphrasing Armstrong, he wrote:

> But this is not all. We tread softly here. With bated breath, we read in 1 Cor. 6:17, "He that is joined to the Lord is one spirit." The union goes beyond a mere formal functional or idealistic harmony or rapport. It is an organic unity, an organic relationship of personalities (Sauer). Through the new birth we become bona fide members of the original cosmic family (Eph. 3:15), actual generated sons of God (1 John 3:2), "partakers of the divine nature" (2 Pet. 1:4), begotten by Him, impregnated with his "genes," called the seed or "sperma" of God (1 Kings 5:1, 18; 1 Pet. 1:3, 23), and bearing his heredity.
>
> Thus, through the new birth, and I speak reverently, we become the "next of kin" to the Trinity. A kind of "extension" of the Godhead. . . . This group outranks all other orders of created beings.[13]

The difficulty with Billheimer's imprecise terminology is that, while admitting human finitude, he asserts that man is an extension of the Trinity itself—therefore implying, if not outright claiming, a union with God by nature or essence. This, of course, can never be reconciled with Scripture. The finite (man) cannot be an extension of the infinite (the Trinity), since any extension of the Trinity's nature would be by definition deity. And yet, Billheimer proposes just that:

12. Kenneth Copeland, "Praise the Lord," Trinity Broadcasting Network. Text and tape on file with CRI.
13. Paul Billheimer, *Destined for the Throne* (Minneapolis: Bethany House, 1983), pp. 35, 37.

According to 1 John 3:2, that is just what they are, true genetic sons of God, and, therefore, blood brothers of the Son. Christ is the divine Prototype after which this new species is made. They are to be exact copies of Him, true genotypes, as utterly like Him as it is possible for the finite to be like the infinite. As sons of God begotten by Him, incorporating into their fundamental being and nature the very "genes" of God, they rank above all other created beings and are elevated to the most sublime height possible short of becoming members of the Trinity itself.[14]

As noted, such language resembles that of Herbert W. Armstrong, who maintained that it was possible for redeemed men and women to be members of the "god family," and, in effect, members of the god class—something Billheimer, Copeland, Paulk, and Tilton affirm. Such teaching puts man on the throne and makes him an extension of the Trinity! It is a serious error, therefore, to use such terms. Man is not now, nor can he ever be, in "God's class." The fact is that man was created "a little lower than the angels" (Hebrews 2:7) and is subject to death as a mortal. If he were a "little god," he would outrank the angels (which faith teachers believe) and human death would *now* be swallowed up in victory without the necessity of a future resurrection. This is a patent error, as Paul reminds us in 1 Corinthians 15.

MISAPPLIED TEXTS AND TERMS

JOHN 10:34-35, WITH PSALM 82:6

Those who embrace the "little gods" doctrine almost universally cite these verses, wrested from their contexts. In Mark 12:28, Christ was asked the question, "Of all the commandments, which is the most important?" to which Jesus replied, "Hear, O Israel, the Lord our God, the Lord is one." And yet, Jesus claimed deity, union with the Godhead, on numerous occasions. Nevertheless, the faith teachers appeal

14. Ibid.

to Christ's remark in John 12:48-50: "Is it not written in your Law, 'I have said you are gods'? . . . and the Scripture cannot be broken" (John 10:34- 35).

In the beginning of this story in John 10, Jesus states, "I and the Father are one" (v. 30). Furious, the Jews picked up stones. Jesus asked them, "For which of these [good works] do you stone me?" to which the Jews responded, "We are not stoning you for any of these . . . but for blasphemy, because you, a mere man, claim to be God" (v. 32-33). His citation of the eighty-second Psalm perplexed them. "Is it not written in your law, 'I have said you are gods'? . . . and the Scripture cannot be broken"—*why on earth did He quote* that *one?* they wondered. Was Christ, in fact, teaching that man was a god? And if so, how can this be reconciled with the extreme monotheism (one-God-ism) of Judaism, which He both believed and taught as a rabbi?

There can be no doubt from the history and theology of the Old Testament that the judges of Israel and rulers of the people were representatives, or mouthpieces, for God. Such individuals were accorded great respect and assumed in the eyes of the people the outward appearance of "mighty ones" (in Hebrew, *Elohim,* "gods").

This should not come as a surprise to us when we remember Exodus 7:1, where God, speaking to Moses, says, "I have made thee a god to Pharaoh" (KJV). Now, there can be no doubt that Moses was no more than a mortal man—in no sense divine, by nature or in essence. Nevertheless, since Pharaoh was a pagan and God was addressing him in that context, He was, in effect, saying, "When I finish with Pharaoh, through the power that will be revealed in you, Moses, My representative, he (Pharaoh) will think you are a god." The plagues of Egypt were evidence to Pharaoh and to the occultic priests who surrounded him, that this was indeed the "finger of God" (Exodus 8:19).

Moses did *not* lay claim to being a deity. Instead, he manifested the *power* of deity as a gift from the *only* Deity —God the Father, Son, and Holy Ghost. Similarly, the judges of Israel fulfilled the same role and so *appeared* to be gods.

But in reality, they were sinful men who abused their office, and as a result God mocked them, saying, "I have said, Ye are gods. . . . ye shall die like men" (Psalm 82:6-7). Here were men who were supposed to emulate God's own character but who had become corrupt rulers. They were supposed to be defenders of "the poor and fatherless . . . the afflicted and needy" (v. 3, KJV), but instead they were proud men, who—though they looked like gods in the eyes of the people—would nevertheless demonstrate their frail mortality in the judgment of death.

In Genesis 3:5, we can clearly see that the teaching that man is "a god" or can become "like God" in relation to the divine essence originates not with God, but with Satan, who brought about the fall of man by deceiving Eve and then Adam into believing they would be like "gods."

Bible scholars have pointed out that Christ's statement, then, in John 10, is in the form of irony. God, they say, was stating something that would be recognized by anyone as an absurdity. Paul did the same with the Corinthians, mockingly referring to them as "kings," when both he and they knew they had not become kings at all. Instead, they were abusing their spiritual gifts. Similarly, in John 10, Jesus mocks the people as if to say, "You all think you're gods yourselves. What's one more god among you?" Irony is used to provoke us, not to inform us. It is not a basis for building a theology.

It is also pertinent to an understanding of John 10 that we remember that Satan is called "the ruler of this world" by no less an authority than the Lord Jesus Christ (John 14:30, NASB). And Paul reinforces this by calling him "the god of this age" (2 Corinthians 4:4). We can make a "god" out of anything—money, power, status, position, sex, patriotism, family, or, as in Lucifer's case, an angel. We can be our own "god." But to *call* something deity or to worship it or treat it as divine is quite another thing than its being by nature and in essence deity.

The Bible insists that there is but one Creator: "Besides Me there is no God" (Isaiah 45:5, NASB). We need only compare Deuteronomy 32:21, where God charged the Israelites with provoking Him to anger by the worship of "what is not God" (NASB), with Galatians 4:8, where Paul reminds the church that they served pagan deities before their conversion to Christ and "were slaves to those which *by nature* are no gods" (v. 8, NASB; italics added).

There is, therefore, only one God by nature, one God who is omnipotent, omniscient, omnipresent, one God who possesses characteristics and attributes that may be *imitated* but never *duplicated* in finite creations. When it is said, then, that man is or can be "a god," we must remember that Christ is stating (John 10, with Psalm 82) that only He, the incarnate Word, has the right to the title of deity among men, since He alone is designated "the only begotten God" (John 1:18, Greek text). What we worship then may become "a god" to us, but it is not deity, as it is written, "'You are my witnesses,' declares the Lord, 'and my servant whom I have chosen, so that you may know and believe me and understand that I am he. Before me no god was formed, nor will there be one after me" (Isaiah 43:10).

If this were not enough, such passages as Isaiah 44:6, 45:22, and Deuteronomy 6:4 would close the issue forever.

SECOND PETER 1:4

Another passage often seized upon by "little god" proponents, 2 Peter 1:4, reads:

> Whereby are given unto us exceeding great and precious promises: that by these ye might be partakers of the divine nature, having escaped the corruption that is in the world through lust (KJV).

The first word, "partaker," is interpreted by faith teachers to mean that man actually takes the divine nature for himself, that he actually participates in the divine nature or essence. It could be pointed out that on my last birthday, I partook of my birthday cake, but I did not become *part of* the cake. Similarly, Peter is certainly not teaching, in violation of all divine revelation, that man—a finite being—actually becomes one with the substance of deity. Let us find out what he *was* saying.

Hebrews 1:3 in the original Greek reminds us that Jesus Christ is the incarnate "character" of God, and herein lies the answer. Because of Christ's death in our place, we have figuratively "died" to sin (Romans 6:2) and are to live in the glory and power of His resurrection (Romans 6:5). We are to seek those things that are above where Christ dwells at the right hand of God, since we are "seated . . . in the heavenly realms in Christ Jesus" (Ephesians 2:6). We, like Jesus before us, are to reflect the character of God in our lives. We have been redeemed. God has recorded to our account the righteousness of His Son and has charged His Son with our guilt (Romans 4:4-8). The Christian, therefore, is justified by faith in Jesus Christ because he has become a partaker of the divine nature and character of God.

The image of God in man, which was shattered, marred, and defaced by sin, due to the first Adam, is restored in the last Adam, the Lord from heaven. We have become recipients of a *new* set of attributes patterned after the last Adam, motives and affections that are constantly at war with our fallen nature (Romans 7; Galatians 5:17).

We partake of the divine nature in the sense that we imitate, not duplicate, His character in our own lives. We were "predestined to be conformed to the likeness of [God's] Son" (Romans 8:29). As we were partakers of the fallen, Adamic nature, so now we are partakers of the resurrected Christ's character—not partakers of His divinity but of His sanctifying grace. We are being conformed to Christ's moral *image* (likeness), not to His essential *deity*. We are called to *resemble* Him in our life-style, but we cannot *become* Him (deity) in any way, shape, or form.

JOHN 1:12-13

"Yet to all who received him," says the gospel, "to those who believed in his name, he gave the right to become children of God—children not born of natural descent, nor of human decision or a husband's will, but born of God."

This text is usually offered, along with other passages referring to man as "begotten" by God, to erroneously prove that the believer, through a direct creative act of the Holy Spirit, becomes a god-bearing person, as Christ Himself was. (This is known in church history as the Apollinarian heresy.) But do such texts really teach that, as "born again" children of God, we ourselves share God's divinity?

In the same text cited by the faith teachers (John 1:12-13), John is urging for the uniqueness of Christ's relationship to the Trinity as "the only begotten (*monogenes*) Son of God." As believers, we are *adopted* children (Romans 8:15, 23; 2 Corinthians 5:20; Ephesians 1:5). When, for instance, Kenneth Copeland states, "God begets gods," he is ignoring the meaning of the term *begotten* and therefore falsely concludes, "You are all little gods."[15]

Jesus Christ is the unique, one-of-a-kind, incarnate Son of God and is, therefore, different from believers. "In the beginning was the Word," says John. "And the Word was with God, and the Word *was* God" (John 1:1, italics added). John the Baptist, our Lord's elder in age, nevertheless said of Christ, "He who comes after me has surpassed me because He was before me" (v. 15). The Baptist recognized that Jesus' origin was eternal. "No one has ever seen God, but God the One and Only, who is at the Father's side, has made him known" (v. 18). We are adopted in time; Jesus is God's eternally-begotten Son, whose origin and deity never began but have always been.

Kenneth Hagin, therefore, is gravely mistaken when he asserts that the Christian "is as much an incarnation [of God] as is Jesus of Nazareth."[16] And Kenneth Copeland is wrong when he insists, "Jesus is no longer the only begotten Son of

---

15. Kenneth Copeland, "Praise the Lord," Trinity Broadcasting Network, Text and tape on file with CRI.
16. Kenneth E. Hagin, "The Virgin Birth," *Word of Faith*, December 1977, p. 8.

God."[17] When the Word became flesh, God the Son remained what He always was—the second Person of the Trinity. Man is *not* an incarnation. He is *never* spoken of as such in Scripture—limited as he is to finite humanity.

None of these texts in any way suggest that redeemed men are or ever will be gods. As we have noted, Scripture forbids this as idolatry and blasphemy, in both testaments. We can see, then, that from their very language those who maintain the "little gods" doctrine are affirming a type of pagan polytheism over against classic monotheism. This constitutes, by any measurement, heretical doctrine.

FALSE PROPHECIES AND A "BORN AGAIN JESUS"

Those who teach the "little gods" heresy have also embraced other serious errors. Among them are (1) the teaching that Jesus never claimed to be God when on earth and (2) the belief that Jesus died on the cross spiritually as well as physically, assuming the nature of Satan, going to hell, suffering punishment at Satan's hand, and being "born again" in the resurrection. All of this had to happen, it is said, for our Lord to be our complete Savior. Deriving such blasphemies from E. W. Kenyon, Kenneth Copeland offered his followers an alleged prophecy from Jesus Christ Himself: "Don't be disturbed when people accuse you of thinking you are God. . . . They criticized me for claiming that I was God. But I didn't claim that I was God; I just claimed I walked with Him and that He was in me. Hallelujah, that's what you're doing."[18]

Elaborating on this later, Copeland declared, "I didn't say Jesus wasn't God. I said He didn't *claim* to be God when He lived on earth."[19] In response to his critics, Copeland said, "Search the Gospels for yourself. If you do, you will find what I say is true."[20]

17. Kenneth Copeland, *Now Are We in Christ Jesus* (Forth Worth, Tex.: Kenneth Copeland, n.d.), p. 24.
18. Kenneth Copeland, *Believer's Voice of Victory*, February 1987, p. 9.
19. Ibid., August 1988, p. 8.
20. Ibid.

Having done just that, we find that what he says is *not* true and that Jesus contradicted him in the gospel of John by affirming that He was the great I AM of Exodus 3, for which the Jews sought to stone Him, claiming blasphemy as their ground. They understood what apparently escaped Kenneth Copeland (i.e., that Jesus claimed deity). Prophecies such as Copeland's do not originate with Christ or the Holy Spirit, and Scripture flatly rejects them as false. We are, therefore, warned not to fear false prophets (Deuteronomy 18:22).

In his Philippian epistle, Paul confirms Christ's own self-understanding: "Let this mind be in you, which was also in Christ Jesus: Who, [existing or never ceasing to be in the form of God] [Greek participle, *huparchon*]" nevertheless "took upon him the form of a servant" (2:5-7, KJV).

The "born again Jesus" concept perverts, on the other hand, the doctrine of Christ's finished work on the cross, as demonstrated in the following quotations:

> It was not sufficient for Christ to offer up only His physical life on the cross. His human spirit had to "descend into hell". . . . While Christ was identified with sin, Satan and the hosts of hell ruled over Him as over any lost sinner. During that seemingly endless age in the nether abyss of death, Satan did with Him as he would, and all hell was "in carnival."[21]

> Jesus is the first person ever to be born again. Why did his spirit need to be born again? Because it was estranged from God. . . . What is spiritual death? The opposite of spiritual life. . . . Spiritual death means something more than separation from God. Spiritual death also means HAVING SATAN'S NATURE. . . . When one is born again, he takes upon himself the nature of God. Jesus tasted death —spiritual death—for every man. Sin is more than a physical act; it is a spiritual act. He became what we were, that we might become what He is. . . . His spirit was separated from God. And He went down into hell in our place.[22]

21. Billheimer, *Destined for the Throne*, pp. 83-84.
22. Kenneth E. Hagin, *The Name of Jesus* (Tulsa, Okla.: Kenneth Hagin Ministries, 1979), pp. 29-32.

If Jesus paid the full penalty of sin on the cross only, that is, by His physical death alone, then sin is wholly a physical act. . . . *Jesus' work was not finished when He yielded up His physical life on the cross* [italics added].[23]

It is unnecessary to analyze this error further. It proclaims itself. When Scripture speaks of Christ's being made sin for us (2 Corinthians 5:21), both the context and grammar indicate that He became a "sin *offering*," of which Isaiah spoke (Isaiah 53:4-7, 10) and which is duly recognized by a footnote on the passage in the *New International Version*.

The Multiplication of Error

Since the early 1970s, the same people who today espouse the "little gods" teaching have forged a virtually unbroken chain of serious doctrinal deviation. We were first told that the church had forgotten the "proper" concept of authority, so it was necessary for us all to have "shepherds" to disciple us. Thus, the "shepherding movement" spread and divided many churches across America. When this failed, the so-called "faith teaching" or "positive confession" was resurrected from the writings of Kenyon. The Christian church was then informed (and still is) that God can be "commanded" to respond to our prayers of faith and that we can create with our tongue both good and evil, prosperity or poverty, health or sickness. Such a position presupposed, in effect, that our faith (not God's sovereignty) was seated on the throne of heaven.

With great speed, these teachings expanded to the dictum that Christians are "little gods." As the faith movement is embraced by leaders within the Christian Reconstruction movement, the "little gods" are given a "dominion theology." One key reconstructionist leader, Gary North, boasts, "It has already begun: bringing together the postmillennial Christian

23. Billheimer, *Destined for the Throne*, p. 94.
24. Gary North, *Unholy Spirits* (Fort Worth: Dominion Press, 1986), pp. 392-93.

reconstructionists and the 'positive confession' charismatics. . . . A new fundamentalism is appearing."[24] Dominion theology, as it is called, states that until we do indeed subdue the creation, the return of the Lord Himself will be delayed.

The multiplication of erroneous doctrine is now complete. Unlimited faith, unlimited health, unlimited wealth, unlimited power, unlimited divinity, and now unlimited dominion.

The study of the kingdom of the cults has taught me many profitable lessons, and this is one of them—error begets error; heresy begets heresy and always in the name of truth, always in the name of the gospel. Those who propagate these erroneous views (the "little gods," the "born again Jesus," and so on) have sadly crossed over into the kingdom of the cults and stand in need of genuine repentance, lest they come under the inevitability of divine judgment.

It is dangerous, in the presence of God, to affirm oneself as a deity—even with a small "g." It is blasphemous to speak in the name of God and utter false prophecies. It is the height of theological folly to reduce God the Son, second Person of the holy Trinity, to a lost sinner with the nature of Satan and then send Him to hell with the requirement of regeneration before He can complete the work of redemption.

The words of the apostle ring true, "From such turn away" (2 Timothy 3:5, KJV). "Keep away from them. For such people are not serving our Lord Christ, but their own appetites. By smooth talk and flattery [what could be more flattering than being told you are a god?] they deceive the minds of naive people" (Romans 16:17-18).

DON'T TAKE THE BAIT!

One of the great paradoxes of Holy Scripture is Satan's desire to be "like the Most High" (Isaiah 14:14). He was hurled from the pinnacle of glory to eternal judgment as a result. When God created man in His own image, jealous Lucifer tempted Adam and Eve with the luscious bait, "You shall be as gods." Even after they had fallen, humanity was promised a Redeemer. Through faith in Him, believers could have the relationship with God that Lucifer so desperately craved. It is no wonder that Satan hates the church, the bride of Christ, the building of God, because within it God has been pleased to dwell (1 Corinthians 3:16). Remarkably, He has described that relationship as "the body of Christ," built upon an unshakable, enduring foundation (Ephesians 2:20).

We are then, as believers, in a union of fellowship with the Trinity. We are joint-heirs with Christ (John 17:11-26; Romans 8:17), eternally subject as He is Himself to the Father of spirits (1 Corinthians 15:28) in love and by choice. The church is not her own; she has been purchased by the sacrifice of Calvary. Our identity is greater than any human concept of "godhood." We are the heirs of eternity, recipients of an indescribable gift.

Let us not cheapen that inheritance or dilute it with perverted theology. The cost is far too great.

For we do not preach ourselves, but Jesus Christ as Lord, and ourselves as your servants for Jesus' sake. For God, who said, "Let light shine out of darkness," made his light shine in our hearts to give us the light of the knowledge of the glory of God in the face of Christ.

—2 Corinthians 4:5-6

We have seen his glory, the glory of the One and Only, who came from the Father, full of grace and truth.

—John 1:14

6

Who Do TV Preachers Say That I Am?

Rod Rosenbladt

Two Foundational Facts of Human Enlightenment: (1) There is a God; (2) You are not He!

So reads the caption of a popular poster.

Among [the] Jews there suddenly turns up a man who goes about talking as if He was God. He claims to forgive sins. He says He has always existed. He says He is coming to judge the world at the end of time. Now let us get this clear. Among Panthesists, like the Indians, anyone might say that he was a part of God or one with God: there would be nothing odd about it. But this man, since He was a Jew, could not mean that kind of God. God, in their language, meant the Being outside the world Who had made it and was infinitely different from anything else. And when you have grasped that, you will see that what this man said was, quite simply, the most shocking thing that has ever been uttered by human lips.[1]

So reads a passage in C. S. Lewis's book *Mere Christianity.* There *is* a qualitative difference between the Creator and the creature. Following the great doctors, Luther and Calvin were clear in stressing that point. If there was one thing about which they left no question, it was that man is not a part of

1. C. S. Lewis, *Mere Christianity* (New York: Macmillan, 1964), pp. 54-55.

107

God, a subset of the divine, "a small spark of the larger flame."

Walter Martin has already pointed out the failure among many televangelists to make such a Creator-creature distinction. It will be the purpose of this chapter to understand the sort of heretical Christology (view of Christ) we discover when men try to become gods. A survey of the statements included in my analysis will demonstrate beyond doubt that many popular media evangelists are preaching what amounts to blasphemy in their references to Christ's Person and work. Not only do they sacrifice the orthodox view of God and twist the Scriptures, but in their lust for godhood they also challenge the biblical, historic definitions of Christ's person .

Christianity Is Christ! reads the title of a small volume by a British writer. And so it is. Whatever else we may say about historic Christianity, it centers on the Person and work of Jesus of Nazareth: His deity, His humanity, and His atoning death as a substitute for sinners. To fool around with the biblical material at *these* points is to engage in error at the level of eternal loss.

Popular theologian J. I. Packer is correct in calling Christians to guard against "any fragmenting of the seamless robe of scriptural testimony to Jesus' person and place." Yet, it is precisely at such key doctrinal junctures where a host of contemporary American media preachers and teachers are denying Christ. Their list of heresies is a relatively substantial one, given the short list of televangelists, but some distinguish themselves by embracing more than one.

A MAGICAL CHRIST

Like the Gnostics of old, today's "faith teachers" stress a metaphysical, mystical, magical Christ. Of course, all orthodox Christians believe in a *supernatural* Savior, but Gnostics view Jesus as a power-dispensing fetish who gains them access to both mystical and material treasures.

These "faith teachers," also known as "positive confessionists," often remake or ignore the most basic biblical assertions about Christ, assertions proclaimed in the Nicene and Chalcedonian Creeds. Says the Nicene, "We believe . . . in one Lord Jesus Christ, begotten of His Father before all worlds, God of God, Light of Light, very God of very God, begotten—not made—being of one substance with the Father by whom all things were made. . . . " How could the clear message of the gospel be twisted into the categories proclaimed so often by certain TV preachers?

Sociologists tell us that the appeal of power is almost irresistible during those periods in which a country's basic values seem to be in recession, times in which a people's power over their own destinies seems to be falling through their fingers as so much sand, eras in which a culture seems to be in decline rather than ascendancy.[2] What the American televangelists offer is power in an era of impotence, magic in a time of fear, divinity in a time of human weakness. One need only turn to the television to observe gatherings of thousands listening to the message of power by means of magic. By many measures, these preachers are succeeding in their proclamation. To this phenomenon many mainline evangelicals seem sublimely indifferent.

But regardless of sociological factors, how could it happen that large Christian denominations that consider themselves biblical and evangelical (one is forced by recent memory to think first of the Pentecostal ones) would allow their people to be bombarded by such esoteric teachings as we hear from so-called faith teachers? What would entice the preachers of a Christ-centered church body to exchange the historic Christ for what Luther called a "theology of glory?"

Could it be that the "upward" tendency (that is, the desire to climb up toward or even into the divine) in some American evangelical or Pentecostal circles is similar to the "upward" tendency Luther saw in the medieval church, with all of its superstition, mysticism, and magic?[3] It is quite possi-

2. Max Weber, "The Sociology of Charismatic Authority," in *From Max Weber: Essays in Sociology*, ed. H. H. Gerth and C. Wright Mills (London: Oxford Univ. Press, 1946), pp. 246-52.
3. Philip Watson, *Let God Be God* (Philadelphia: Fortress, 1970), pp. 73, 148.

ble that the magic powers attributed to the purchase of alleged relics (a martyr's tooth, a piece of the cross, a patch of cloth from Jesus' robe) is parallel to the offering of modern-day prayer cloths, "holy oil," and similar gimmicks.

Martin Luther attacked medieval superstition, insisting that Jesus was *not* a mystical ladder one climbed to health, wealth, and happiness—or glorification. What he called the "theology of glory"—the desire for deification—is characterized by three approaches, or three "ladders." One historian explains:

> The medieval interpretation of Christianity [says Dr. Nygren] is marked throughout by the upward tendency. This tendency asserts itself no less in the moralistic piety of popular Catholicism than in the rational theology of Scolasticism and the ecstatic religiosity of Mysticism. . . .
> They all know a Way by which man can work his way up to God, whether it is the Way of merit known to practical piety, the Way of mysticism, or the Way of speculative thought . . . Man must mount up to God by means of one of the three heavenly ladders. Against this upward tendency or ascent Luther makes his protest. He will have nothing to do with this "climbing up into the majesty of God." In place of this *'theologia gloriae'* [theology of glory] he demands a *'theologia crucis'* [theology of the cross].[4]

The only way we can know God is by the Son's becoming a lowly servant. Sinners cannot climb up to God through "revelation knowledge" (as the heretical Gnostics, ancient and modern, espouse) or through mystical experience any more than by merit. Instead of climbing up to God in His glory, they must embrace the God who came down to us in humility.

THE TWO NATURES OF CHRIST UNDERSTOOD HISTORICALLY

At the heart of the church's understanding of Christ is the belief in His two natures: human and divine. The great

4. Ibid, pp. 94-93.

bishop Athanasius (A.D. 328-73) argued that Jesus was not some mixture of "God substance" and "human substance," as the "faith teachers" assert. Athanasius faced heresy in the form of Arianism (the belief that Jesus was the first created being, not of the same eternal essence as God), subordinationism or semi-Arianism (the belief that Jesus was of similar divine essence, but subordinate to Him), and adoptionism (the belief that Jesus was adopted by the Father at His baptism—or in hell, as the "faith teachers" insist. He *became* the Christ, they taught).

The key question was this: Is Jesus of (1) a different substance from the Father, (2) a similar substance, or (3) the same substance as the Father? The church made clear the biblical teaching: Jesus is singularly, uniquely, solely, exclusively, with the Holy Spirit, of the *same* substance with the Father.

The Catholic church resisted the mounting heresies with regard to the Person of Christ, and when the Protestant Reformers came along it was clear that Protestants would continue to affirm Catholic Christology. Radical sects (some Roman, some Protestant), similar in both theology and spirit to today's "faith teachers," did drink from the heretical wells of the past, but they were immediately recognized as heretics and excluded from the common Christian fellowship.

The Reformers knew, unlike Copeland, Hagin, and the others, that unless Jesus was true God and true man—indeed, history's *only* God-Man, united and preserved in one single consciousness—we were still in our sins. Luther and Calvin would agree with Anselm (A.D. 1033-1109), in his major orthodox volume, *Cur deus homo [Why the the God-Man]:* If Jesus Christ were not God in human flesh, He could not have functioned as our Redeemer, and we are all lost. Very simply, only a man could stand in the place of sinful persons and bear their punishment; but if Jesus were only man, His sacrifice would be insufficient. Our redemption rests particularly on His deity. Thus, Christ's saving *work* is our best guide to determining His *nature.*

CONTRASTED WITH THE TV PREACHERS

Virtually all of the leading American TV ministers have drunk at the trough of the esoteric, Swedenborgian, theosophical speculations of the late E. W. Kenyon. As one writer put it, "It's one thing to argue with a speculative philosopher who knows that he is one; it's quite another to argue with a speculative philosopher who is *too ignorant* to realize he *is* one!" Kenyon would be of the latter type—a writer who would condemn philosophy as worldly, yet use it on his audience whenever it was needed.

One finds a common theme, or motif, in many of the televangelists, one which should surprise no student of church history (particularly American church history). It is this: *All of "denominational" Christendom has been in the grip of confusion, but the truth has finally been revealed to the television listeners through the revelations given directly to the true leader.*

Sadly, those who "have the ear" of the masses as far as evangelism goes (if sheer numbers are our guide), could not care less for careful scriptural exegesis and being in line with ancient Christianity. To the average observer, they appear to care much more about larger offerings, visions, signs, and flattering teachings. As we now engage in an analysis of the statements of the televangelists themselves, remember that no one ever promised that television entertainers had to (1) make sense, or (2) tell the truth.

KENNETH HAGIN

"Physically we are born of human parents and partake of their nature. Spiritually we are born of God and partake of His nature."[5] "You are as much the incarnation of God as Jesus Christ was. Every man who has been born again is an incarnation and Christianity is a miracle. The believer is as much an incarnation as was Jesus of Nazareth."[6]

5. Kenneth E. Hagin, *How You Can Be Led by the Spirit of God* (Tulsa, Okla.: Kenneth Hagin Ministries, 1978) p. 94.
6.. Kenneth E. Hagin, *Word of Faith*, December 1980, p. 14.

FRED PRICE

In an interview with Trinity Broadcasting Network president Paul Crouch, televangelist Fred Price said the following:

Crouch: Do you believe that believers can literally call things into existence just as God did by the word of His mouth?

Price: Now you have to qualify that because we are not God, like God is God. We are (and some people have a problem with this) only to the extent that we are the son of God. [Turning to Paul and Jan] Don't you have a son?

Crouch: Two sons: Paul, Jr., and Matthew.

Price: They're both Crouch. . . . They're Crouch. In fact, if we dissected them, you'd find some of you in them.

Crouch: Exactly.

Price: All right, we're the children of God. We've been recreated and have been made new creatures in Christ Jesus. So I'm God as much as your sons are Crouches. But certainly I'm not God God, the Creator God. . . . "[7]

KENNETH COPELAND

It is highly unlikely that anyone in the "faith movement" has done more to popularize the ideas of E. W. Kenyon than Kenneth Copeland. Let us follow him through his rationale, his "systematic theology," invented by Kenyon and defended by the "faith teachers." We will limit our examination to its teaching on the Person of Christ.

Stage One: Who was Jesus before the incarnation?

This is one of the most difficult questions to answer, it seems, for the faith teachers. The bulk of their theology centers on the incarnate Jesus, the divinized man. It is unclear from our research as to the faith teachers' position with regard to Christ's preincarnate state. Was He the eternal Son of

7. Paul Crouch and Ted Price, "Praise the Lord," Trinity Broadcasting Network, Jan. 10, 1986.

God, uncreated, sharing equal deity, equal infinity with the Father and the Holy Spirit, as the Scriptures teach?

Stage Two: Who was Jesus in His incarnation: divinized man or the God-Man?

Whatever their view with regard to our Lord's preincarnate state, their position *is* clear with regard to His *incarnate* state. "This man—Jesus," says Copeland, "was a carbon copy of the one who walked through the Garden of Eden."[8] In other words, Jesus was no different from Adam. If that analysis sounds a bit too hasty, take a look at the following Copeland remark:

> He [Jesus] referred to God as His Father (which enraged the Pharisees), but He never made the assertion that He was the most High God. In fact, He told His disciples that the Father God was greater and mightier than He (John 14:28). Why didn't Jesus openly proclaim Himself as God during His 33 years on earth? For one single reason. He hadn't come to earth as God, He'd come as man.[9]

All of this was in response to questions raised by a supposed revelation Copeland alleges to have had from Jesus Christ. Our Lord is alleged to have said:

> Don't be disturbed when people accuse you of thinking you're God. . . . they crucified Me for claiming I was God. But I didn't claim I was God; I just claimed I walked with Him and that He was in Me. Hallelujah. That's what you're doing.[10]

Since this alleged revelation, a number of Christians have sought to confront Copeland. In fact, Walter Martin sent a detailed letter expressing great concern over the comment.

8. Kenneth Copeland, "Jesus Our Lord of Glory," *Believer's Voice of Victory*, April 1982, p. 2.
9. Kenneth Copeland, *Believer's Voice of Victory*, August 1988, p. 8.
10. Kenneth Copeland, "Take Time to Pray," *Believer's Voice of Victory*, February 1987.

Copeland refused correction or even correspondence on the subject and reissued his position, standing by his alleged revelation.[11] "Jesus hadn't come to earth as God; He'd come as man. He'd set aside His divine power and had taken on the form of a human being—with all its limitations," he said. He said Jesus lived on earth "not as God but as a man"[12] and prayed "not as the divine One who had authority as God but as a man, . . . "[13] arguing that Jesus never believed Himself to be "the Most High God."[14]

Known as kenotic theology, the view that Christ emptied Himself of deity in the incarnation is heretical, and Dr. Martin confronted both Copeland and Crouch on just this point.[15] In correspondence on file with the Christian Research Institute, Copeland has refused to even discuss these issues. According to the *Evangelical Dictionary of Theology,*

> all forms of classical orthodoxy either explictly reject or reject in principle kenotic theology. This is because God must be affirmed to be changeless; any concept of the incarnation that would imply change would mean that God would cease to be God.[16]

During a crusade, Copeland gave his audience a familiar lesson: "I say this and repeat it so it doesn't upset you too bad. . . . When I read in the Bible where He [Jesus] says, 'I Am,' I say, 'Yes, I Am, too!'"[17] But when Shirley MacClain is shown in a television movie giving in to her New Age instructor's charge to repeat, "I am God" (which is what is meant by

11. Kenneth Copeland, in Christian Research Institute (CRI) correspondence. Copies are available upon request.
12. Kenneth Copeland, *Believer's Voice of Victory,* August 1988, p. 3.
13. Ibid., p. 4.
14. Ibid., p. 8
15. Walter Martin, in CRI correspondence, May 5, 1988. Copies are available upon request.
16. Walter A. Elwell, ed., *Evangelical Dictionary of Theology* (Grand Rapids: Baker, 1984), p. 607.
17. Kenneth Copeland, tape of crusade, July 19, 1987, on file with CRI.

"I Am"), evangelicals get up in arms! Why the reaction to the one but not to the other?

In yet another prophecy, Jesus is alleged to have told Copeland, "Pray to yourself because I'm in yourself and you're in Myself. We are one Spirit, saith the Lord. . . . Many of you are going to have visitations from the Spirit realm. Many of you will have divinely appointed visions and dreams. . . . You're just part of the times. It's time for spiritual activity to increase."[18]

In fact, he asserts, historic Christianity is mistaken in believing that the incarnate Christ was any different from any other human being. "They mistakenly believe," Copeland asserts, "that Jesus was able to work wonders, to perform miracles, and to live above sin because He had divine power that we don't have. Thus, they've never really aspired to live like He lived."

"They don't realize," says Copeland, "that when Jesus came to earth, He voluntarily gave up that advantage [deity], living His life here not as God, but as a man. He had no innate supernatural powers. He had no ability to perform miracles until after He was anointed by the Holy Spirit as recorded in Luke 3:22." "He ministered," Copeland insists, "as a man anointed by the Holy Spirit."[19]

In other words, Jesus' power came not from His being the second Person of the Holy Trinity, but from His being indwelt by the Holy Spirit and anointed. Since believers are filled with the Holy Spirit and anointed, they too possess the same supernatural powers. According to the faith teachers, there is no qualitative difference between the believer and the incarnate Christ, according to the faith teachers. With training from the evangelist, you, too, can become a Jesus. The faith teachers take this one step further, however.

18. Kenneth Copeland, tape of "Victory Campaign," Dallas, Texas, on file with CRI.
19. Kenneth Copeland, *Believer's Voice of Victory,* August 1988, p. 8.

Stage Three: Is Jesus a born-again man?

According to the "faith" message, Jesus "surrendered to the lordship of Satan" on the cross. "Jesus accepted the sin nature of Satan in His own spirit," says Copeland. God allegedly told Copeland, "You don't know what happened at the cross" (one of Copeland's prophecies I'm inclined to accept).

Then Copeland tells us how Jesus surrendered to Satan's lordship:

> Why do you think Moses, obeying the instruction of God, hung the serpent up on the pole instead of a lamb? That used to bug me. I said, "Why in the world would you want to put a snake up there—the sign of Satan? Why didn't you put a lamb on that pole?" And the Lord said, "Because it was the sign of Satan that was hanging on the cross." He said [Jesus speaking to Copeland], "I accepted in my own spirit spiritual death and the light was turned off."[20]

Gloria Copeland adds to this metaphysical myth:

> After Jesus was made sin, He had to be born again. . . . Once again, He was the righteousness of God, and once again, eternal life was His nature.[21]

Thus, Jesus was, says Kenneth Copeland, the first born-again man:

> .It is important for us to realize that a born-again man defeated Satan. . . . Colossians 1:18 refers to Jesus as the firstborn from the dead. . . . He was the first man to be reborn under the new covenant.[22]

Copeland concludes, "God turned to a man [Jesus] and called Him God. He is in a higher position now than He was

20. Kenneth Copeland, "What Happened from the Cross to the Throne," tape, side 2, on file with CRI.
21. Gloria Copeland, *God's Will for You* (Fort Worth: Kenneth Copeland, 1978), p. 5.
22. Kenneth Copeland, *Believer's Voice of Victory,* September 1980, p. 6.

before He headed to the cross."[23] Hence, God turns to other born-again men and calls *them* gods, too.

The theory that Jesus died both physically and spiritually is equally damning. Of course, in biblical and historic Christianity it has been believed that Jesus was God and if He were to have died spiritually, there would be a time when the second Person of the Godhead ceased to exist. Of course, if Jesus were not God anyway, His dying spiritually would present no problem to the "faith teachers."

In the new birth, the believer is said to become an incarnation of God. We have already seen, particularly in Walter Martin's chapter, the numerous statements referring to the believer's being "as much the incarnation of God as Jesus of Nazareth." E. W. Kenyon claimed, "The Lord Jesus was not, however, a 'one-of-a-kind.' 'Incarnation' can be repeated in each and every one of us. Every man who has been 'born again' is an Incarnation."[24]

Kenneth Copeland expounds on this idea in another alleged encounter with God:

> And the whole New Testament calls Him the first-born. Born, born, born, born, born, born again. I was born again. Born, born, born, born. The word "born" began to ring in my spirit; it just began to roll around: born, born. I never had let Him go through that in my own thinking. . . . And while I was laying there thinking about these things, the Spirit of God spoke to me. And He said, "Son, realize this: Now follow Me in this, don't let your tradition trip you up." He said, "Think this way: A twice-born man whipped Satan in his own domain."
>
> And I threw my Bible down. I said, "What?" He said, "A born-again man defeated Satan. The first-born of many brethren defeated him." He said, "You are the very image and the very copy of that one." I said, "Goodness gracious, sakes alive!" And I began to see what had gone on in there, and I said, "You don't mean—you couldn't dare mean, that I could have done the same thing?" He said, "Oh, yeah, if

23. Kenneth Copeland, "What Happened from the Cross to the Throne," tape, side 2, on file with CRI.
24. E. W. Kenyon, *The Father and His Family*.

you'd had the knowledge of the Word of God that He did, you could've done the same thing, 'cause you're a reborn man, too."[25]

Finally, by reducing Jesus to the first born-again Christian, these new Gnostics have found their entrance to the "naked God" and to their own deification. Hence, Copeland's remark "You need to realize that you are not a spiritual schizophrenic—half-God and half-Satan—you are all God. The problem area is not in your spirit; it lies in your mind and body."[26]

Copeland's remarks, therefore, reiterated, paraphrased, and restated by the other faith teachers, demonstrate that this movement is self-consciously heretical. That is, its leaders are aware that they are teaching views that are contrary to historic, orthodox, mainstream Christianity, but, of course, that's nothing more than "tradition" that can "trip you up."[27] Most of these faith teachers even glory in their being at odds with historic Christianity.

PAUL CROUCH

At the time of this publication, founder, president, and host of the Trinity Broadcasting Network, Paul Crouch, has resisted frequent attempts at correction. "I AM A LITTLE GOD. I am a little god." "Critics, be gone!"[28] he says.

ORTHODOXY VERSUS HERESY

It does not take a theological wizard to recognize the heresy represented by those statements. In almost every point of Christology, these televangelists have deviated from orthodoxy and have promoted their own fantasy savior. They have confused the only infinite Creator with His finite creation.

25. Kenneth Copeland, "Substitution and Identification," tape, on file with CRI.
26. Kenneth Copeland, *Believer's Voice of Victory,* March 1982, p. 2.
27. Kenneth Copeland, "Substitution and Identification," tape.
28. Paul Crouch, "Praise the Lord," Trinity Broadcasting Network, July 7, 1986.

They have mingled the divine and human natures of Christ, creating a muddy mess that is neither fully divine nor fully human but which conveniently allows them to exalt themselves to divine status. Ignoring the many Scriptures affirming Christ as the unique and *only* essential ("begotten") Son of God, they have shunted Him aside, granting Him only elder-sibling status.

Liberal theologian D. M. Baillie wrote, "Jesus is the One in whom human selfhood fully came into its own and lived its fullest life . . . because His human selfhood was wholly yielded to God." When the "liberals" were spouting this stuff, we balked—and rightly so. When Mormons and Jehovah's Witnesses reduce Jesus to *a* god and exalt themselves to equality with Him, we write them off as cults. But when self-proclaimed "evangelical" preachers offer the same deception, we insist that judgment partakes of disunity. Indeed it does, and that is why judgment must be restrained by the parameters of Scripture, not by the whims of self-proclaimed inquisitors. Nevertheless, in this case there can be no unity. Until these heretics repent, the evangelical church must declare them spiritual outlaws.

I am astonished that you are so quickly deserting the one who called you by the grace of Christ and are turning to a different gospel—which is really no gospel at all. Evidently some people are throwing you into confusion and are trying to pervert the gospel of Christ. But even if we or an angel from heaven should preach a gospel other than the one we preached to you, let him be eternally condemned! As we have already said, so now I say again: If anybody is preaching to you a gospel other than what you accepted, let him be eternally condemned!

—Galatians 1:6-9

7

The TV Gospel

Michael Horton

Of course, the obnoxiousness of offering salvation for money is itself heretical, indeed, pagan. Nevertheless, the gospel heralded by some of the television preachers is even more perverted than that proclaimed by Tetzel's indulgences at the time of Luther. For this new message moves beyond the "prosperity gospel" and promises salvation in terms of the Gnostic heresy we have already described in previous chapters. It is not only crass and ugly; it is *overtly* blasphemous and anti-Christian. We have seen that some TV pulpits are occupied by those who are preaching another Word, another God, and another Christ. But in this chapter we will see how they preach another *gospel.*

THE GOSPEL OF HEALTH, WEALTH, AND HAPPINESS

It is appropriate that a prosperity gospel be born in the hedonistic, self-centered, get-rich-quick milieu of modern American society. We are, by nature, pagan. Either our religion will transform us or we will transform our religion to suit our sympathies.

But the "prosperity evangelists" are not just odd merchandisers. They have worked out a whole theological scheme for what they believe.

"By his wounds," Isaiah prophesied concerning the coming Messiah, "we are healed" (Isaiah 53:5). That verse is the key proof text used by the "name it and claim it" teachers, or "faith teachers," as they call themselves. When Jesus died on the cross, these teachers say, He carried both our sins and sickness; therefore, healing is available now for those who will "name it and claim it."

But the apostle Peter did not handle the prophecy so carelessly. Rather, when he referred to the passage, he placed it within its context: "He himself bore our *sins* in his body on the tree, so that we might die to *sins* and live for *righteousness; for by his wounds you have been healed*" (1 Peter 2:24, italics added). In chapter 4 of this book, pages 67-70, Henry Krabbendam reminded us of a cardinal principle of interpretation: Scripture interprets Scripture. If one passage is unclear, let the other parts of Scripture clarify it. If the prosperity evangelists had done that, they would have recognized that Isaiah's reference to our being healed by Christ's wounds concerns His sacrificial death for our sins, not the healing of our physical body.

But the prosperity Bible does not deal only with freedom from sickness. It would have us read, "He Himself bore our sickness *and poverty* in His body on the tree, so that we might die to *infirmity* and *lack*; for by His wounds you have been healed." In contrast, there was no question in the mind of the apostles that the gospel promised "spiritual riches in heavenly places in Christ" (Ephesians 1:3), not earthly ones. Our Lord was afflicted so that we could be healed. But that is a metaphor for the wonderful truth that the penalty justly meant for us was endured instead by Christ, our substitute. The rod of justice that dealt the Lamb of God such bitter blows declared *us* righteous!

It is to trivialize greatly the work of Christ to suggest that God the Father sent His only-begotten Son into the world to bear the world's blasphemy, insults, and violence, and, most of all, to bear the Father's wrath—all for increased cash flow and fewer bouts with asthma. It is to make a joke out of the great displeasure, anger, and wrath God has toward sin and sinful persons. God's real problem, say the faith teachers, is not that we are wicked, selfish, God-hating rebels who deserve eternal punishment, but that we aren't enjoying ourselves!

For the faith teachers, sickness is "all in the head." Much like Christian Science (whose origins are shared by the "faith teachers"), this philosophy denies the reality of negative things—sin, sickness, poverty, and depression. The supposed reality of their existence is blamed on the failure of the believer to speak the word of faith—a sort of "abracadabra" recited to decree health and prosperity. Kenneth E. Hagin, commenting on Christ's remark, "If you ask Me anything in My name, I will do it," asserts, "Here, the Greek word translated 'ask' means 'demand'. . . . Let that soak in a little. You're not demanding anything of the Father. . . . You're demanding of the Devil."[1]

Hagin to the contrary, the same apostle who recorded Christ's promise also recorded a clarification of that promise. Jesus informs us that "If we ask anything *according to his will*, he hears us" (1 John 5:14, italics added). Moreover, to suggest that we are demanding health, wealth, and happiness *from the devil*, is, once again, a revival of Gnosticism. Those ancient heretics, too, believed that the physical, natural world, belongs to Satan. As a result, two camps developed within Gnosticism: the *ascetics,* who renounced the world and all earthly possessions and lived in monastic communes; and the *antinomians,* who indulged themselves in every possible license—for was not God concerned only with the spirit, not the body? One could indulge the physical monster while staying close to the Lord "in His spirit." And because the devil ruled the physical realm, men were merely indulging themselves at his expense when they demanded this or that.

But what if a Christian *doesn't* experience prosperity? What explanation do the faith healers give when that happens? Though they cite a number of explanations, two are most frequent: a lack of knowledge and a lack of obedience.

1. Kenneth E. Hagin, *Faith Food for Winter* (Tulsa, Okla.: Kenneth Hagin Ministries), p. 58.

By lack of knowledge the faith healers do not mean intellectual or rational knowledge, mind you, but a mystical, Gnostic, direct knowledge through which the believer plugs into the spiritual realm and discovers his inner powers, a parallel to the "gnosis" of the mystery religions. By lack of obedience the faith healers mean that the truly obedient believer must decree things into existence. If a believer "insists" on "allowing" Satan to hold his goods, he is being disobedient. Hagin tells of an alleged conversation he had with God that was periodically interrupted by Satan. Hagin asked God to silence the devil, but God said He couldn't. So Hagin commanded Satan to be quiet. "Jesus looked at me," Hagin says, "and said, 'If you hadn't done anything about that, I couldn't have.'"[2]

Since God's hands are tied, it is up to the believer to decree prosperity. So, to ask the question once more, what happens when the believer "decrees" it but nothing happens?

Pat Robertson asserts that poverty "is a curse that comes upon those who either have not served God properly, or who are not following certain laws of God, or are temporarily in transit to one of God's destinations."[3] The father of the faith movement, E. W. Kenyon, states, "You are suffering . . . because you have refused your place in Christ."[4]

It is amazing that the faith teachers could miss such clear statements as Paul's, who said he wanted to know "the fellowship of sharing in [Christ's] sufferings" (Philippians 3:10). "For," said the apostle, "suffering produces perseverance; [and] perseverance [produces] character" (Romans 5:3). By seeking to escape rather than enduring our trials, we short-circuit the sanctifying, character-building process. Furthermore, Peter commanded, "Those who suffer *according to*

2. Kenneth E. Hagin, *Having Faith in Your Faith* (Tulsa, Okla.: Faith Library, 1980).
3. Pat Robertson, *Answers*, Christian Broadcasting Network (CBN) Partners' Edition (Virginia Beach: Christian Broadcasting Network, 1984), p. 155.
4. E. W. Kenyon, quoted in Judith Matta, *The Born-Again Jesus* (Fullerton, Calif.: Spirit of Truth, 1987), p. 33.

God's will should commit themselves to their faithful Creator and continue to do good" in spite of their adversity (1 Peter 4:19, italics added). But "Jesus was not poor in His ministry," Copeland insists. "He had a treasurer!" And Oral Roberts has just published his treatise *How I Learned that Jesus Was Not Poor.*

In connection with this failure to "decree" prosperity, one must point out the important distinction the faith teachers make between *rhema* and *logos.* The Greek language offers two terms for "word," whereas English has only one. In the original Greek, *rhema* and *logos* are little more than synonyms. There is very little difference between the two words as they were used. The parallel in English would be the words "big" and "large." We select the word most appropriate to the sentence, but both are essentially the same in meaning. The same is true of *rhema* and *logos.*

But the faith teachers have invented a false distinction in meaning between those two Greek words. *Rhema,* they say, is the "word" believers are to "decree" or "speak forth" in order to bring prosperity or healing into this dimension. It is the "abracadabra." Then there is the *logos,* or "revelation word," which is the mystical, direct word that God speaks to the initiates. The term can refer also to the Bible but is usually spoken of in the context of dreams, visions, and private conversations between God and His "agent." Hence, when one reads references in the faith-teacher literature to "God's Word," or "acting on the Word," and so on, the author is most likely intending, not the written Word of God, the Bible, so much as either his own "decree" *(rhema)* or God's personal word to him *(logos).*[5] Pat Robertson states, "Most people ask God for a miracle but many omit a key requirement

---

5. Charles Capps, *Authority in Three Worlds* (Tulsa, Okla.: Harrison House, 1980), pp. 81-83. See also Capps, *The Tongue: A Creative Force* (Tulsa, Okla.: Harrison House, 1977), pp. 32, 34; Robertson, *Answers*, pp. 215, 219; E. W. Kenyon, *Jesus the Healer*, 19th ed. (Lynnwood: Kenyon Gospel Pub. Society, 1968), p. 6; Gloria Copeland, *And Jesus Healed Them All* (Fort Worth, Tex.: Kenneth Copeland Ministries, 1981), p. 18.

—the *spoken word*. God has given us authority over disease, over demons, over sickness, over storms, over finances. We are to declare that authority in Jesus' name." "We are," says Robertson, "to command the money to come to us. . . . "[6]

A further lack of obedience can be demonstrated by failing to "seed" one's faith. This requires payment of a certain sum of money to a particular ministry. Those who are on the mailing lists of the televangelists referred to in this book receive numerous testimonies along the lines of "I seeded $300, decreed my husband's salvation, and he got saved last Sunday!" Tetzel would have loved it!

Oral Roberts was the first to popularize the "seed faith" concept, but many since have seized upon the notion as a "You give me a check and, in turn, I'll 'agree' with you so that you will get what we decree" sort of arrangement. A point of contact between the evangelist and the believer is established through holy oil, water from the Jordan, a photocopy of a napkin on which the evangelist traced his hand (Roberts, Tilton, and others), and the "seed" money is but a token or pledge of just how earnest the believer is in his faith. Hence, one's failure to receive what one decrees can also be charged to the disobedience of withholding the appropriate contribution.

THE GNOSTIC GOSPEL

Throughout this chapter, as indeed throughout this book, we have made references to "Gnosticism" and its revival among some televangelists. At this point, it is essential that we understand the Gnostic view of salvation. If we can read labels, we are less likely to consume poisonous substances! And if we can recognize the key features of the ancient Gnostic heresy, we can more easily avoid those errors in our own thinking.

It is also essential that we recognize that something here goes beyond a crassly materialistic, exploitative, and greedy gospel. Gnosticism is a tremendously warped system of

6. Robertson, *Answers*, p. 76.

beliefs. The promises of prosperity are bad enough. But other promises, far more treacherous, are made by television's "faith teachers." Let us compare the ancient Gnostic heresy to the modern version at key points directly touching the gospel.

CREATION

Gnosticism is marked by a *dualism* in which the world is divided sharply between "spiritual" (good) and "material" or "physical" (bad) realms. Thus, Gnosticism emphasizes the spiritual realm to the denigration or exclusion of the natural realm. Reason, earthly passions, or other elements that make us "human" are dismissed as corrupt. In that the spiritual is seen as divine, it is regarded as the only genuinely good aspect of our being. The spirit realm is regarded as being closer to God; consequently, the more one moves into the physical or natural realm, the further one moves from God Himself.

This understanding of the nature of things does not, of course, keep many of the leading televangelists of the prosperity gospel from being materialistic, for, as you remember, cars, boats, and planes are regarded as simply stolen goods the believer is reclaiming from the devil. Nevertheless, the faith teachers work out their sharp division between the spiritual and natural realms.

For instance, according to Kenneth Hagin, "the mind is something that will trip you and cause you to fall."[7] The believer must learn to control the mind with his spirit and feed it with positive confessions rather than allowing it simply to accept the reality it perceives. The mind is seen as evil because it is human, and, therefore, satanic.

Kenneth Copeland insists that believers do not even possess Adam's nature. That is, it is not because humans inherit Adam's fallen moral nature that they are fallen. Then why are they fallen? Whose nature *do* they possess? Copeland comments: "Now, some folks claim that you still got Ad-

7. Kenneth E. Hagin, videotape 1, on file with Christians United for Reformation (CURE)

am's nature in you. Well, you didn't have Adam's nature in the first place. You had Satan's nature in you."[8] In line with his Gnostic presuppositions, Copeland rejects the historic Christian view that humans are fallen as the consequence of inheriting original sin. Instead, the Fall is the consequence of there being a defect in human nature apart from human sin. We actually possessed a satanic nature, Copeland says.

Copeland argues that when we become believers, we escape the natural realm, with its physical laws, and become engaged to spiritual laws. "You need to realize," Copeland says, "that you are not a spiritual schizophrenic—half-God and half-Satan—you are all-God. *The problem area is not in your spirit; it lies in your mind and body*" (italics added).[9] Before one is born again, then, he is satanic (by virtue of his humanity); upon conversion he becomes a spirit-god inhabiting a physical body.

To get an idea of just how foreign this thinking is to orthodox Christianity, compare it to the pagan Roman mythology. An ancient paganism adopted extensively by Gnostic sects, the Roman mystery cults held that a race of giants, called Titans, stalked the earth. Zeus, of course, was the most important god in the Roman pantheon. When the Titans killed Zeus' son, the powerful deity destroyed them. From their decaying flesh, the flesh of animals and humans emerged. But humans also had spirits, which were "bits of Zeus," as a drop is a part of a pool of water. Hence, humanity in its physical dimension is due to monsters, whereas mankind's spiritual origins are divine. These creation mythologies, in which human wickedness and viciousness are blamed on a defect in his creation rather than on sin, abound in ancient pagan folklore. And they are revived in some of American televangelism.

That is why Kenneth Copeland argues, "Don't center upon that body of yours; your spirit's where your nature is."[10]

8. Kenneth Copeland, "Substitution and Identification," tape, on file with Christian Research Institute (CRI).
9. Kenneth Copeland, *Believer's Voice of Victory*, March 1982, p. 2.
10. Kenneth Copeland, "Substitution and Identification," tape.

The spirit, after all, is divine, as a drop is a part of the pool. The Bible, presumably, shows us "how to take authority over that [our mind and body] and get out from under it."[11] This "Platonic" view of man, which became the creed of Gnosticism, depreciates that which is human about us.

Throughout history, Christianity has had to fight Platonizing tendencies even within its own orthodox ranks. Hoping to escape the world's contaminating influences, monks fled to the desert, placing meditation, regimented schedules, and spiritual techniques above active, physical involvement in and communication with the world. Nevertheless, such tendencies (which we might well view as erroneous) are not *heretical*. They may indeed be unfortunate expressions of theological misunderstandings, but they are affirmed and practiced in orthodox circles, among those who would recite the creeds with whole-hearted devotion.

What concerns us is not a Platonizing *tendency* but the adoption of Platonic *heresies*—the same heresies that became central in the Gnostic cult against which the apostles fought so vigorously. By attributing our essential humanity to Satan, today's faith teachers have articulated the Gnostic doctrine of man in terms so outrageous they would have made the heretic Marcion blush.

The biblical view of creation is quite different. When God created the world, He gave the benediction, "It is good." To what was He referring? The angels? Prayer? Spirits? No. He was speaking of rocks, trees, birds, the oceans and mountains, the creatures He had brought into existence—at the pinnacle of which stood humans. God pronounced the *material* or *physical* world good! He then went on to declare the goodness of human activity (government, culture, education, labor, leisure, and so on) and articulated the mandate for encouraging it. Therefore, in the biblical perspective, *this* world is of profound importance to God and His people.

After the Fall, the world became the theater in which the divine drama of redemption is acted out. History became

11. Ibid.

"His-story," the unfolding of God's plan in time and space. He builds no monasteries and condemns no creature *except* on the basis that such a creature is engaging in open hostility to His reign.

God did not create man with a good (spiritual) and evil (physical) composition. Man does not sin because he is human, but because he is a sinner. The biblical account states, "And the Lord God formed man from the dust of the ground and breathed into his nostrils the breath of life, and man became a living being" (Genesis 2:7). Notice the unity of the human composition here. The dust that formed man's physical dimension was sculpted by God Himself. How could we consider something God formed evil? Furthermore, notice that God did not just form man's *body* from the ground, but "the Lord God formed *man* from the dust of the ground." In other words, it is impossible to talk about human identity apart from man's physical or material identity. Man is intrinsically physical, earthly—and that's good! One cannot say, therefore, as Copeland does, "Don't center upon that body of yours; your spirit's where your nature is."[12]

THE FALL

Rocks fall on cars, trees rot, birds fall from the sky, the oceans become polluted, illness and death stalk the earth —not because of intrinsic defects in the creation, nor because humans possess a satanic nature. The problem is not nature (as God created it), but the *corruption* of nature that occurred when our race, represented by Adam, decided to declare its independence from its Creator. The world is filled with evil, not because it is filled with minds and bodies, reason and intelligence, passions and drives, but because man has decided to turn his mind and body, reason and intelligence, passions and drives against God.

As I mentioned earlier, the faith teachers maintain that when Adam sinned, the world was turned over to Satan. The devil became the legal owner of the planet. The faith teach-

12. Ibid.

ers' position accommodates the Gnostic view (particularly evident in Zoroastrianism, a Persian Gnostic religion), in which a good god rules the spiritual world and a bad god rules the physical realm. In such a philosophy the problem of evil is solved by blaming everything that goes wrong on the bad god (the devil); the good god is seen as no more than a counterbalance. One is left with the impression that the two gods each possess equal power both in quality and quantity. Everything that is wrong in the world is the fault of the bad god. And it's up to the initiate or believer to make sure the good god wins.

When Jimmy Swaggart defied the orders of the Assemblies of God to refrain from preaching for one year, he assured the public that he was free of moral defect, for, he said, Oral Roberts had cast out the demons from his body over the phone. Oral Roberts confirmed Swaggart's report, insisting he saw the demons with their claws deeply embedded in Swaggart's flesh. Now that the rascals were gone, Swaggart and Roberts asserted, Swaggert could get on with preparing the way for Christ's return. Evidently, personal responsibility for sin can be dismissed by blaming it on an external force. Yet Flip Wilson's famous quip, "The devil made me do it" is hardly comedy when we're talking about the biblical view of sin.

For these metaphysical evangelists, even personal sins can be attributed to the bad god, since he is, after all, sovereign over this earthly realm as the good god is relatively in charge of the spiritual domain. Here again, then, is the echo of the Gnostics of old. When that heresy was revived toward the end of the medieval period, Calvin said, "They made the devil almost the equal of God."

In this way, the problem of sin is replaced with the problem of Satan. It is facing Satan, not my own sin and rebelliousness, that becomes the great task of the Christian life. *I'm* not the problem—*the Devil* is!

According to Copeland, "We should take the name of Jesus and drive out this sin consciousness. . . . A good example [of sin consciousness] is [the statement], 'Well, I'm just an old sinner saved by grace.""[13] Similarly, Fred Price states, "When you say you're a sinner saved by grace, you're still confessing that you're in the same state you were in before Jesus saved you." "No!" Price shouts, "I am no longer a sinner. You may be a sinner, but *I am not a sinner saved by grace*" (italics added).[14] Kenneth Hagin adds, "Sin is only what I think. There is a higher Knowledge."[15] Remember, the name *Gnostic* is derived from the Greek word, *gnosis*, or "knowledge," because its adherents believed they had access to a higher knowledge far superior to mere human insight. The higher knowledge of today's Gnostics is no less deadly, for it teaches them that they are *not* "sinners saved by grace."

There is still another doctrine at stake in the faith teachers' view of the Fall. Classical Christianity has always affirmed the biblical doctrine of original sin. It is a fundamental belief of Roman Catholicism, Orthodoxy, and all orthodox Protestant bodies. From time to time, believers have failed to take the doctrine as seriously as they should have, but it has always been considered an act of heresy actually to deny it. The Princeton theologian Charles Hodge noted that "These two great truths, namely, the imputation of Adam's sin and the imputation of Christ's righteousness, have graven themselves on the consciousness of the Church universal." Though these truths "have been reviled, misrepresented, and denounced by theologians, . . . they have stood their ground in the faith of God's people . . . [and] have been and still are maintained by the people of God wherever found, among the Greeks, Latins, or Protestants."[16]

And then Hodge gives us the definition of original sin that has been accepted historically by the whole church:

13. Kenneth Copeland, in Matta, *The Born-Again Jesus*, p. 82.
14. Fred Price, quoted in Matta.
15. Kenneth Hagin, quoted in Matta.
16. Charles Hodge, *Systematic Theology* (Grand Rapids: Eerdmans, 1946), 3:154.

> The fact that the race fell in Adam; that the evils which come upon us on account of his transgression are penal [i.e., imputed guilt]; and that men are born in a state of sin and condemnation, are outstanding facts of Scripture and experience.[17]

The idea meant by the expression *original sin* is that all humans are born sinners. There is no such thing as "an innocent little baby." From conception, each of us merits the wrath and judgment of God (Psalm 51:5). Some of us may have grown up with the saying, "Sinners by birth and sinners by choice." That's exactly what is meant here. Due to original sin, I am bent toward myself and I am charged with Adam's guilt. I can be sent to hell whether I have personally committed a sin or not. Adam's guilt was imputed to the whole human race, just as Christ's (the second Adam's) righteousness was imputed to believers apart from their own actions.

The doctrine of original sin is hardly ever taught from our pulpits, much less from the electronic pulpits. Although many media evangelists do in fact accept the doctrine in theory, one would hardly know it from their preaching. Nevertheless, our concern is even greater than the *neglect* of the teaching of the doctrine of original sin. It is the outright *denial* of the doctrine, always considered an act of heresy, that has commanded our attention.

Robert Schuller is not, strictly speaking, a "faith teacher." He represents the "positive *thinking*" rather than the "positive *confession*" school. He is not a Gnostic. But in spite of all that, Schuller contributes his own distorted view of human sinfulness, for though the positive thinkers and the faith healers are not related historically, they are never far apart and view each other as partners in the battle.

Schuller, concurring that the notion of original sin opposes the concept of positive thinking, seems to agree that what is needed is a denial of sin-consciousness: "Reformation theology failed to make clear that the core of sin is a lack

17. Ibid.

of self-esteem." "The most serious sin," he says, "is the one that causes me to say, 'I am unworthy. I may have no claim to divine sonship if you examine me at my worst.'" "For once a person believes he is an 'unworthy sinner,'" says Schuller, "it is doubtful if he can really honestly accept the saving grace God offers in Jesus Christ."[18]

Never mind that Jesus told us of a Pharisee and a publican, the latter of whom, beating his chest, cried, "God, be merciful to me, the sinner!," while the Pharisee boasted, in effect, "Lord, I thank you that I've got my act together, that I have a healthy sense of self-esteem." Jesus commented, "I tell you, [the publican] went down to his house justified rather than the other; for everyone who exalts himself shall be humbled, and but he who humbles himself shall be exalted" (Luke 18:13-14, NASB).

Furthermore, when Schuller suggests that "once a person believes he is an 'unworthy sinner,' it is doubtful if he can really honestly accept the saving grace God offers in Jesus Christ," he fails either to understand or to accept the idea that "the saving grace God offers" is available *only* to "unworthy sinners." Isn't that the whole idea of grace: unmerited favor?

Although we can appreciate Schuller's frustration with oppressive, legalistic religion, we must remember that that is not actually biblical faith. Far from being an oppressive, legalistic religion, biblical faith is exactly the opposite. The most serious sin is *not* the one that causes me to say, "I'm unworthy if you examine me at my best," but the one that causes me to say, "I *am* worthy, not only if you examine me at my best, but even if you examine me at my worst!" For the second I think I *do* have a claim to divine sonship, I have eliminated grace from the gospel. Here we have a clear example of the principle that weak views of sin always include weak views of grace.

18. Robert Schuller, *Self-Esteem: The New Reformation* (Waco, Tex.: Word, 1982), p. 98.

Pat Robertson also denies original sin in unmistakable language, defining it in deficient terms: "From that moment [the Fall] on, man's awareness of God became dimmer and dimmer. It is as if man is now born with a moral handicap. He is lame in the most important part of his being—his spirit. This is original sin."[19] What Robertson describes is, of course, *not* original sin. Original sin says nothing at all about man being born "with a moral handicap" or about his being "lame." It is not a "tendency." Rather, it speaks of our being "dead in trespasses and sins" (Ephesians 2:1, KJV), charged with Adam's guilt. This element of being charged with Adam's guilt—even before we have actually committed our own first sinful act—is the heart and soul of the doctrine of original sin.

It seems that Robertson knows what the historic doctrine of original sin teaches, but simply redefines it to suit his preference. For, he says, the reason babies will not go to hell is not because of divine mercy but "because they are not guilty of anything."[20] That view is similar to the one held by the heretic Pelagius, who was condemned by more church councils than anybody in history. Like Pelagius, Robertson believes the Fall somehow affected humans, inasmuch as it provided a weakness in their moral character. But unlike Pelagius, Robertson believes that the effect of the Fall went beyond more than a poor example. Robertson, it would appear, wants to be more orthodox. Nevertheless, he still denies original sin. "There is," he says quite clearly, "no such thing as original guilt."[21] But original guilt, after all, is the whole point of this biblical teaching.

Although Swaggart does not deny the reality of human sinfulness, he does attack the doctrine of "total depravity." Humans, he says, are not so lost that they cannot perform certain acts to improve their spiritual condition. Even in their fallenness, men and women move toward God by their free

19. Robertson, *Answers*, p. 32.
20. Ibid., p. 33.
21. Ibid.

will. Such doctrines as total depravity, Swaggart teaches, have actually "sent more people to hell than any other teaching.[22] The position Swaggert adopts is semi-Pelagian and was condemned by the Council of Orange in 529.

In short, there are televangelists who do not accept the teaching on human fallenness that has been held by catholic Christianity for nearly two millennia. Though Protestants and Roman Catholics, Calvinists and Wesleyans, have disagreed with each other over substantial questions regarding the doctrine of human fallenness and divine grace, I would argue that never have Pentecostals, evangelicals, and fundamentalists been so confused with regard to the notion of human helplessness. The views of sin and grace censured in this book would be equally condemned in the past by Calvinists and Wesleyans, Protestants and Catholics.

Perhaps this modern nervousness with regard to human impotence is due to the fact that it confesses a moral weakness and inability that undermines the self-confident piety and self-righteous moralism of our churches and their political crusades. If we tell people that salvation "does not . . . depend on man's desire or effort, but on God's mercy" (Romans 9:16), they will give up trying to be better people. Of course, that is just what the gospel commands: that people give up trying to secure God's favor by becoming better people. Jesus "came to save sinners," not to help good people become better.

Although individual *sins* are often condemned by religious groups, the sinful *condition* is rarely explained or understood from a biblical, theological perspective. Again, I believe that the omission is due to the fear many have that, in things pertaining to salvation, a pessimistic view of human potential and an optimistic view of Divine omnipotence will take too much away from human strivings.

The Scriptures teach, "And you . . . were *dead* in trespasses and sins" (Ephesians 2:1, KJV, italics added) and "slaves to sin" (Romans 6:20). "What is man, that he could

22. Jimmy Swaggart, *The Evangelist*, September 1983.

be pure? And he who is born of a woman, that he could be righteous?" (Job 15:14, NKJV). "Who can say, 'I have made my heart clean, I am pure from my sin'?" (Proverbs 20:9, NKJV). "The natural man does not receive the things of the Spirit of God . . . nor *can* he know them, because they are spiritually discerned" (1 Corinthians 2:14, NKJV, italics added). "Can the Ethiopian change his skin or the leopard its spots? Then may you also do good who are accustomed to do evil" (Jeremiah 13:23, NKJV). "No one can come to Me unless the Father who sent Me draws him" (John 6:44, NKJV). It is the gravity of our condition that requires the immense measures God has taken in redemption.

REDEMPTION

The gospel was never intended to show people how to save themselves with God's help. The law was designed to drive them to despair of saving themselves so that they would give up their self-improvement struggle for salvation and cast themselves entirely on God's mercy. *Jesus did not come to make people redeemable, but to actually purchase those who were wicked, alienated, and hostile to that redemption.* He does not "help those who help themselves," but saves those who are entirely helpless to lift a finger.

All of the televangelists censured in this book tend to trivialize the plan of salvation. There is rarely any serious attempt to explain to the masses such basic redemptive truths as the substitutionary atonement, propitiation, or sacrifice and satisfaction. The general impression is given that Jesus died on the cross to show the world how much God loved us (the "Governmental Theory") and to make it possible for us to follow Christ's loving example ("Moral Influence Theory"), but the "offense of the cross," reminding us of our debt to grace, is hardly a footnote.

One thing the viewer comes away with is the sense that the purpose of evangelism is not to satisfy God and His purposes, but to satisfy the consumer with the product. An effort is made to package a likable God, one who helps us without getting in the way—a genie who can appear when we rub the bottle but otherwise is corked inside. But the issue is not a matter of getting the sinner to like God but of getting God to like the sinner. Over and over in the Bible we read that God "maintains his wrath against his enemies" (Nahum 1:2) and that "God's wrath remains on" the unbeliever every day of his life (John 3:36). Paul says to unbelievers, "You are storing up wrath" (Romans 2:5). The Bible speaks vividly of "the fury of the wrath of God Almighty" (Revelation 19:15) and of the "wrath of the Lamb" (Revelation 6:16).

Clearly, the God of the Bible is not a genie who can't wait to fulfill our hopes and dreams. God cannot accept us the way we are. He is perfect and we are wicked, self-centered to the very core of our being. In order for His wrath to be propitiated, His justice must be satisfied. Jesus Christ, the second Person of the Holy Trinity, was sent to bear the wrath of God for believers. Thus, the issue in evangelism is not one of attracting sinners to divine benefits (the question, "Don't you want to accept Christ?"), but to bring them face to face with this issue: "Do you want God to accept *you?*" Then the cross becomes more than a symbol of God's love and becomes love *in action* actually accomplishing something significant.

JUSTIFICATION

Though it is fundamental to any presentation of the gospel, the doctrine of justification is virtually unknown in much of popular media evangelism. Jimmy Swaggart, in fact, says it is "a lie" to believe that "the believer's sins are already forgiven—past, present, and future," and that "his sins are not taken into account."[23] Yet Paul joined David in singing, "Blessed is the man whose sin the Lord will not take into account" (Romans 4:8, NASB).

Furthermore, Swaggart teaches that justification, rather than being a once and for all declaration of righteousness in Christ, requires constant renewing. Each time the believer

23. Jimmy Swaggart, *Questions and Answers* (Baton Rouge, La.: Jimmy Swaggart Ministries, 1985), pp. 291-95.

fails morally (How often could *that* be in one day!), "these same acts of grace are available. . . . And *again*, instantly, the Lord cleanses him and *justifies* him" (italics added).[24] That is precisely the sort of language against which the Protestant Reformers launched their polemics.

According to Swaggart, God will continue to justify believers "if they will cooperate."[25] The durability of this justifying grace is "on the basis of obedience to God." Thus, "a person can lose his salvation through neglect and disobedience," can "fall back into sin and lose [his] sonship." Believers can "stay free and pure in Him, but only by that continued cooperation."[26]

The evangelist even characterizes justification by the heading, "A Twofold Work." "So actually," he says, "a twofold work takes place here: God's redemptive work in our heart and our cooperation in that work."[27] "We teach and believe," he says, "that all of God's promises are conditional. Nothing, as far as God's dealings with mankind are concerned, is unconditional."[28]

Such a concept, of course, eliminates any scriptural understanding of salvation by grace. It also places Swaggart beyond semi-Pelagianism and, therefore, beyond orthodoxy. Even the Roman Church, which opposed the Reformers' insistence on "grace alone," would condemn such a view as heretical.

Pat Robertson holds a view similar to Swaggart. Robertson promises, "Your future depends *entirely* on your obedience to God" (italics added).[29] Christians, says Robertson, should have "a healthy fear of falling."[30] But how can a Christian have a "healthy" fear of God's promises failing? Aren't we told in Scripture, "You did not receive a spirit that makes

24. Ibid.
25. Ibid.
26. Ibid.
27. Ibid.
28. Jimmy Swaggart, *The Evangelist*, September 1983.
29. Robertson, *Answers*, p. 14
30. Ibid., p. 58.

you a slave again to fear, but you received the Spirit of sonship" (Romans 8:15)?

"Why are some people closer to God than others?" Robertson asks. "Some people are wiser than others, some are more learned than others, some are more diligent than others, and some work harder than others. Some people have a godly ancestry, as I do."[31] To the contrary, the Bible assures us, "Not many of you were wise by human standards; not many were influential; not many were of noble birth. But God chose the foolish things of the world to shame the wise; God chose the weak things of the world to shame the strong. He chose the lowly things of this world and the despised things —and the things that are not—to nullify the things that are, so that no one may boast before him" (1 Corinthians 1:26-29).

Much of Paul's epistle to the Romans is devoted to the explanation of justification. God, says the apostle, is in the business of declaring wicked people guiltless and, in fact, righteous. He does that not by overlooking their sins, not by having them do penance or by having them write "I will never do it again" a thousand times, not by giving folks an "A" for effort. Rather, God *imputes*, that is, charges or credits to the believer's account, the life-long obedience, death, resurrection, and victory of Christ. We are not saved by *our* "victorious Christian life," but by *His*! Of course that means that even though the believer will sin many times (in one day!), God has nevertheless declared that person to be a perfectly law-abiding citizen. The basis for our relationship with God is Christ's track record, not our own.

That status does not change with our moral ups and downs. The believer continues to sin and "fall short of God's glory," even though he stands in Christ's righteousness. As Luther put it, the believer is "simultaneously a sinner and justified." Therefore, when the faith teachers tell us they are *not* "sinners saved by grace" because they are "no longer sin-

31. Ibid., p. 200.

ners," they deny both the nature of sin and the nature of grace.

The radical gospel of grace, as it is found throughout Scripture, has always had its critics. Jimmy Swaggart told me a few years ago that by trusting in God's justifying and preserving grace, I would end up living a life of sin before long —and thus, lose my salvation and be consigned to hell. Paul anticipated that reaction from the religious community of his own day after he said, "Where sin abounded, grace abounded much more" (Romans 5:20, NKJV). So he asked the question he expected us to ask: "Shall we continue in sin that grace may abound?" (6:1) Should we sin so that we can receive more grace? In other words, "If people believed what you just said in Romans 5, Paul, wouldn't they take advantage of the situation and live like the dickens, knowing they were 'safe and secure from all alarm'?" That's a fair question. But it reveals a basic misunderstanding of the nature of God's saving grace. Paul's response is unmistakable: "Certainly not! How shall we who died to sin live any longer in it?" (Romans 6:2, NKJV).

Someone confronted Martin Luther, upon the Reformer's rediscovery of the biblical doctrine of justification, with the remark, "If this is true, a person could simply live as he pleased!"

"Indeed!" answered Luther. "Now, what *pleases* you?"

Augustine was the great preacher of grace during the fourth and fifth centuries. Although his understanding of the doctrine of justification did not have the fine-tuned precision of the Reformers, Augustine's response on this point was similar to Luther's. He said that the doctrine of justification led to the maxim, "Love God and do as you please." Because we have misunderstood one of the gospel's most basic themes, Augustine's statement looks to many like a license to indulge one's sinful nature, but in reality it touches upon the motivation the Christian has for his actions. The person who has been justified by God's grace has a new, higher, and nobler motivation for holiness than the shallow, hypocritical self-righteousness or fear that seems to motivate so many religious people today.

Paul insisted that salvation "does not . . . depend on man's desire or effort, but on God's mercy" (Romans 9:16), and Jesus confirmed, "The Spirit gives life; the flesh counts for nothing" (John 6:63). That gives too much to grace, say heretics such as Pelagius, Coelestius, Abelard, and Finney. And so say many of our modern televangelists.

It is reported that Anselm, one of the greatest doctors of the church, had this to say concerning salvation:

> Dost thou believe that thou canst not be saved, but by the death of Christ? . . . Put all thy confidence in this death alone, place thy trust in no other thing, commit thyself wholly to this death, cover thyself wholly with this alone, cast thyself wholly on this death, wrap thyself wholly in this death. And if God would judge thee, say, Lord, I place the death of our Lord Jesus Christ between me and thy judgment; and otherwise I will not contend, or enter into judgment with thee. And if He shall say unto thee, that thou art a sinner, say, I place the death of our Lord Jesus Christ between me and my sins. If He shall say unto thee, that thou hast deserved damnation, say, Lord, I put the death of our Lord Jesus Christ between thee and all my sins; and I offer his merits for my own, which I should have, and have not."[32]

Justification is *objective*. Its reality depends on an already completed historical event in which we in no way participated or contributed. Yet much of our religion these days is tremendously subjective. We talk about feeling holy, becoming holy, yielding, surrendering, and on and on. And to be sure, there is a subjective application of Christ's work. Nevertheless, when we emphasize what Jesus does *to* us and *within* us without grounding that on what He has done *for* us, our faith degenerates into sentimentalism.

And if our faith has degenerated in sentimentalism, when feelings of guilt build up inside us we will have no ob-

32. Quoted in Charles Hodge, *Systematic Theology*, 3:154-55.

jective fact to use as a weapon against those insecurities. If we cannot point to a historical moment outside of ourselves, when two thousand years ago our guilt was charged to another person (namely, Christ), then we can never experience the *relief* of pardon. In other words, we cannot *experience* or *feel* justified, redeemed, adopted, chosen, accepted, and secure unless we *believe* and *understand* in some measure the doctrines that produce such joy.

Insofar as a televangelist obscures, ignores, or denies basic biblical teachings, he is a purveyor of "another gospel" and merits the apostle Paul's condemnation: "If we or an angel from heaven should preach a gospel to you other than the one we preached to you, let him be eternally condemned!" (Galatians 1:8). That, of course, is a grave charge—indeed, it is a grave threat.

"But these people love the Lord," we are told. "They are zealous for God's work. Just because they aren't theologians doesn't mean they should be outcasts." But is a doctrine like justification nothing more than a pet project for theologians, concerning which well-meaning Christians may disagree, so long as they love the Lord and have zeal? Evidently, not, according to the apostle: "For I can testify about them that they are zealous for God, but their zeal is not based on knowledge. Since they did not know the righteousness that comes from God and sought to establish their own, they did not submit to God's righteousness [i.e., justification]" (Romans 10:2-3).

CONVERSION AND FAITH

In his pamphlet *How to Have Faith in Your Faith*, Kenneth E. Hagin ("Daddy Hagin," as he is known by the faith teachers) argues that "faith" is a synonym for "positive thinking" or "positive confession" or "positive mental attitude." The *act* of believing is more important than the *object* of belief. Thus, the power lies not in the One believed, but in the one believing. But that amounts to little more than self-worship or will-worship. It sees our good fortune as being determined by the degree to which we can believe something into existence and not by the One who alone spoke the worlds into being.

There are faith teachers in the electronic church who often "speak to" money, success, and health as though those things were personal gods. Similarly, they "speak to" Satan and demonic forces, "binding" them by their "word of faith."

Once again, it seems that the object of faith for those teachers is not the God of Scripture, but the gods of health, wealth, and happiness. Faith is seen not as a matter of believing *in* God but a matter of believing *for* things. Hagin speaks of decreeing his brother's salvation. Thus, he makes God the absentee landlord who leaves the decreeing and application of salvation, as well as health and wealth, to the "authority of the believer."

Faith, according to such teachers, is not faith *in* God, but the faith *of* God. In other words, God is not the *object* of faith but is a *model* for the kind of force our faith can have. Just as He spoke things into being, so too can we. "Faith is a power force," says Copeland." "The force of faith is released through words. Faith-filled words put the law of the Spirit of life into operation."[33] Thus, faith is not "the gift of God" to trust God with one's eternal welfare (Ephesians 2:8-9).

Like other spiritualists, the faith teachers point adherents to their own inner spirit rather than to a Savior outside of them. But according to Scripture, God gives faith to whom He will (John 1:13; Acts 13:48; Romans 9:18; Ephesians 1:5; Philippians 2:13). Furthermore, the object of that faith is always God and His grace, not faith itself. We are saved, not by believing, but by believing in Christ. Faith in *faith* is idolatry.

There is a further, and more distorted, element in the faith teachers' view of conversion. In orthodox Christianity, conversion is the product of regeneration (i.e., the new birth). Groups within the orthodox community have debated the details, but it has been generally recognized that conver-

33. Kenneth Copeland, *The Force of Faith* (Fort Worth, Tex.: Kenneth Copeland, 1980), p. 6.

sion is the result of a miraculous intervention of God's grace. As the Bible puts it, at some point during a person's life, the Holy Spirit turns the heart of stone into a heart of flesh. That may be a gradual process, beginning from the youngest stages of childhood, or it may be a radical, transforming experience. But either way, God is turning us from ourselves to Him. As Augustine put it, "Turn me and I will be turned."

This conversion (whether instantaneous or gradual) turns an unbeliever into a believer; the sinner becomes a saint, the rebel becomes a servant and faithful child.

Yet for the faith teachers, conversion turns the new believer into "a new species of being that never existed before."[34] Fred Price says, "You, as a Christian are supposed to be the master of your circumstances. . . . There is no way in the world you can reign as a king in life and be poverty-stricken."[35] Hence the Christian life now begins as a process, not of serving Christ and others, but of "decreeing" health, wealth, and happiness for oneself. Conversion thus produces a superman who can live above it all.

But Price's first comment—that the believer becomes "a new kind of being that never existed before"—is an even more sinister perversion of the idea of conversion than that summed up in the doctrine of the believer's being able to "decree" health, wealth, and happiness. It is related to the faith teacher's assertion that, whereas the unbeliever is no more than a physical being, the believer has become somehow non-earthly; he has been miraculously transformed from human to spiritual. "When we are born again," says Gloria Copeland in *Christian Life* magazine, "we become a spirit being in a flesh body."[36] That, of course, is sheer Gnosticism. It has absolutely no basis in Scripture—and historically, whenever such an obvious departure from orthodox faith has occurred, the proponent was charged with heresy.

34. Jerry Savelle, *The Established Heart* (Tulsa, Okla.: Harrison House, 1977), p. 15.
35. Fred Price, *How to Obtain Strong Faith* (Tulsa, Okla.: Harrison House, 1977), p. 104.
36. Gloria Copeland, "A Fast Brings New Direction," *Christian Life*.

The metamorphosis Scripture discusses is not at all the metamorphosis the faith teachers propound. The new birth converts unbelievers to believers—not physical beings to spirit beings in a flesh body. Believers and unbelievers alike share a common nature. In fact, both bear the image of God. The new birth does not change a person in terms of his created composition. Rather, it converts us from rebellious humans to believing humans. As touching our humanity, there is no difference between the person who is born again and the person who is not. What conversion intends to correct is not our humanity, but the *corruption* of our humanity by sin and guilt. God does not want to *eradicate* that about us which is human, but *redeem* it.

As though this distorted, science-fiction metamorpho sis were not enough, the errant televangelists add a greater blasphemy. The new birth, they say, not only converts the believer to "a spirit being in a flesh body," it changes the believer from a mere human to a god. Reference has already been made in this book to the teaching by some televangelists that the believer is "as much the incarnation of God as Jesus Christ," so the point will be made in passing here. Nevertheless, it is important to see that the physical to spiritual, rational to mystical "conversion" the faith teachers talk about is a conversion from mere humanity to deity. Having been given the very nature of God, we are to "walk as Jesus walked, without any consciousness of inferiority to God or Satan."[37] Hence, by their own admission, these teachers, many of them leading televangelists whose growing followings number in the millions, deny being "conscious" of their sinfulness, their need for grace, and, now, of their inferiority to God. Clearly, such "confessions" can be anything but "positive."

CONCLUSION

In many ways, TV evangelism is nothing more than a large-screen projection of certain segments of evangelicalism

37. E. W. Kenyon, *The Blood Covenant* (Lynnwood: Kenyon's Gospel Pub. Society, 1969), p. 53.

generally. Indeed, all those whom we have been forced to characterize as "heretics" in this volume cheerfully claim for themselves the designation "evangelical," and the secular media takes their word for it that they speak for the rest of us. We must admit that the crisis of truth we have seen in the televangelists condemned in this book is only a microcosm of the disarray present in Christendom generally. Paul never said, "If anyone visits a prostitute, let him be eternally condemned." Nor did he say, "If anyone steals millions of dollars from unwary victims and engages in immoral sexual activities, let him be eternally condemned." No indeed. Christ "came not to call the righteous, but sinners." A televangelist who preaches a false gospel can repent of his exploits, but that is not enough. He must repent of his heresy. For Paul *did* say, "If [anyone] preach *any other gospel* . . . let him be accursed" (Galatians 1:8, NKJV, italics added).

But are such doctrines as those we have considered in this chapter essential for the average person? Need we burden the viewer with such theological details? Indeed we must. We *must* burden the viewer with his rightful sense of guilt. The viewer must sense that the issue at stake is not how satisfied he is with God and His plan, but how satisfied God is with him. And God can only *be* satisfied with the sinner if he is covered by the righteousness of Christ. Such doctrines are not theological details. They are the *big picture*—the form and substance of what the gospel promises and what the Christian confesses as his or her faith.

Salvation is God-centered, not human-centered. The viewer must not be flattered, but confronted. That is true not only for God's honor, but for the good of the unbeliever. After all, a little bit of sugar might help the medicine go down—but not if you're a diabetic! Attempts to cajole the unbeliever into accepting a gospel that does not place his self-centered appetites under arrest will lead to eternal loss.

The biblical gospel offers freedom from sin, not sinlessness, liberation from guilt, not from sin-consciousness, salvation from spiritual, not material, poverty. It offers peace with God won by Christ's bloody sacrifice—not success won by our incessant "decrees." It promises salvation from God's wrath, not freedom from the unhappiness common to all humanity from time to time. And it hides us—in the midst of our pain and grief—in the wounds of Christ, who has made us worthy to share in His suffering.

I, for one, have been deeply impressed with the relevance and comfort of these truths. Our guilt-ridden, maligned, depressed, oppressed society cries out for a *real* solution to its perennial problem. It is tired of artificial solutions. Although our weak and feeble natures tend to reach for cotton candy before meat and potatoes, we all know which is better for us in the long run. We need to rediscover for ourselves the richness of biblical, historic Christian truths, and then integrate those truths into our daily practice and share them with our neighbors. And if we pastors are too busy to feed ourselves on a steady diet of Scripture and sturdy Christian classics, we are indeed too busy.

Those we have been critiquing throughout this book are guilty of the greatest of all sins: distortion of the gospel. While we were looking for air-conditioned dog-houses, the real scandal, the scandal of *eternal* weight, went uncontested. It is time we—all of us—gave serious thought to what the content of the gospel really is. The world has never more desperately needed the it. Tragically, the same could be said of the electronic church.

They devoted themselves to the apostles' teaching and to the fellowship, to the breaking of bread and to prayer.

—Acts 2:42

8

The TV Church

W. Robert Godfrey

We have seen in these last several chapters just how important a clear and correct view of God, the Scriptures, ourselves, and salvation are to the health, peace, and advancement of the Christian faith. Our view of the church—its nature, its role, and its mission, is also essential for that health. Many of the scandals and distortions of biblical faith we have been discussing point up a skewed ecclesiology (doctrine of the church).

What *is* the "electronic church"? If you turn on your TV, you will find a variety of religious broadcasting, from Roman Catholic masses to traditional Presbyterian services to charismatic talk shows. Some programs are rather amateurish local broadcasts of local worship services. Others are sophisticated and expensive programs syndicated all over the world. Some of these programs are produced by honest, earnest people trying to be helpful to others. Others seem, at best, questionable as to their message and methods. In one sense, all of these programs are part of the electronic church.

Usually, though, "electronic church" is used to refer to those programs distributed beyond a single local area and supported by the contributions of the viewers. For the purposes of this chapter, the "electronic church" will refer to any TV broadcast that becomes a central part of the religious experience and practice of its viewers.

My objective here is not to analyze the TV church in any detail. That has been done and will be done throughout this book. My concern is to argue that the electronic church at its very best can only be a religious *supplement* in the life of a Christian. There are indeed many useful supplements for Christians today, including Christian bookstores, radio stations, and a host of local, national, and international organizations for various educational, evangelistic, and welfare goals. But the purpose of this chapter is to maintain that all of those supplements must remain subordinate to and supportive of the Christian's commitment to the local church.

The necessity of the local church is clearly taught in Scripture and is indispensable for the life of the Christian. Before we critique the idea of an "electronic church," we should understand the nature of the institutional church.

THE INSTITUTIONAL CHURCH

God has a great redemptive purpose in the world. He intends to save a people from the judgment and wrath to come and has sent His Son, Jesus, into the world to fulfill all righteousness and to die for sinners that such a people might be redeemed. God's saving work, however, is not concerned with individuals in isolation. Rather, God is redeeming a people whom He calls the Body of Christ, the church: "And God placed all things under his [Jesus'] feet and appointed him to be head over everything for the church, which is his body, the fullness of Him who fills everything in every way" (Ephesians 1:22-23).

What is this "church" about which the Scriptures speak so highly? In the Bible, the word *church* is used in one of two ways. The first usage refers to the universal or organic church —all believers in all times who are united to one another and reconciled to God by their union with Christ. The second usage refers to the institutional expressions of that universal church.

Many Christians today seem to assume that all God requires is a relationship to the universal church that occurs automatically for the believer. In other words, it is often said that "the church is people." Hence, belonging to the church means belonging to Christ, not to an institution. That is, however, not true. The Bible is clear that Christians are also required to be part of the life of the institutional church, particularly the life of the local church, which God Himself has brought into being and structured by His Word.

God's structuring of the local church began with the apostles. Jesus chose from among His disciples twelve apostles (Luke 6:12-16). He sent them like the prophets of old to preach God's Word (Luke 11:49). These apostles—specially chosen leaders who had been eyewitnesses to Jesus' life (Acts 1:21-25)—became the foundation of the life of the new church, and their teachings were authoritative for the church (Ephesians 2:20).

The apostles were not the only officers appointed in the earliest church. In Ephesians 4:11 there is mention of pastors and teachers, and in Acts 14:23 the apostle Paul is described appointing elders in each church he founded. In 1 Timothy 3 Paul gives some of the qualifications for the offices of overseer and deacon.

It is clear that the apostles themselves established two or three offices as continuing offices of leadership and authority in the life of the church. Those officers have important responsibilities for the Christian community given to them by the Lord through the apostles. Look, for example, at the solemn charge Paul gave to the Ephesian elders concerning their care for the church at Ephesus. Elders are to guard the flock as a shepherd protects the sheep from wolves (Acts 20:28-29). They have hard work to do to protect the weak (20:35). The danger is real, sometimes arising from within the church itself. The officers of the church are able to nip false teaching in the bud because of their official role in the church.

The care Christ and the apostles took to provide us with officers and an institutional church should make a great impression on us. Christ and His apostles established an institutional church to help us in our need and weakness. Elders are appointed for our sakes, and we need to submit ourselves to their authority in the local church if we are to be obedient to the Lord and His vision of the Christian life.

Submission to elders is closely tied to the question of "church membership." Some people today object to the idea that Christians must be church members, suggesting that such a requirement is unbiblical. But it is surely an implication of the eldership that Christ has appointed in His church. Elders are necessary to teach and admonish and discipline us. But how can elders carry out that work unless we submit to them? What is church membership but our joining our local congregation and submitting to the authority of the elders?

To be sure, elders are not infallible. Sometimes they can deviate; indeed, they have, from time to time, been known to leave the faith entirely. But the fact that some elders are unreliable does not eliminate our responsibility to find godly elders and submit to them.

The subject of the authority of pastors and elders, and church membership, is closely related to the matter of church discipline. The topic of discipline is not a popular one in America today. Parents may talk regretfully of a lack of discipline among the young, but many parents seem short on a willingness to insist on discipline at home or to support it in the schools. Adults in our society certainly often fail to discipline themselves. Think of the misuse of drugs or alcohol, the high divorce rate, and irresponsibility on the job, to name only a few. In such a society, church discipline has almost disappeared. Churches often are so eager to attract people that they make very few demands upon them.

But the Bible teaches the importance of a disciplined church life. After all, the church is a hospital for sinners. Its members are going to continue sinning, even though they are Christians. They need the support and discipline of older and wiser Christians as they mature in their faith. Setting aside responsibility in the interest of independence is no healthier for growing Christians than for growing children. Of course, there is Christian liberty, and the church cannot command the conscience where Christ has freed it. Nevertheless it can and must care for the flock in the way its Chief Shepherd has proscribed.

Jesus taught that when informal attempts to handle problems among Christians have failed the church must proceed formally, even to the point of expelling someone from the church (Matthew 18:15-18). There are examples of this in the New Testament (1 Corinthians 5:1-7; 2 Thessalonians 3:14-15). The hope in such discipline is to restore the sinner to the Lord and to the church by repentance (2 Corinthians 2:5-8). But if that does not happen, at least the church has been protected and purified from scandalous and unrepentant behavior.

Many people do not like the idea of a disciplined church. They believe they should be able to do whatever is right in their own eyes. Such an attitude reflects the militant individualism of our society. But it does not reflect Christ's teaching about the life of His church. Proper discipline by the officers of the church is necessary for the well-being of individual Christians as well as for the church as a whole. Such discipline can take place only in the context of membership in a local church.

Christ's structuring of the church is not limited to offices and discipline. Christ also directs the church as to its life and worship. From its earliest days after Pentecost the church gathered with eagerness and devotion (Acts 2:42). When some became negligent in worship and fellowship, a stern warning was issued: "Let us not give up meeting together, as some are in the habit of doing, but let us encourage one another—and all the more as you see the Day approaching" (Hebrews 10:25). This warning stresses Christian worship as one source of the encouragement needed to lead the Christian life faithfully.

THE WORSHIPING CHURCH

Space does not permit a full look at the teaching of the New Testament on the way in which the church should worship. But it is essential to reflect on one text that relates worship to the priority of the local church. That text is Acts 2:41-42: "Those who accepted his [Peter's] message were baptized and about three thousand were added to their number that day. They devoted themselves to the apostles' teaching and to the fellowship, to the breaking of bread and to prayer." This text promotes at least four elements of worship: the apostles' teaching, fellowship, the sacraments, and prayer.

THE APOSTLES' TEACHING

The first element is *the apostles' teaching*. Those early believers had the opportunity to hear the apostles themselves as they taught and directed the lives of the new converts and those growing into Christian maturity. Today the church finds the teaching of the apostles faithfully recorded in the Bible. It is in the study and preaching of the Bible that the contemporary church has access to that authoritative teaching of the apostles. That is why, historically, the reading and preaching of the Word of God has been such an important part of Christian worship. That is also why Christians have devoted so much time and energy to establishing colleges and seminaries. They have wanted well-educated pastors who could responsibly teach them the Scriptures.

Is the teaching of the Bible one area where the electronic church can do the job of the local church? Surely television can provide instruction in the Bible. But it would be a good test to measure on any given religious broadcast how much time is actually spent in preaching or teaching the Bible. On too many programs, entertainment and fund-raising greatly diminish the time spent in opening God's Word.

Even if the Bible is taught on a TV program, how is the listener to evaluate the reliability of what is taught? There are many programs on which the teachings of the believer's local church are undermined or rejected. Many televangelists mock the institutional church—it is clear that the dominant attitude toward the institutional church among many leading televangelists is cynicism. There are also programs where outright heresy is taught under the name "Christianity." Who monitors and evaluates these programs and their teaching? How can the Christian be sure that what is taught is not blatantly or subtly undermining the faith? Surely it is the responsibility of the local church and its officers to ensure that God's people are fed with apostolic truth. Once again we see the necessity of the local church and how, at best, the electronic church can only supplement the local church's ministry.

Even if the electronic church gives good time to reliable teaching of the Word, it still cannot effectively fill the shoes of the local church. The church can see to the *pastoral* preaching of the Word—the teaching of Scripture applied to the particular needs of the local group of believers. However faithful a televangelist might be, he cannot know the special direction that a particular local church may need to take the way a faithful pastor can. It is in the local community, uniquely, where the encouragement to good works of which Hebrews 10 speaks can take place. Devotion to the apostles' teaching can best take place in the local church.

FELLOWSHIP

The second element mentioned in Acts 2 is *fellowship*. The word "fellowship" here is *koinonia*, and it means sharing in common. It means being together and participating together in various concerns and activities. It means hearing and responding to the Word together. It means supporting one another in prayer. It means sharing financial resources to provide for the poor and to accomplish the work of the church. The central form of fellowship is found in the public worship of God. As we join our voices, hearts, ears, and minds together, fellowship takes place in the highest degree.

Can the electronic church provide such fellowship? At first glance, some may think so. People from all around the country are united in hearing the same songs and sermons. TV as a medium seems to be personal, immediate, intimate.

The speaker can seem close and concerned. But is this really the fellowship that our text describes? There is nothing genuinely personal about television fellowship. There is no human contact with fellow believers. The TV preacher cannot possibly meet his viewers on a personal, immediate, intimate level, since he has no personal contact with them at all. Once again, TV may supplement the fellowship of the church, but it cannot be a substitute for it.

THE SACRAMENTS

The *sacraments* constitute the third element. For many Christians today, the sacraments are not a central, vital part of Christian life. They may believe that the sacraments are peripheral to Christianity, but if they want to be biblical, they must hold the sacraments in high esteem. The Bible clearly makes the sacraments an important, even necessary, element of Christian experience.

Luke tells us, for example, that when Peter finished his Pentecost sermon, his listeners asked what they had to do to be saved. Peter gave a two-fold answer: "Repent and be baptized" (Acts 2:38). The apostles regularly linked the inner response of faith and repentance to the outward act of baptism as the beginning of the Christian life.

The brief summary of Christian devotion in Acts 2:42 includes "the breaking of bread." That expression can mean nothing more than having a meal together, but in this religious context it surely means the unique breaking of bread that Christians share in the Lord's Supper. When our Lord instituted the Supper, He commanded the church: "Do this" (Luke 22:17-20). Paul gave careful direction to a church on how this sacrament must be observed for spiritual benefit (1 Corinthians 10 and 11).

Can the electronic church administer the sacraments? Some TV ministers would readily admit that they cannot administer Holy Communion over the airwaves. There certainly can be no proper supervision of the sacrament over television, nor can there be genuine fellowship. After reading the apostle's warnings in 1 Corinthians 10 and 11, I cannot imagine any evangelist having the courage to offer the Holy Supper via television. Yet Pat Robertson, Oral Roberts, and Paul Crouch are among those who have offered Communion over the airwaves. In fact, Roberts has sent packets of Communion wafers to his donors to be taken during a telecast. This is sacrilege!

Most TV preachers either implicitly or explicitly minimize and trivialize the importance of the sacraments. But the Scriptures make baptism and the Lord's Supper indispensable to any church, and without them such a ministry is incomplete. Again we see the necessity of the local church.

PRAYER

The final element mentioned in Acts 2 is *prayer*. All Christians recognize the importance of prayer, of personal and corporate communication with God. Prayer is one way in which the Christian cultivates a living relationship with God. In the worship of the local church, significant time is spent in prayers of adoration, confession, thanksgiving, and intercession.

Can the electronic church lead Christians in prayer? There is again the problem of what it means to pray with a videotape. There is also the problem of how such prayer can be personal and particular. Some programs have tried to solve that problem by having viewers send in cards with prayer requests. But is it genuine intercessory prayer for a preacher to put his hands on thousands of cards and just ask God to grant those requests? That is not true prayer but is more like spinning a prayer wheel or lighting candles and calling it prayer. Further, since all believers are priests, there is more benefit in having a fellow-Christian (whether clergy or laity) intercede personally on one's behalf than to send a card to a preacher. A TV celebrity preacher is no closer to God than one's Christian neighbor. In fact, quite a contrary conclusion might sometimes be drawn.

Beyond the problems of praying over television is the question of how much *time* is spent in prayer on TV programs. In reality, very little effort is given to prayer on TV because prayer is not the kind of activity (dare I say entertainment?) that broadcasts well.

Once again we can see that prayer that carefully, thoughtfully, and intimately communicates with God is not possible on TV but is part of the ministry of the local church.

The Attractive Church

If the biblical case for the local church is so strong, why are so many people attracted to the electronic church? The TV church is so attractive because it fits many of America's cultural characteristics. It serves America's search for the easy, the individualistic, and the interesting.

EASY

The electronic church is *easy*. It requires no more effort than turning on the TV. It does not require the discipline of getting dressed, driving somewhere, and arriving on time. Since some religious broadcasts are available at many different times throughout the week, one is not required to set aside Sunday as the day of worship. Almost any time will do. It is also easy in that the only involvement required is the writing of a check. There is no pressure to attend meetings or to undertake any of the tasks necessary to maintain a local church.

In many ways "easy" can also mean shallow. It's easy to grasp the music and message of the electronic church because it is so shallow. The tunes are often insipid, and the lyrics are usually centered on human emotions rather than on divine attributes and actions (which genuinely *inspire* human emotions). The message does not often stimulate the mind to reflect on anything profound. Immediate emotion rather than gradual growth in grace seems to be its goal.

The easy church is often the undisciplined church. The pursuit of genuine holiness is a life-long, arduous task. It is not easy. Holiness easily attained is easily lost. Religion that feeds immediate emotional gratification will encourage immediate gratification of other appetites as well. Financial and sexual scandals are the logical outcomes of such religion.

INDIVIDUALISTIC

The electronic church is *individualistic*. America, especially since the 60s, has greatly stressed the rights and prerogatives of the individual. Linked to that concern for the individual has come a distrust of institutions. Institutions are often seen as the bastion of hypocrisy, bureaucracy, and opposition to the individual's freedom. The church has doctrines and ethical requirements and services that interfere with the individual's freedom of thought and action. The electronic church provides an ideal alternative. The viewer says, "I can watch the show that says what I want to hear and that encourages (or at least tolerates by its silence) my life-style. I do not have to participate in any genuinely human communal life. I can just do my own thing."

INTERESTING

The electronic church is *interesting*. Perhaps the most common charge brought against the local church is that it is boring. The TV church, by contrast, is fast-paced, exciting, and engaging. It has attractive people and personalities, professional music and effective communicators.

Probably the single word that most viewers believe best describes the broadcasts is "inspirational." But what does it mean to be "inspired"? It is a feeling of being moved religiously. What determines the genuineness of the feeling of inspiration? What separates inspiration from entertainment? Perhaps the dividing line can be described this way: Genuine inspiration is an emotional response to a genuine encounter with the living God. Inspiration, therefore, is not an end in itself or even something we should seek. It is rather a result of seeking and meeting God in His way. Inspiration is the result of something profoundly God-centered. Entertainment is profoundly man-centered. In entertainment a person looks for what pleases and excites himself or herself.

Entertainment gratifies the viewer emotionally. Whether it pleases God may be quite a secondary matter. Error can inspire. It can make people feel good, though it displeases and angers God. The electronic church too often is in the entertainment, not inspiration, business. One is more likely to meet and be moved by singers and personalities than by God. And to mask the quality of their programs with the ambiguous term *inspiration* is quite dishonest.

One of the great tragedies of our time is that so many local churches are choosing to try to copy the electronic church. Many local churches are seeking to be attractive by emulating some of the easy, individualistic, and interesting features of the electronic church. This strategy is self-defeating because usually the local church cannot match the professional production and slick graphics of television. But more important, the strategy dishonors God by failing to be what He wants the local church to be.

The local church will fail to teach in depth, or discipline, or spend time in prayer. It will lose touch with the great hymns of praise. It may adopt a style of worship that contradicts the reverence before God that Scripture commands (Hebrews 12:28). The local church is a divine institution that has fallen on hard times, and it must once again learn to devote the greatest care to pleasing God and serving Him according to His Word.

THE SUCCESSFUL CHURCH

Frequently, the electronic church is defended on the basis that it is, after all, successful. That attitude is a beautiful summary of American pragmatism, but it must not be applied to religion. Truth is not established by majority vote, and the religion with the largest number of adherents is not necessarily true. It is especially ironic when Protestants accept such pragmatism, since on that basis we should all be Roman Catholics.

Yet, the argument often runs, the electronic church is not just successful in terms of numbers of viewers and funds raised, but is successful in evangelism. For many Christians that is the ultimate test of success. Is not the Great Commission of our Lord (Matthew 28:18-20) a charge that makes evangelism the most important responsibility of all Christians?

Without a doubt some people have been evangelized by the electronic church. The number actually converted, however, is very difficult to determine. It seems that most of the viewers of televangelism already consider themselves Christians. On a purely pragmatic basis, one might ask if the millions of dollars spent on TV time and production costs could produce more effective results if they were invested in home and foreign missions. Someone might respond by saying that without television those millions would not have been raised. That may be true. But if it is true, it probably means that money was raised more by entertainment than out of a genuine concern for evangelism. And that brings us back to the basic question of what the electronic church is really all about.

It is not enough, however, to examine these questions from a purely pragmatic point of view. Again, we must ask about the biblical guidelines. What does the Great Commission really *say*? It certainly begins with a challenge: "Go!" Christians need always to be reminded of their responsibility to look beyond themselves to the many who need the saving message of Jesus Christ. But in their "going," Christians are not just to evangelize—if by "evangelize" we mean some minimal communication about Jesus and some minimal response. Our Lord said we are to "make disciples." We are to lead people into a life-long commitment to learn from and follow the Lord Jesus Christ. The electronic church cannot make the personal contact necessary to discipleship.

The Great Commission itself specifies what the discipleship entails. It first mentions "baptizing them." The initial phase of instruction in the gospel and response with faith and repentance culminates in baptism in the missionary setting. Baptism represents not only the promise of God to wash away sin, but the sinner's commitment to look to Jesus alone as his Savior. Baptism is the public break with the old life as a rebel against God and the beginning of the new life as a follower of Jesus.

For many Americans, the drama and central importance of baptism may seem foreign to their experience. But they should listen to the missionaries' stories from places where it is fine to "believe" whatever you want about Jesus as long as you are not baptized. Once baptized, however, family, friends and perhaps the government see you as one who has rejected his own religion and culture. Baptism is a powerful testimony to the unique claims of Jesus to be the Way, the Truth, and Life. One is not truly a disciple, is not truly evangelized, until one will make that kind of commitment. Evangelism includes incorporation into the church.

Second, the Great Commission specifies that making disciples involves "teaching them to obey everything I have commanded you" (Matthew 28:20). Here again we see nothing minimal about genuine evangelism. Evangelism is not a matter of rousing songs and repetitious, but empty, references to Jesus. Our Lord wants us to be carefully and deeply instructed, and He wants us to seek to be obedient in all things.

The electronic church cannot fulfill the Great Commission. At the very best it can provide some assistance to the local church. The electronic church must be secondary to the local church in the interest and support of Christians. It is the local church that can and must fulfill the Great Commission.

CONCLUSION

The danger posed by the TV church is two-fold. The first is that it threatens to replace the local church as the central focus of religious life for many people.[1] Such a threat is seri-

---

1. According to Ben Armstrong in *The Electric Church* (Nashville: Thomas Nelson, 1979), televangelism has not discouraged or replaced church attendance for its viewers. Nevertheless, to the degree that it performs any function reserved for the local church, it undermines that institution.

ous because it is the local church that has been established by Jesus Christ as the center of the religious life of His people.

The second danger is, if possible, more serious. Since the electronic church will not and cannot do all that Christ has commissioned the local church to do, the TV church as one's sole church will teach a religion that is sub-Christian. The electronic church will be sub-Christian in doctrine because, even if the doctrine is not wrong (as it often is), it will surely be incomplete. What is not entertaining or commercially appealing will be ignored. And the electronic church will be sub-Christian in ethics, since it will not be a disciplined church.

The danger posed by televangelism is also an opportunity for all Christians and local churches for examination. Churches that have failed in teaching, or in worship, or in outreach or hospitality, should repent and, by God's grace, renew themselves for service. And Christians should realize that they must be more involved, not less, in the local church, reforming it and making it, by God's grace, what it should be.

Christians *are* the church, after all. It is to Christians in a local church that Paul said, "Now you are the body of Christ, and *each one of you* is a part of it" (1 Corinthians 12:27).

As the crowds increased, Jesus said, "This is a wicked generation. It asks for a miraculous sign."

—Luke 11:29

Many will say to me on that day, "Lord, Lord, did we not prophesy in your name, and in your name drive out demons and perform many miracles?" Then I will tell them plainly, "I never knew you. Away from me, you evildoers!"

—Matthew 7:22-23

9

Faith-Healing and the Sovereignty of God

C. Everett Koop, M.D.

I don't know how many operations I actually performed in my surgical career. I know I performed 17,000 of one particular type, 7,000 of another. I practiced surgery for thirty-nine years, so perhaps I performed at least 50,000 operations. I was successful, and I had a reputation for success. Patients were coming to me from all over the world. And one of the things that endeared me to the parents of my patients was the way my incisions healed.

Now, no one likes a big scar, but they are especially upsetting to mothers when they appear on their children. So I set out early on to make my scars small, as short and as thin as possible. These "invisible" scars became my trademark. But was I a *healer*?

The secret of thin scars is to make the incision precise —no feathered edges—and in the closing, get the edges of the skin in exact apposition. I would do this by sewing the stitches inside the skin, but not through it, and the knots were tied on the bottom. All you have to figure out is how I crawled out after doing that.

I was the one who put the edges together, but it was God who coagulated the serum. It was God who sent the fiberblasts out across the skin edges. It was God who had the fiberblasts make collagen, and there were probably about fifty other complicated processes involved about which you and I will never know. But did God come down and instruct the fiberblasts to behave that way?

In a sense, He did. But He did it through His *natural laws,* just the way He makes the grass grow, the rain fall, the earth quake. The question, then, is not, Does God heal? Of course He heals! We are concerned with this question: Granted that God heals, is it *normally according to natural laws* or an *interruption* of those laws (i.e., a miracle)?

Natural Law

It is natural law that keeps the sea at the edge of the shore, or an airplane in the sky, or that makes cats out of kittens. When the twenty-three chromosomes of the sperm and the twenty-three chromosomes of the egg are put together, it is God's natural law that turns a baby into a child, a child into an adolescent, an adolescent into an adult, and an adult into an elderly person. It is also His natural law that brings about the death of a person, set off by one phenomenon or another. Nevertheless, the phenomenon is part of God's natural law. Can you interrupt or alter God's law of nature? It may indeed appear that you can. You might accelerate the process or slow it, but you cannot avoid it. Whatever happens, it is according to God's natural laws.

Suppose you get tonsillitis. Your doctor recommends penicillin, and your condition improves. You say to your doctor, "You're a magician!" Not so. He was an instrument, just as I was an instrument in putting the skin together. I used instruments to do it, but *I* was an instrument in so doing. You might say at this point, "What makes *you* so special?" And the reply is, "I'm not." Nothing makes me special. God uses instruments who will spend eternity with Him. I'm one of those instruments. But He also uses instruments who curse Him and people who never even acknowledge Him.

I remember well an incident that occurred during my days in training. A woman was recovering from gall bladder surgery. She said to her surgeon as he made his rounds, "I thank God for making me well." The surgeon angrily grabbed the foot of the bed with both hands and shouted, "God didn't do that; *I* did!" But whether this doctor acknowledged it or not, he was an *instrument* of God's natural law.

Now, back to the tonsillitis. God created a fungus that a man named "Penicillin notatum." It has been around, I presume, since the beginning of time. But I was well into my residency before Alexander Flemming noted its properties. Penicillin killed bacteria, and it did so through a very complicated process: all part of God's natural laws. Penicillin killed the streptococcus in your tonsils, and you were healed in accordance with the process and timing of God's law.

Maybe you have had a severe illness. Let us say you have "hovered at death's door," as they say. Then you slowly improved, and here you are today, fit and healthy. I can just imagine that when you recovered someone told you, "It's a miracle!" Not necessarily. God's natural law was again at work.

Let me offer another illustration that should be familiar to most city-dwellers. I missed the entrance to the expressway and wandered all around parts of San Francisco I had never seen before. Finally, I got back to where I wanted to be, got on the expressway, and arrived at the airport with no time to spare. It was a miracle that I caught my plane! Miracle? Not so. Just a loose use of a word that is rarely employed in its authentic meaning. That was no more a miracle than the recovery from tonsillitis. Now, I can hear somebody say, "He doesn't even believe in *miracles*!" But I *do* believe in miracles, and that is why it is worthwhile hearing me out in this matter.

If the surgeon who had reacted so arrogantly to the praise attributed to God were writing this chapter, you would be wasting your time to continue reading. But I have credentials in this matter. I am a Bible-believing, evangelical Christian, steeped in the doctrines of the Reformed faith. I am absolutely committed to a belief in the sovereignty of God in all things, and because of my understanding of the art and science of medicine, I do have a perspective on the process of healing as it ordinarily takes place.

SUPERNATURAL INTERVENTION

Having defended my supernaturalism, let us turn our attention to a case-study that *does* circumvent or interrupt God's *natural* laws. It is the account of a man who never attended medical school. On one occasion, he encountered a homeless person who had been unable to walk since birth. The man's heart went out to that disabled individual and, looking the man straight in the eyes, the non-credentialed physician said, "Silver and gold I do not have, but what I do have I give to you. In the name of Jesus of Nazareth, stand up and walk."

Of course, this is an excerpt from Acts 3:6, and the unlettered physician was the apostle Peter. The next verses tell us, "And he took him by the right hand, lifted him up, and immediately his feet and ankle bones received strength. And he, leaping, stood up, walked and entered with them into the temple, walking, and leaping, and praising God." *That was a miracle!* An apostle uttered those words of healing. It was performed before there was a written New Testament, and the healing was immediate, radical, and demonstrable to those who knew the man when he was disabled.

Was this healing in accordance with God's natural laws? Either it was, or His natural law was interrupted. If by God's natural law, the difference between that and the tonsillitis case was only a matter of *time*. The healing of the lame man was instantaneous, and that is what made it a miracle. However, a miracle is more than a matter of time. It is an act of God produced in unusual circumstances in which He uses means unfamiliar to us but which are perfectly normal expressions of His character. Miracles may be a departure from

God's usual way of acting (as we understand it), but we can never say they *contradict* God's nature.

Over the years I have had innumerable people say that I am wrong, that they have witnessed numerous miracles. For example, after I had spoken in a church service one night, a woman came to me and said, "God can do anything! . . . I once knew a woman who went into the hospital to be fitted for a glass eye and while the surgeon turned his back to get an instrument, he turned back to find a new eye in the empty socket where there had been nothing before, and the woman could see!"

I said, "Did you say you knew this woman?"

"No. I knew someone who knows her," she conceded.

"Well," I said, "could you tell me who he or she is? I would like to have a conversation with *that* person."

"Well, I don't really know that person either, but I know someone who knows *her*."

"Even so," I persisted, "I would like to meet *that* person."

"I don't really know that person, but she knows someone who knows someone. . . . " And so it goes.

Is It Faith or Faithlessness?

A surprising number of Christians are convinced God will not be believed unless He makes tumors disappear, causes asthma to go away, and pops eyes into empty sockets. But the gospel is accepted by God-given faith, not by the guarantee that you will never be sick, or, if you are, that you will be miraculously healed. God is the Lord of healing, of growing, of weather, of transportation, and of every other process. Yet people don't expect vegetables without plowing. They don't expect levitation instead of getting in a car and turning a key—even for extraordinarily good and exceptional reasons.

Although God *could* do all of this, Christian airline pilots do not fly straight into a thunderstorm after asking God for a safe corridor, although He could give them such safety. We do not have public services and ask God to remove all criminals, prostitutes, and pornographers from our midst, although He could do that too. God *could* eliminate AIDS from our planet. While we pray for a speedy discovery of successful treatment, I must do all I can to employ medical science in its task, as all health care professionals must do.

We live in a fallen world and the afflictions of our bodies and souls are the result of that Fall (not the immediate work of Satan). Disease and death are "givens" in this fallen world. They are the expectation. All will be straightened out only after the return of Jesus Christ—and not before. God is sovereign. By "sovereignty" I mean that God is in total control of this universe, at all times. If you and I could determine human circumstances by our "faith" (as it is called), God would not be sovereign, and I do not think, indeed, that he would be God. He did not create us and drop us down here, withdrawing control to see how we would make out. He does not act capriciously nor arbitrarily. It is all in line with the grand plan that you and I can only see in pieces now but will see in its completeness in the future.

Presumptuous Christian writers claim to know God's intent, such as the author of the book that insists, "God wants you well." Who says so? Why should He want *you* well when He did not want the apostle Paul well? Paul apparently had a serious eye disease to which he refers in his letters to the young churches. And indeed, Paul asked God to remove his thorn in the flesh several times. But God chose not to do so. Timothy, Paul's protégé, had something in the way of a gastrointestinal complaint. Paul didn't respond with the command "Be healed!" Instead, he told Timothy to stop drinking only water and to drink a little wine!

Affliction is part of the Christian's life just as much as the nonbeliever's (sometimes more so). The proper response of Christians to affliction is not to demand healing but rather to witness to the world that through the grace of God a Christian is able to accept affliction, trusting in the sovereignty of God. We are called to witness to the sovereignty, grace, and mercy of God *in time*, knowing that all of these things will be removed *in eternity*.

You will recall that soon after the Sermon on the Mount, Jesus Himself began to perform miracles. And those miracles, no doubt, authenticated Christ's claims and His mission. Thereafter, He invested His twelve apostles with these same healing capabilities in order to authenticate this "new" religion, which we call Christianity. But after serving their purpose, these gifts ceased. With the completion of the canon of Scripture, the total revelation of God has been given (that is, not all that *can* be known about God, but all that God has *decided* to let us in on).

If miracles were commonplace, they would cease to be miracles. And I repeat what I said earlier: It is God who does the healing, but He does not regularly do so in a *miraculous* way. He heals according to His own natural laws. God can be, and should be, glorified when healing of illness takes place. But He should also be glorified when healing does not take place—and even when death ensues, in spite of the pain and grief it may cause. I don't say that flippantly. I lost my own son to a rock-climbing accident, and I have learned how essential the doctrine of God's sovereignty is in such circumstances. God was greatly glorified by that tragedy in ways I could never have predicted.

Miracles, then, were the credentials of Christ and the apostles, to whom He gave the gift of healing. And one can assume, I think, that the cessation of these gifts came at the end of the apostolic age. Tertullian, one of the great early church Fathers, studied this issue carefully and analyzed the miracles that had taken place among the apostles. He came to the conclusion that the phenomena that we call "miracles" today, the sort of astounding signs carried out by the apostles, came to an end about two hundred years after the death of Christ.

A few biblical statements would seem to promise, at first glance, that God will do whatever we ask of Him. Obviously, these cannot be taken as absolute promises in an unconditional sense, because, if this were true, God could not possibly be sovereign (hence, God). Besides, is there a Christian anywhere who can say he or she has received every single thing he or she has requested?

Furthermore, such conclusions are reached hastily, before the statements can be analyzed within their surrounding context. For instance, we read in John 15:7, "If you abide in Me, and My words abide in you, ask whatever you wish, and it shall be done for you" (NASB). Nevertheless, there is a condition to this promise, given in 1 John: "If we ask anything *according to His will,* He hears us" (5:14, NASB).

When a faith healer commands God to perform a miracle, in the absence of a prayer that says, "Thy will be done," it is, as far as I am concerned, the most rank form of arrogance. No doubt some have said that it is the will of God for every affliction of man to be healed, but you know that this could not possibly be true. Otherwise, we would have to conclude that God falls far short of His plans. He is, in this case, not sovereign, not God at all, and hence unworthy of our worship and praise.

The faith healer may say that faith makes God act. If you follow that line of reasoning, God is in His heaven, but Bosworth rules the world! In Matthew 8:2-3, where Jesus heals a leper, we read:

> Behold, a leper came and worshiped Him, saying, "Lord, if You are willing, You can make me clean." Then Jesus put out His hand and touched him, saying, "I am willing; be cleansed." And the leper departed. *And slowly, over the course of the next several weeks, his symptoms began to disappear.*

I am sure you realize that this is not what the Bible says. I put it in those terms because that conforms to a lot of "miraculous healings" today. The healing takes place next month. But what the Word of God says is this: "'I am willing; be cleansed.' And *immediately* his leprosy was cleansed" (NKJV, italics added).

Now I know that all healing comes from God, but if we are to pursue this matter of faith healing so that I do not have any questions, this is what I want to see: I want to see a person with one leg suddenly ("immediately") have two. In fact, I want to see a person cold, flat-out dead, get up and walk. Now it is not that I want to see these miracles take place just to satisfy my own curiosity. I want to see them happen in such a way that there is no praise attributed to the faith healer. And I want to see it done in a situation that is not a carnival. Now if all of those conditions were in place, I suspect that a healing service would occur very much in private.

The rise of the professional faith-healer is one of the seamiest sides of this whole business. It is also important to remember that a number of diseases come from psychosomatic stimuli. There is no question about the fact that what we think has tremendous effects on our bodies. If we can change our thinking, the body frequently "heals itself," as the saying goes.

If it were the sovereign will of God that humans be healed of all illness and of all afflictions, all humans would be immortal. Isn't death, after all, the ultimate illness?

Giving that great Reformed theologian from Princeton, B. B. Warfield, credit for his contribution to my thinking on this subject, let me summarize in the following way. There is no promise anywhere in the Scriptures of miraculous healing for those who will claim it. Anywhere. No facts exist that compel us to believe that such miraculous healing should be expected. Such *miraculous* healing is unnecessary, because God is perfectly capable of healing people by natural means. The employment of such a method is contrary to the way God works in other modes of dealing with us. Miraculous healings of the type I have been describing would be contrary to the very purpose of "miracle." If miracles were commonplace, they would soon lose their significance.

DOES SIN CAUSE SICKNESS?

Contrary to what many televangelists will tell you, there is no connection between specific sin and the judgment of God, in the sense of retributive justice.

Miraculous gifts of the New Testament were the credentials of the apostles. Faith healing arguments presuppose or lead to many false doctrines: for example, to the erroneous notion that sickness and sin are somehow connected. It can lead us into the situation where we can trip over perfectionism. If sinfulness is not to be removed entirely in this life, neither is sickness. If we can be led into completely unscriptural views of the function of suffering and the uses of pain, we will inflict deeper pain on timid souls, and we will actually cause people to give up on God (or their "faith") when they do not receive what they were convinced God promised. After all, God lied to them, if the faith teachers are correct.

All sickness and suffering are spoken of by faith healers as though they came from Satan, or as if they were surely the result of God's displeasure, as if they were a particular fruit of sin. But the Bible says, "Whom the Lord loveth he chasteneth, and scourgeth every son whom he receiveth" (Hebrews 12:6, KJV).

Sickness is often the *proof* of God's special favor, and it always, in His loving pleasure, is coordinated with everything else that befalls the believer to achieve ultimately positive goals (Romans 8:28). The faith healer's contention leads to dissatisfaction with God's natural method of healing and, therefore, with God Himself. As Warfield put it, we are not to demand to be fed by miracles but by Christ Himself. Faith healing leads to the proliferation of professionals who stand between man and God (an error the Reformation challenged). This is a grave danger for the afflicted individual and a source of great spiritual pride for the man who calls himself a healer.

If Christians ought to be spared illness, whether cancer or a cold, anybody would jump on the Christian bandwagon just to avoid sickness. Therefore, the demand to come to Christ through faith alone would also be nullified. "Faith alone" is negated when it depends on outward signs for its existence. "Faith," according to Hebrews 11:1, is "the evidence of things not seen" (KJV). Faith trusts God *in spite of* pain, suffering, and even death, knowing that it is all part of a scheme that is destined to serve His glory and our good.

In the thirty-five years I was in the practice of pediatric surgery, I had many children who died, primarily from cancer. I used to tell my residents that the cases were rare indeed where the parents would not find cause in their own minds to justify one of two positions: either blaming God or blaming themselves. But I think Scripture is clear that God does not punish people for individual sins. "Who sinned," the disciples asked Jesus, "this man or his parents, that he was born blind?" Jesus answered, "Neither this man nor his parents sinned . . . but this happened so that the work of God might be displayed in his life" (John 9:2-3).

And if the parents could not blame themselves for sin, they blamed themselves for a lack of faith. It is always difficult to assuage the feeling of desolation experienced by a parent who says, after the death of a child, "I guess I didn't have enough faith."

Did I Have Enough Faith?

Along these lines, you must allow me one anecdote that goes back many years to the time when I was president of the Evangelical Foundation. We hired an investigative writer to look into some of the cults and into faith healers specifically. Our investigator traveled to a Southwestern city where a healing campaign had been advertised some weeks in advance. Adjacent to the huge tent into which thousands would pour for the services was a smaller tent. For the whole week prior to the services, those who had physical infirmities came to this smaller tent in order to be screened by associates of the healer. After all, they had to pick the proper specimens for their "chief" to heal on television. They chose people with such conditions as asthma, which has a very strong emotional overlay. They dealt with hysterical people, with those who are very suggestible. With others, they tried to see if they could find samples of psychosomatic illness that could be altered by suggestion.

Among those who applied for healing was an elderly Christian gentleman who lived out on the prairie. His vision was becoming dim, and he most likely was developing cataracts. The only lighting in the little cabin where he lived was a kerosene lamp. He was a devout Christian, read his Bible daily—or tried to—and had all the faith necessary for healing, if faith indeed does secure healing. His major complaint was that his sight had deteriorated to the point where he could no longer read his Bible.

On the night of his appearance before the healer, the old man was brought up in the atmosphere of a sideshow. The faith healer said, "Well, Pop, you can't see anymore. You've gotten old, you can't even see with your glasses. Your vision is failing." Then he reached over and took off the old man's spectacles, threw them on the platform, stamped on them, and broke them. He then handed the elderly gentleman a large-print Bible, which, under the lights necessary for television in those days, enabled the gentleman to read John 3:16 out loud, to the astonishment and applause of the audience.

The elderly gentleman praised God, the healer praised God, the audience praised God, and the old man went back to his dimly lit cabin and could not *find* his Bible, because his glasses were destroyed. The man went back to the healer but was told the most discouraging thing a godly man like that could possibly hear: "You didn't have enough faith, or the healing would have stuck."

Now, obviously, this makes two classes of Christians: those who have enough faith to be healed—the first-class Christians—and those who don't have enough faith to be healed—they, of course, are second-class. There is great poverty in that kind of religion. One's willpower, not divine grace, is suggested as the basis for faith and life. I prefer the biblical faith, expressed in the words of a hymn:

> When through the deep waters I call thee to go,
> The rivers of sorrow shall not overflow,
> For I will be with thee, thy trials to bless,
> And sanctify to thee thy deepest distress.

That is what God expects of you and me as He asks us to commit our way to Him, to trust Him completely, and to put our future into His hands. His way may be completely contrary to what we would like it to be. But whether it is sickness we are talking about, or infirmity, or deformity, or approaching death, God will indeed sanctify to us our deepest distress.

Part Two
Facing The Future

Again, the devil took [Jesus] to a very high mountain and showed him all the kingdoms of the world and their splendor. "All this I will give you," he said, "if you will bow down and worship me." Jesus said to him, "Away from me, Satan! For it is written: 'Worship the Lord your God, and serve him only.'" Then the devil left him, and angels came and attended him.

—Matthew 4:8-11

10

TV and Evangelism: Unequally Yoked?

Quentin Schultze

Malcolm Muggeridge once called television the "Fourth Great Temptation." He imagined TV as the devil's final attempt to appeal to the vanity of the Savior before He went to the cross. Roman tycoon and television promoter Gradus offers to make Christ the star of a new show sponsored by Lucifer, Inc. Gradus will "put Christ on the map, launch him off on a tremendous career as a worldwide evangelist, spread his teaching throughout the civilized world, and beyond. He'd be crazy to turn it down." Christ overcomes the temptation to trade "fantasy and images" for "truth and reality," and mankind is saved.

Ben Armstrong, recently retired executive director of the National Religious Broadcasters, describes a far different scenario. God "raises up" communications satellites in the final days to proclaim the gospel around the globe before Christ returns. Satellites are the angels prophesied in the book of Revelation: "And I saw another angel fly in the midst of heaven, having the everlasting gospel to preach unto them that dwell on the earth, and to every nation, and kindred, and tongue, and people" (Revelation 14:6). In *The Electric Church*, Armstrong argues that broadcasting has "broken

Portions of this essay first appeared in *Christianity Today*, March 18, 1988. Copyright 1988 by *Christianity Today*. Used by permission of the publisher.

through the walls of tradition we have built up around the church and . . . restored conditions remarkably similar to the early church."

Muggeridge and Armstrong represent opposing views of technology held by the church throughout the ages. From the resurrection of Christ to the present, Christians have both loved and hated, venerated and condemned, celebrated and vilified various technologies. Television is the latest object of attention in a long line of technologies that included radio, the telegraph, printing presses, and even church organs.

On the one hand is the optimism of Armstrong, which links broadcasting to the second coming of Christ and the salvation of the world. Like Francis Bacon (*The New Atlantis*, 1626) and other religious visionaries of Renaissance Europe, Armstrong challenges humanistic views of technology by baptizing them in romantic language. Like nineteenth-century American poet Walt Whitman, Armstrong hears the seductive music of the machines. This is an appealing image for the hopeful throngs of Christian believers.

On the other hand is the pessimism of Muggeridge, which associates mass communication, especially TV and film, with the fall of humankind into sin in the Garden of Eden. Here is an example of a modern Luddite who would prefer to see picture tubes smashed because of their demonic potential. Here as well is the Christian who seeks a life of simplicity and peace without the worldly influence of the one-eyed monster.

These contradictory views of television appeal to the Christian community and the wider culture. Both of them capture something of the impact of TV. Unfortunately, neither gives us a clear sense of the inherent nature of television as a medium.

The truth lies somewhere between these exaggerations of the medium's demonic and redemptive characteristics. TV is not a "neutral" communications medium; its message is always shaped by the technology and by those who use it. Neither is television inherently good or evil. Its benefits to Kingdom and society depend both on the inherent biases of the technology (the equipment itself) *and* on how it is used (its social institutions). In other words, to evaluate the potential of television for communicating the gospel we must examine both the people who make the messages and the equipment they use.

Given the medium's dual nature of technology and institution, every televangelist should approach TV with hope and fear, and the church should demand accountability for the message as much as for the finances.

At stake is not just the popularity or stature of individual televangelists, but the public image of the church of Jesus Christ. For many unchurched people around the globe, religious broadcasts are their only contact with the gospel. Just as gangster films created an international picture of life in Chicago during Prohibition, televangelism has spread its own portrait of the Christian life—for good and ill. There is no neutral ground.

In America, televangelism is the major public window for viewing the sights and hearing the sounds of evangelicalism. Scandals of the 1980s made that abundantly clear. Scripture holds spiritual teachers to a high standard of truth-telling. Might not the Lord hold televangelists and their supporters especially accountable for their public teachings in the name of Christ?

TV CREATES CELEBRITIES

On television, the evangelist is immediately the focus of audience attention. The nature of the medium requires this focal point. The small screen always accentuates his personality as the camera returns repeatedly to his face. No medium is more pervasively dependent upon the human face for message and meaning. The television industry has built an empire out of the successful imaging of the heads of news reporters, sports celebrities, commercial characters, and especially dramatic actors. Even situation comedies and soap operas are little more than strings of acting and reacting faces.

Close-ups and panoramic shots are almost meaningless on a nineteen-inch set. Unlike still photography, which often thrives on the detail of particular, close-up images, TV must use grimaces of pain, smiles of joy, and tears of sorrow. And unlike film, which can project enormous panoramic scenes on a large screen in a darkened room, television feeds us several feet of flashing phosphorescence on a relatively small set. The TV screen collapses the splendor of the Austrian Alps in the opening and closing scenes of *The Sound of Music* into an unexciting picture. It focuses more on the *characters* than on the magnificent scenery.

In order to hold viewers' attention on the television set, TV programs must be fast-paced and must center on colorful, dramatic characters. That is the nature of the medium. If we seek to visually communicate the miracle of Creation, either in molecules or mountains, television is hardly the best technology.

In nearly all religious broadcasts the evangelist becomes the attraction. Christian talk shows typically turn discussion into chats among various personalities—usually celebrities. And the focus of conversation is usually the life and times of the celebrities themselves. Church broadcasts transform the space and ambiance of a church sanctuary into a ministerial stage. The gospel may be presented, but cameras promote the preacher, sometimes unwittingly, like the latest Hollywood star. On the tube, the person and the message are so thoroughly intertwined that it is often difficult to determine where one stops and the other begins.

Partly because of the technology itself, then, successful televangelism often results in religious personality cults. Few TV ministers are willing to de-emphasize their own role in the broadcasts because a weak personality usually guarantees poor ratings and fewer contributions. The televangelist, typically, is more important than the message.

Television's institutions—the organizations that use it —further accentuate personality cults. Education requires institutions: grade school, college, publishing houses, and so on. So, too, television has, in a short period of time, created its own institutions, from networks to production houses and local stations. And these institutions also engender personality cults.

First, the drive for ratings and contributions encourages televangelists to emphasize the person over the message. As in commercial TV, highlighting individuals simply makes for greater success—if one wishes to define success in traditional broadcasting terms, such as audience ratings and revenues. People like to watch other people.

Many broadcast ministries emphasize the televangelist because they wish to achieve the notoriety and celebrity status of their secular counterparts in Hollywood. They realize that more people will watch and support a person than will view serious theological discussion or even direct, exegetical preaching. On TV an evangelist can say little and attract many. For years news anchors and sports commentators have made a living out of creating the impression of personal wisdom and knowledge. Walter Cronkite, the former anchor of the "CBS Evening News," was the most believable man in the United States, according to public opinion polls. Yet few Americans knew this grandfatherly interpreter of world events.

Emphasis on the Celebrity Appeals to Fallen Human Nature

Second, focus on a leader appeals to fallen human nature. Like the early congregation at Corinth, television audiences seek human leaders to follow. They wish not only to be instructed in the faith but to become disciples of TV's own mediators of the gospel. As a result, many viewers tenaciously cling to the beliefs and doctrines espoused by their favorite televangelist. Although the televangelists might be biblically illiterate, these viewers come to trust the apparently authentic images of their friendly pastor on the home TV set. The results are strife and division within the church—cultivated by appealing, charismatic personalities. The apostle Paul faced this problem at Corinth and wrote, "Let him who boasts boast in the Lord" (1 Corinthians 1:31).

PRIVATE VIEWING HEIGHTENS
TV'S EMPHASIS ON CELEBRITIES

Third, television's emphasis on celebrities is heightened even more by private viewing. TV celebrities enter our homes like relatives and neighbors. The televangelist, along with the soap opera star or the news anchorperson, soon is a friend of the family. He is trustworthy and compassionate, concerned about our spiritual condition, and taken to prayer on our behalf. Through personalized direct-mail appeals and carefully planned camera shots, the televangelist wins a privileged place in the homes and hearts of the viewers. If television were viewed in public, like a play or a theatrical film, the influence of the persons viewed would not be nearly so strong. Instead, we view TV privately, and the medium's celebrities become the inhabitants of our private worlds.

Finally, the private viewing creates an artificial relationship between televangelist and viewer. Seeking personal peace, the viewer tunes to one of the few constant sources of encouragement and friendship in modern life. The televangelist always accepts us as we are, regardless of our mood, looks, or actions. Unlike a spouse or an employer, the TV preacher loves us no matter what we say or do. He faithfully accepts us every week, if only we return to the same channel at the appointed time.

PERFORMANCE

Television packages nearly everything as performance. Over the decades it has spun its dramatic web to include commercials, news and game shows, and traditional comedies and adventure series. Even real life is packaged for the tube on "Divorce Court" and "People's Court." Advertisements depict tales of lonely hearts who found love through toothpaste and mouthwash. News reports portray a world in conflict where the major characters are public officials and disaster victims. Nature programs create a fictional animal kingdom where these creatures battle for survival. From

Westerns to detective programs, television is an enormous stage where everyone performs for the living-room audience.

As a technology, then, television does not accurately or easily communicate abstract or complex ideas. Unlike the printed word, which the reader can ingest intellectually at his own pace, the images on the tube keep running regardless of the ability of the viewer to make sense of them. The viewer cannot stop to reflect upon what he has seen and heard except after the program is over. Unless he uses a videocassette recorder, the program is gone. All that remains is his memory of the show and its passing images. Therefore, all types of highly logical, rational, linear messages are poorly communicated on television. This is as true for systematic theology as for mathematics and physics.

It should not surprise us, then, that television has never been a particularly effective educational medium. In the 1950s many professional educators championed the new medium as the answer to the nation's growing educational problems. There was grand talk of putting a TV set in every classroom, and some schools did exactly that in spite of the protests of many teachers and more enlightened educational theorists. Television was even supposed to greatly lower educational costs by reducing the number of teachers required for each school district. That rhetoric was remarkably similar to the unsupported claims by televangelists that TV is the most efficient and effective means of communicating the gospel to the nation and to the world.

The history of the medium clearly shows that it is no educational panacea. Simply put, the tube does not teach as well as it entertains. The moving images, locked into their own rhythms, do not easily communicate abstract or complex ideas. Television best communicates simple, straightforward, and dramatic messages. In fact, the medium has increasingly based its programming philosophy on the concept of entertainment—not just because people like to be entertained, but because television entertains so much more effectively than it educates and informs. As both a technology and an institution, television has learned the rules of entertainment.

Therefore, we should not think of television as a book but as a stage. Also, we should not view the tube as the great *communicator* but as the great *performer*. Whatever the TV camera captures, it turns into a performance. This is as true for television drama as it is for talk shows and the news.

Televangelism, too, is gobbled up by the medium's insatiable appetite for performance. The medium demands more than entertaining characters. It wants lively action to engage sleepy viewers and boost the ratings. Often, preaching is not enough—unless it is dramatic and entertaining. There must be tearful soliloquies and maudlin renditions of gospel songs.

Soon the pulpit becomes a stage for histrionics of all kinds. On some shows the devil is chased off the set, broken bodies are healed, and spirits are slain. Prophecies and special knowledge about unidentified viewers are dramatically uttered by talk-show hosts. On other broadcasts, the performances are packaged more acceptably for middle America as testimonials, conversion stories, and revivals. Even appeals for contributions are cast as cosmic struggles to "fight Satan and deliver the gospel to every living human being."

The trend is clear: television is turning religion into public entertainment, making religious programs increasingly indistinguishable from secular fare. Today there are few distinctly Christian national broadcasts. Nearly all of them combine show business and religion.

For this reason, television is theologically biased toward more emotionally dramatic formulations of the Christian faith. Charismatic worship visually overshadows traditional Protestant liturgy on the tube. Historic Protestantism is often dull and sleep-inducing on television unless it is packaged for the visual medium. Although there remains a significant audience for clear, exegetical preaching, television ministries will always be tempted to dramatize the message visually for the small screen. Biblical exposition is rarely as entertaining as sheer performance.

Reformation theologies are an interesting case in contrast. Few preachers of the Reformation heritage have become successful on television without changing both the content of the message and the style of presentation. Calvinist theology, for example, is highly logical and systematic. Moreover, although it emphasizes the fundamentals of the historic Christian gospel (e.g., salvation through faith and *sola Scriptura*), it was formulated during an age of written and eventually printed communication. Luther, Calvin, and others challenged the church primarily through the written, not spoken, word. They were certainly preachers, but they were also scholars and writers. Calvin was trained in the law, and even his well-known *Institutes of the Christian Religion* reads like a legal tome.

Luther or Calvin might have made interesting television guests on talk shows or preaching programs, but would their message have been effectively communicated on the tube? Probably not, for they were not performers of their Reformation messages. Their ideas were driven by biblical consistency and theological conviction, not by popularity or entertainment value. They sought the truth, not the most appealing doctrines or the most exciting messages. In short, Reformation theology was the product of a search for truth in and through the written word, from biblical exegesis to theological formulation. The message was never the servant of visual performance.

Television's fundamental religious bias, then, is toward experientially validated theologies—those theologies whose veracity is communicated through the *experiences* of believers, not through doctrinal or even biblical certainty. For this reason, many televangelists use their lives to interpret the Bible, not their Bible to interpret their lives. This is obvious in programs that talk at length about "what God is doing with this ministry" while spending little time actually discussing God or His Word. Viewers get celebrities' autobiographies instead of biblical history. Also, experiential theologies are obvious in the ways various televangelists use letters and telephone calls from viewers to convince audiences that a ministry's work is effective. Rather than relying on the historic Christian gospel as narrated in the Old and New Testaments, these teleevangelists effectively create their own scriptures based on the success stories of the ministry. The seemingly personal words of televangelists become more believable than the written words of Scripture.

As a result, televangelism suffers from a rhetoric of hyperbole that exaggerates and accentuates the power of the Holy Spirit in the life of the TV preacher. On a twenty-inch screen these television preachers stand larger than life. They are portrayed as spiritual giants who have a special relationship to God. The viewer supposedly can capitalize on the power of the televangelist by watching the program, sending contributions, and reading additional literature offered "free of charge." TV has given rise to new media papacies with power vested in particular religious leaders. American Protestantism has replaced one Roman Catholic pope with many Protestant popes who claim special insight and profound religious experiences that qualify them to rule their See. Those experiences, not Scripture, seem to validate their authority and their infallibility.

The drama on religious broadcasts often has little to do with the gospel itself. Instead, the programs frequently are stories about the ministries and ministers. Every week the preacher dramatically updates the expectant audience on the latest work of the ministry. If funds are low, the drama is nearly a tragedy, sometimes even replete with tears and pleadings for support. At other times, the contributions are beyond expectations, morale is high, and the program becomes almost comedic. There is much singing and rejoicing. But the party won't last; eventually donations will decline or ministry expansion will tax the resources. Then the preacher will once again dramatize the plight of the ministry. Some ministries have new financial crises every week because they lend themselves so well to the kinds of fund-raising performances that elicit large donations. TV fund-raising is indeed a performing art in many of today's largest ministries.

Of course, in the broadest sense, any presentation of the gospel is a performance. Even the church pulpit is like a stage for the local pastor, who uses his voice and body to communicate the message. Liturgies and worship services of all kinds must include human action, and even the sacraments of Communion and baptism can be interpreted as religious drama. Throughout the ages, the church used drama, from morality plays to tropes, to build congregational life and witness to the wider culture. Indeed, the story of salvation itself is dramatic and life-changing.

But the use of popular dramatic devices to communicate the gospel and depict the Christian life can easily confuse message and method. If the "performance" of the gospel on TV imitates the secular programs, the Good News loses its distinctiveness. Then the message is not from God but from Hollywood. There is no authenticity because there is no difference in the message. Christianity is simply another expression of the Hollywood culture and the entertainment industry.

The most difficult job ahead for televangelism is capturing the inherent drama of the gospel without succumbing to the same techniques of the entertainment industry.

Is the Message Authentic?

Nothing should concern religious broadcasters more than the authenticity of their message. Modern TV ministries, taking their cues from Madison Avenue, frequently define success in terms of audience ratings and viewer response. They tabulate telephone calls, letters, and, of course, contributions. Some even attempt to keep a running total of the number of viewers saved. All of this leads some televangelists to be far more concerned with the size of the audience and the apparent scope and power of the ministry than with the authenticity of the message. In this way, many television ministries mimic the standards of success championed by secular broadcast institutions.

Televangelists easily slip into a marketing mentality that adjusts the message to the hopes and dreams of the audience. This would not be a problem except for the selfish desires of the viewers. What *are* the hopes and dreams of unbelievers? Health, wealth, and happiness? So give it to them! TV leads to market-driven gospels, not to the historic gospel of salvation from sin.

Some of the gospels preached on television today are cleverly disguised distortions of the biblical message. They offer solutions for sickness and poverty, showing viewers how to overcome unhappiness and to create a positive attitude toward life. They inform audiences concerning enjoyable ways to spend their time and money. But often they skip over the heart of the gospel. Christ is merely a friend—a "buddy," a healer, a rich uncle, or a great teacher. He is a cosmic lawyer or psychologist, a positive thinker or a helpful neighbor. But He is not the Son of God who died on the cross for our sins.

Compared to counterfeit gospels of success or happiness, the real one is not nearly so flashy and interesting. Even commercials offer far more compelling messages and seductive products: sex appeal, automotive power, popularity, self-confidence. The historic Christian gospel calls for faith and perseverance, whereas the culture preaches instant gratification and sensual pleasure. The forgiveness of sins hardly makes for great TV; there is nothing spectacular to show. Either the gospel must be altered, or it will lose out in the cacophony of media voices.

It is a strange fact that in a nation loaded with Bibles and churches, the counterfeit "health and wealth" gospels should thrive on the airwaves. Clearly, religiosity is not religious faith, and the outward appearance of piety bears little resemblance to true faith.

The fund-raising gimmicks employed by some televangelists are incontrovertible evidence that superstition is alive and well in the modern world. It is all there for the asking: sand, dirt, twigs, and stones from the Holy Land, prayer-blessed cloths, anointed oils, sanctifying soap, and even lucky pennies. For $15 or more the viewer can stand with the superstitious people of all ages who had their own icons to venerate and images to adore. Television, the latest mass communication technology, is now a servant of superstition, cant, rumor, and hearsay. Authenticity is but a stumbling block for the opportunistic preachers of the tube.

CONSULTING THE WIZARDS

Today, television evangelism is big business, and many ministries turn to various marketing and media consultants, another institution created by the medium.

These wizards work their financial magic, advising thousands of nonprofit organizations what to do on and off camera to attract viewers and maximize contributions. The major ones work on a fee basis, but some will accept contracts that guarantee them a percentage of the income generated by their direct-mail appeals. Some of these wizards are truly committed servants of the gospel, but others are merely cogs in the institution of religious television programming. Some of them give realistic and helpful advice to ministries that are struggling to make ends meet. However, there are also consultants who divine little beyond the spirits of fame and fortune. Emulating their counterparts in secular broadcasting, they give pagan advice for capturing a pagan world with a pagan gospel.

GODS OF GROWTH

Modern TV evangelism is influenced strongly by the American preoccupation with expansion and growth. Like corporate America, religious broadcasting frequently defines success solely on the basis of size. Ministries are often committed more to expansion—more stations, larger audiences, additional cable TV outlets—than to ministry.

Like secular broadcasters, who erroneously assume that audience ratings and advertising revenues correlate with program quality or public service, televangelists assume that worldly measurements of success correlate with service to

God. Although growth itself is not evil, neither is it alone a worthwhile purpose for any Christian organization. Too often growth is simply a quest for power and recognition within evangelicalism and the wider society. The important question is whether God is pleased, both by the size of a TV ministry and the words and actions behind that growth.

As a result of their penchant for growth, fledgling national television ministries rapidly become major deficit spenders. Often, they buy equipment on credit and start purchasing time on dozens of television stations around the country. Thirty or sixty days later the bills are due, and the funds must be raised to cover the costs of air time. Of course, a ministry might drop from a station or time slot a program that draws fewer viewers and contributors. And any ministry could reduce the number of stations until the income and expenditures are about equal, but that "defeatist" attitude runs against the thinking of most TV ministries, which are geared toward optimistic expansion and unlimited growth, even if that means being millions of dollars in debt.

THE CULT OF SECRECY

Probably nothing has tarnished the image of televangelism in recent years more than the secretive mentality of the ministries. Scandals come and go, but the cult of secrecy goes on. Televangelists project a public image of dishonesty and paranoia by refusing to provide contributors and especially the media with accurate and comprehensive information about their ministries. Some ministries even refuse to grant interviews and provide information to Christian publications. In this sense, too, TV ministries have emulated the secular programs, producers, and networks. Like Hollywood institutions, many televangelists secretly plan their program strategies and protect the privacy of their financial dealings.

Why should television ministries be so secretive? Why should the electronic church fear exposure to the light? Is there any justification for such an attitude toward the church and the public? In American society, personal salaries are considered private information. This might be a strong reason for not releasing the salaries of all ministry employees. But televangelists are public figures and, more important, public representatives of the church of Jesus Christ. Although there is no law or specific ethical responsibility for salary disclosure, secrecy creates the public impression that the church is more concerned about building a self-serving, worldly corporation than a godly kingdom of service and peace.

Disclosure must go beyond salaries to perks of all kinds —bonuses, homes, royalties, and automobiles. There is no doubt that some ministries have taken elaborate measures to "protect their privacy." The PTL and Swaggart scandals opened a few doors in 1988, but others were shut tighter than ever. Such secrecy works against the church regardless of whether or not TV ministries actually have anything to hide. Secrecy suggests that the church is a cult, not the servant of fallen humans. Secrecy also suggests that TV ministries, like their secular counterparts, are competitive, self-interested organizations.

There is nothing inherent in television technologies that requires religious broadcasters to operate in a cult of secrecy. It is purely an institutional decision guided by the norms for secrecy in corporate America. If the church truly wishes to distinguish itself from other institutions in society, it ought to err on the side of openness instead of secrecy. If it fails to do this, televangelism will be increasingly perceived by the public as a self-interested cult of religious entrepreneurship. But then that may well be what much of it actually is.

SITUATIONAL ETHICS

Over the years, Christian ethicists have widely criticized the trend in Western society toward situational ethics. During the same time the church has created its own rationalizations for shifting ethical beliefs and standards. Nothing makes this more evident than contemporary televangelism. In the name of Christ, some televangelists practice a style of "holy deception" that distorts the gospel, legitimizes lavish life-styles,and approves of direct-mail chicanery. This is not an isolated phenomenon. It happens every day in the religious fund-raising letters sent to contributors and the entertaining performances conducted on television.

Holy deception also has its parallel in corporate America: millions of business people treat their employees and clients with entirely different ethical standards than they use with their own families and friends.

In the advertising business, for example, many agencies create commercials that intentionally deceive young television viewers. Do these producers treat their own children with the same ethical laxity? In the same way, some televangelists live multiple ethical lives, treating their audiences, employees, and families very differently. That is because the institution of televangelism takes much of its ethical climate from the secular business culture instead of from the biblical guidelines that should direct all Christians to honesty and integrity.

Of course, accountability is ultimately the relationship of each person to God. Personal accountability cannot be legislated. As Reinhold Niebuhr once said, "There is no easy way of forcing people to be responsible against their own inclination and beyond their capacity." But the church of Christ is not merely a collection of responsible or irresponsible human beings. It is—or *should* be—a community of saints. Individualistic, situational ethics have no place in the church unless one wrongly assumes that the body of believers is little more than a collection of selfish entrepreneurs who are competing for their piece of the pie.

Legalism and lifeless traditions are not the answers. As someone once said, "Tradition is the living faith of the dead, whereas traditionalism is the dead faith of the living." That is precisely why ethical codes are usually so ineffective in the business world, where personal faith is less important than company policy. Instead, the church must take its collective responsibility seriously, creating a living, dynamic community of ethical action. The church should be outraged by the unethical practices of its members, speaking forcefully and directly against wrong and inappropriate practices.

In the end, it is not the televangelists who will keep their own house in order any more than doctors, lawyers, or business executives have done. They, too, carry the burden of the Fall. Professionalism is not the answer; professing faith and obedience to God before the body of believers is part of the solution. Therefore, accountability must be sought by the Christian community, beginning with a televangelist's associates and family, expanding to the local congregation, and ending with the church universal. This was true at Corinth, and it is true on the airwaves today.

GUIDELINES FOR ACCOUNTABILITY

Given the inherent dangers of televangelism, these ministries should consider adopting guidelines that would help them steer clear of the possible dangers of television as both a technology and an institution. I would propose the following:

1. All TV ministries should be governed by a church, a denomination, or a board of directors composed primarily of people greatly respected in the religious and professional communities—whose reputations would not allow for "minor" indiscretions here or there. The churches and boards should review finances and programming in detail. Parachurch ministries are usually more creative and dynamic than churches. But they are also far more likely to become personality cults. They need a strong, independent board of directors composed of people whose own public stature depends upon how well they oversee the television ministry. These directors should be willing to risk their own community standing to ensure that the ministry is run ethically and openly.

2. Each ministry should establish procedures for determining the impact of celebrity and performance on broadcasts. Whenever possible, programming should be shared by a variety of personalities so that the entire ministry will not be

identified with the personality or charisma of one religious celebrity.

3. Televangelists should provide viewers with truthful and informative assessments of the work of the ministry. This would require TV ministries to conduct such assessments and to share them with contributors. Currently, most monthly newsletters and annual reports resemble religious propaganda, which identifies the ministry exclusively with the will of the Lord and greatly exaggerates the actual impact of the ministry through anecdotes or statistical summaries of audience sizes and stations airing the program.

4. Media ministries should provide detailed financial information to all requesting it. In this sense the church of Christ should live by a much tougher standard of openness than does the business community. Secrecy says far more to the public about the inauthenticity of a ministry than does the programming itself, especially in a time of crisis.

5. Every ministry should provide channels for employees to voice significant discontent without retribution. In troubled ministries ethical employees are sometimes the first to leave because they are considered trouble-makers or nay-sayers. How the televangelist is perceived is usually the most important factor: Don't tarnish his image. No one dares question the boss, the one who receives his knowledge and his instructions directly from on high.

6. Television ministries should invite respected leaders from the Christian community to evaluate their programming on a regular basis. These should be neither members of the board nor friends of the televangelist. They must be outsiders to the work of the ministry who would offer a candid evaluation of the authenticity of the message.

We have seen that television and evangelism make for an uneasy marriage. The successful ones may never be the ones with high ratings, large audiences, numerous contributors, and state-of-the-art studios. Rather, they will be the ministries that support the local church, preach the biblical gospel, and avoid dishonest standards.

[Love] is not proud. It is not rude, it is not self-seeking, it is not easily angered, it keeps no record of wrongs.

—1 Corinthians 13:4-5

11

An Atmosphere of Alienation

John Dart

The radio transmission began with a woman's lilting voice. "Hello, Petey. I love you. I'm talking to you—can you hear me? If you can't, you're in trouble."

Indeed, he would have been.

"Petey" was the Reverend Peter Popoff, a Southern California-based evangelist who was on stage in San Francisco's Civic Auditorium and about to start a faith-healing service to be videotaped for broadcast on his weekly television program. The affectionate voice testing the communications was that of his wife, Elizabeth, out of the audience's view but apparently able to see her husband via television monitors. He could hear her through a tiny receiver placed in his ear.

Like many charismatic healers, Popoff would call out the names and ailments of people in his audiences. This "word of knowledge" is supposedly supplied by the Holy Spirit. A Popoff magazine described a beneficiary in one crusade audience as one who has been "called out by the Spirit for healing!" Popoff then would individually call those people forward or approach them. Touching them and praying loudly for healing, he sometimes elicited declarations from his subjects affirming the success of the healing.

Popoff was not a preacher to say that "someone" in the audience has a back problem and that God is healing it right now. He would call out names. People filled out cards with personal information before the service started, and surely some guessed he could call out some people and their ailments after reviewing the cards.

Yet, for his wealth of detail Popoff either had a supernatural memory or supernatural help . . . or so it seemed. In early 1986, a volunteer team of self-described skeptics, led by magician-debunker James Randi, thought otherwise. One member for the Committee for the Scientific Examination of Religion suspected that Popoff was wearing a radio receiver. At a Houston crusade, posing as an usher, he stumbled intentionally into the faith healer and spotted the tiny object in Popoff's left ear.

Employing a scanning receiver and recording equipment at the next meeting in San Francisco, a team member picked up radio transmissions at 39.17 megahertz, a frequency in the range often used by police. The team continued the surreptitious monitoring at Popoff crusades in Anaheim and Detroit. The tapes and transcriptions recorded Elizabeth repeatedly cuing Popoff with names, afflictions, addresses—and occasional ridicule of those seeking healing.

Randi made the findings public April 22, on NBC-TV's "The Tonight Show Starring Johnny Carson." Randi first showed a televised excerpt from a Popoff crusade in which the evangelist gave a man and his wife information about themselves and their eye troubles. Then the excerpt was played simultaneously with a tape revealing that Mrs. Popoff had moments earlier fed the information piecemeal to her husband.

A statement issued the next day by the Peter Popoff Evangelistic Association, in Upland, California, declared cryptically that not everything Randi said was true. Popoff's statement also asked Christians to pray concerning "this attack on Christian organizations," alluding to criticisms by the same skeptics of Jerry Falwell, Oral Roberts, and Jimmy Swaggart. Popoff accused Randi of "using these tactics to get publicity for a book that he is writing to discredit God's word." Randi admitted he was planning to put this into a book, but Popoff also conceded within a few days that he used some rather mundane substitutes for what is commonly viewed in Pentecostal circles as a supernatural phenomenon.

Popoff discussed the "mundane" in an interview with this reporter. The evangelist said there was a precedent: His father, George Popoff, memorized some prayer request cards in his crusades as a way to give "words of knowledge." As for his more modern technique of radio transmissions, Peter Popoff said, "It's not a secret. We've never denied using it." He didn't say whether anyone had ever thought to ask, either.

On the other hand, Popoff pointed to his ministry's average monthly receipts of $550,000 in donations and a growth rate of 35 percent a year as evidence of God's blessings for those on his mailing list. To an audience following him on fifty-one TV and forty radio stations, Popoff wrote promises that he would call them forward if they were to come to the next nearby crusade. "It's just like 'The Price Is Right'; they expect to be called down," he said. "This is a very effective format for television."

The revelations about Peter Popoff did not cause a national stir in the spring of 1986; the thirty-nine-year-old healer was not a well-known name in religious television. And although the evidence for high-tech deception was dramatically obtained, many people already skeptical of faith healers did not find the disclosures all that surprising.

Los Angeles area residents were also treated that year to the saga of another television minister, the Reverend Gene Scott, based in nearby Glendale. His programs have appeared in other cities as well. The maverick broadcaster had been known for his long harangues against the Federal Communications Commission (FCC) and various government officials seeking to investigate, usually to no avail, his operations. He raised large sums of money during that embattled period. In 1986, Scott made a down payment on the downtown Los Angeles building of the Church of the Open Door, once a fundamentalist bastion, but the deal fell through in 1987 amid a flurry of charges and countercharges of bad faith.

The national amazement over the antics of TV preachers, of course, did not begin until March 19, 1987, with a surprise announcement by PTL television network founder, Jim Bakker, who was handing his operations to Jerry Falwell because of a sex-and-payoff scandal he felt could no longer be hidden. Bakker's charges that an unnamed evangelist had attempted a takeover of PTL brought other nationally known TV ministers into an odd debate.

This scene had both a "prelude" and continuing acts to make the whole thing a production both comedic and suspenseful. The early 1987 prelude had two events: first, Oral Roberts's declaration that unless he raised millions God was going to take his life by the first of April, and second, the relatively little noted retreat by Tammy Faye Bakker to Palm Springs, reportedly because of addiction to prescription drugs. As it would turn out, Roberts got his money before April Fool's Day and revelations about PTL excesses steadily emerged as the Bakkers played desert recluses.

Jimmy Swaggart produced a surprising "sequel" to the drama in February 1988 when his dalliance with a prostitute was told. He obtained very little sympathy for his moral failure, partly because he snubbed his denomination's requirements for restoration.

Using stage terms above to describe late 1980s news events may not be inappropriate inasmuch as the most successful TV ministers seem to be those who entertain best. Other contributors to this volume have explored the implications of that observation.

My concern is over the atmosphere of alienation that I believe is cultivated by many TV ministries, and which, unfortunately, is an extension of the prevailing climate in much of the evangelical movement.

This air of alienation, I think, is stirred by winds of resentment against segments of society and by the puffed-up notion that it doesn't matter whether it is *true* just so long as it sounds scriptural. This bombast feeds incivility between believers and nonbelievers.

Falwell fondly defines a fundamentalist as "an evangelical who is mad," an expression that aptly makes the distinction by style and degrees of tolerance rather than by Christian beliefs. But I'm afraid it also reminds me of the vengeful bumper sticker "Don't get mad, get even." The fundamentalist resurgence of the 1980s, following on the heels of the evangelical comeback of the 70s, seemed to be emboldened by secular currents of resentment. The announced targets of the secular and religious right were the excesses in abortion, pornography, homosexual pride, and feminism, but a superior, domineering, separatist, and holier-than-thou mentality shaped the character of the right-wing movements.

The religious right additionally has had an anti-intellectual and authoritarian strain. Conservative evangelicals seem hesitant, if not unwilling, to critique themselves. Even the most clever spoof and perceptive satire often sits poorly with the most serious lieutenants of God. A reading of any letters section of *The Door,* the evangelical humor magazine published in El Cajon, California, shows that some unhappy readers confuse God's self-promoted lieutenants with God Himself.

What does all of this have to do with TV evangelism? George Gerbner, dean of the Annenberg School of Communications at the University of Pennsylvania, has characterized the electronic church as a "conservative, downscale, and generally alienated, but politically active, audience." It has been commonly observed that many TV ministers play on that alienation by suggesting that biblical values are ignored by entertainment and news media, public education leaders, and most governmental figures. Thus, those secular quarters are discredited.

Peter Popoff, as noted, tried to deflect the expose of his radio-transmitted "word of knowledge" by rallying supporters against "this attack on Christian organizations." And certainly Gene Scott's TV ministry has been characterized by his ridicule of government bureaucrats, using toy monkeys for a while on his TV show to represent government officials.

Even before the turmoil of 1987-88, Roberts and Swaggart rarely gave news interviews, and Bakker was known for his running battle with the *Charlotte Observer.* Their behavior contrasted starkly with the openness of Billy Graham and Jerry Falwell over the years to interviews and press inquiries. Any experienced journalist or public relations worker knows that misunderstanding will be minimized when the newsmaker is accessible. The newsmaker also benefits by gaining more listeners for his message.

As later events suggest, some TV preachers may have had reason to fear exposure from an inquisitive press. I don't doubt that these and many other clergy have a deep-seated mistrust of people from what has been labeled the "secular humanist" establishment—media, academia, and government. The latter often have different views and values, but that does not mean biased and unfair treatment will necessarily result.

During his controversy, indeed, Swaggart said that the press was being fair to him. Swaggart never issued denials of the main allegations that surfaced in the news. A national survey of adults by the Barna Research Group in Glendale, California, released in June 1988, demonstrated that most people gave the news media a passing grade on coverage of the controversial TV preachers. People were asked about news reports on Swaggart, the Bakkers, Robertson, Roberts, and Popoff. George Barna, who often does market research for evangelical groups, said "no difference" existed between the responses of born-again Christians and nonevangelicals. The media was "completely fair and objective," said 20 percent, and another 51 percent said news organizations had been usually fair and objective, with some exceptions. Only 7 percent felt the media was usually not fair, and 8 percent said they were completely unfair and biased. The "don't know" responses amounted to 14 percent.

Does this mean the strategy of fostering alienation (vs. non-believing outsiders) might have suffered a blow? I hope so, although I think that fervent fund appeals will continue to employ exaggerated mischaracterizations of "those who want to destroy this ministry." This alienation is often buttressed, it seems to me, by description of "satanic" forces that are open to serious question. This is my second major concern prompted by TV evangelism.

The persuasive preacher, one who is "on a roll" at a given service, one whose ministry has grown by leaps and bounds, and one who has been able to stay out of the news (thus controlling the way he is viewed by the public) can create illusory islands of sanctification. Evangelical leaders have seen the dangers of a powerful preacher accountable neither to a large board or a denomination nor to his donors and the larger evangelical community. The scandals should have made voluntary financial disclosure a very desirable goal.

But that is *financial* accountability and, to some extent, moral accountability—requiring tighter restrictions and oversight. *Now* what might be needed is accountability of *beliefs*. Is fervent faith unerring? Does increasing your power of believing promise health and prosperity? Does it promise that God will provide the sought-after millions for the evangelist's latest ministry? This devotion leads to disillusionment when contradictory evidence appears. It can lead to self-deception in order to keep hopes alive.

The problem peculiar to TV ministries may lie in the popularity of the charismatic movement. Evangelicals have been loathe to damage a remarkably good alliance since the early 1970s with tongues-speaking, Spirit-filled charismatics, who, in turn, have tactfully moderated their display of spiritual gifts in mixed company. But who can deny that the most controversial TV preachers, including Popoff, are charismatic in tradition? Their integrity has been questioned, including their supposed ability to discern what is "of God," what is not, and what they well know is not. (Popoff, by September 1987, was off television and had filed for bankruptcy, though he was maintaining a radio and mail ministry under another corporate name. His attorney attributed the collapse of his TV ministry more to financial mismanagement than to disclosures.)

Had he not striven for the 1988 Republican nomination for president, M. G. (Pat) Robertson, founder-president of the

Christian Broadcasting Network (CBN), might have emerged from the TV evangelists' turmoil as the unscathed statesman of the broadcasters. But under the demands of presidential politics, his life and career were scrutinized with results not always pleasing to him. He also abandoned his ordination and posts with CBN in order to shed the "evangelist" and "religious broadcaster" labels. After quitting the primary races, however, he was forced to break his vow of never returning to CBN in light of the network's drop in donations.

Was Robertson in part a victim of his own alienation from "the real world"? When the Swaggart scandal broke in late February, 1988, Robertson maintained that the delay of more than four months in the disclosure of Swaggart's sin was the work of his principal Republican rival, Vice-President George Bush. Bush, he said, tried to tarnish him with guilt by association only weeks before the Super Tuesday primaries on March 8. Yet Robertson offered no evidence of collusion between Bush's campaign and the Reverend Marvin Gorman, the evangelist who uncovered Swaggart's weakness. Gorman went to Assemblies of God leaders with photographs of Swaggart entering and leaving a motel room only after Swaggart did not act on a promise to Gorman that he would voluntarily confess his failure to the church. Bush was not a party to the drama.

Increased public familiarity with Robertson's charismatic beliefs also may have hurt his chances, and that points up, once again, the theme of alienation. Robertson received a highly negative reaction to his claim that his prayers turned away a hurricane from CBN's Virginia Beach headquarters —and the reaction could not be blamed simply on the obstinance of unbelievers: Christians need not believe that God intervenes to manage the weather.

The *Los Angeles Times* reported on March 4, 1988, that Robertson believed God told him in May 1968, "I have called you to usher in the coming of My Son." This was in a prophecy mediated through a close associate, Harold Bredesen, who laid his hand on Robertson's head and spoke as though God were speaking. Those words are not in any Robertson biography or autobiography. But in an April 1982 letter to CBN contributors, Robertson quoted the prophecy and added, "God has assigned to CBN, in these last days, a ministry of John the Baptist—to prepare the way for Jesus' second coming."

Most important, Robertson also reiterated the prophecy during a televised Dallas Gathering in December 1984, the same month he was interviewed for a highly flattering *Saturday Evening Post* cover story (published in the March 1985 issue) that essentially introduced him as a White House aspirant. In that Dallas talk, Robertson drew a mental picture of a crime-free society in which Christians would be "taking dominion" and reaping the wealth of non-believers. This dominion was only several years away, and the changes would include the election of "a spirit-filled President" and "judges speaking in tongues from the bench."

Robertson added, "Now, you say that is the description of the millennium, when Jesus comes back. Well, some of it is." He urged his audience: "We've got to prepare ourselves and know that God is going to put us in positions of leadership and trust and responsibility." Citing his steady successes with CBN's growth, including the acquisition of a CBN transmitter in the Middle East, Robertson assured his listeners that God has "never failed one thing that He has promised to me."

Did Robertson think God promised him the White House, and if not in 1988, in 1992? Did he feel that he could usher in the second coming better from the District of Columbia? Bredesen told the *Los Angeles Times* that the 1968 prophecy applied to CBN, not to Robertson himself. Yet Robertson's claims of a special intimacy with God made most people uneasy. "There is an innate suspicion of people who hear voices that we don't hear," said historian Edwin S. Gaustad.

Disappointed hopes for a God-anointed President governing a quasi-theocratic nation had the potential to foster resentment within a subculture of believers. That emotion has been attributed to Christians in the past.

In the late nineteenth century, philosopher Friedrich Nietzsche, certainly an antagonist of Christianity, accused members of the faith of thriving on ressentiment. The word can be understood as "marrow-rich resentment," according to historian Martin E. Marty, a Lutheran scholar who applied the word more narrowly a decade ago to fundamentalist Christianity. Marty said it is resentment that "fires and fuels movements like 'scientific creationism,' which is less anti-evolutionist than it is resentful of the way evolutionists seem to get honors and privileges while 'creationists' are 'non-mainstream.'" Failure to understand this bitter resentment will lead to a failure over how to address fundamentalism, he said.

Regardless of what happens on television, I hope that reason and civility in religion might regain respectability. Signs have appeared that more mature religious convictions have become more prominent as the fantasy-and-alienation promoters on religious TV have stumbled. The preliminary statement announcing the convocation of a convention in Philadelphia in November 1988, "To Serve Our Present Age," under the sponsorship of the Institute for the Study of America, is an example of that growing attention to maturity: "Contemporary America's public forum is pluralistic and it demands sophisticated levels of civility from its participants. . . . Evangelicals cannot learn these skills by [simply] talking to each other."

You are the salt of the earth. But if the salt loses its saltiness, how can it be made salty again? It is no longer good for anything, except to be thrown out and trampled by men. You are the light of the world. A city on a hill cannot be hidden. Neither do people light a lamp and put it under a bowl. Instead they put it on its stand, and it gives light to everyone in the house. In the same way, let your light shine before men, that they may see your good deeds and praise your Father in heaven.

—Matthew 5:13-16

12
What Now? Practical Guidelines for Media Involvement

Ken Curtis

Here is an unpleasant thought: the unbelieving world, to a large degree, is forming its understanding of the meaning of Christianity and the nature of the church through what it sees presented by TV religion. Unpleasant? Indeed, but true. We fool ourselves if we think our well-written books or our well-trained pulpits are going to reach the world. Everyone today is taught by television.

We know that God is in control; He saves, we don't, and He doesn't need TV to fulfill His plans. But Jesus took the gospel where the people were. Paul went to Rome, where all roads led. Today, the multitudes are on sofas watching the tube, hour after hour. And who is there to meet them, to introduce them to the "unknown God"? Surely, television deserves the most serious attention of the church.

The church generally is paying dearly for failing to take the medium seriously enough. There are, to be sure, some noteworthy examples of efforts by some denominational agencies and independent groups. But there has not been a well thought-out and concerted approach by the larger Body of Christ to meet the challenge—and opportunity—of television. The field has been left to self-appointed, entrepreneurial celebrities. They have evolved organizations that in many cases are captive to incessant and vulgar fund-raising needs —resulting in methods and messages that tragically distort the gospel.

Beyond the damage done by those who, speaking in the name of Christ on television, distort and discredit the gospel, there is also the matter-of-fact conclusion that the larger secular television industry operates outside of any sensitivities to Christian concerns. The secular industry is in many ways consciously hostile to a Christian view of humanity, life, and society. That should not surprise us. Television, after all, is primarily a business. But it is more than a business; it is a pervasive *cultural institution*, disseminating pictures of reality, shaping values, influencing life-styles, setting social agendas.

It is difficult to sell church leaders on placing television high on their list of priorities. So many other matters press for attention, all screaming for support. Taking on something new might mean cutting something else. Don't the demands of feeding the hungry, missions at home and abroad, and education need all the support we can give them? Of course! However, new support must also be found for television. After all, everything else the church attempts within society is done within the all-pervasive media environment, which is strongly influenced, if not dominated, by television.

The church's mission in this field should be done corporately and collectively as much as possible. This is hard for some church leaders to grasp. We must get beyond the inclination to see involvement in television as merely a means to add to the membership rolls. Such a strategy is short-sighted and self-centered.

At the risk of sounding like an alarmist, I wonder if future generations of Christians will look back upon our half of the twentieth century and see the effects of television on our culture as similar to that of drugs (substantial comparisons could be made). Such generations would surely find it incomprehensible that the church did not work together energetically in dealing with this medium. What follows are some suggestions as to how the church might begin to deal wisely with television.

MEDIA VOCATIONS

We are making a serious mistake in not encouraging young people to go into the secular media—television in particular, as a *Christian* vocation. Evangelicals continually moan that the secular media reveals a clear anti-Christian bias. The complaint is justified. But part of the fault lies in our own failure to challenge our youth to take up responsibilities within this field. What ends up happening is this: we abandon a field almost entirely to unbelievers because we think it is somehow unspiritual, and then complain about the field being run by non-Christians. Talk about wanting to have your cake and eat it too!

We need talented young writers to create scripts, not just tracts; producers to invent new creative programs; executives to shape policy; and actors who leave audiences spellbound by their compelling performances. We need to teach our young people that taking up such a vocation is justified not only by its evangelistic utility but by its cultural significance. God has called us to be salt and light, and we fulfill that purpose by pursuing our calling with excellence.

Christian colleges could become centers for training students in media vocations. A fine interdenominational Christian college dropped its communications major because the leadership thought they couldn't compete with institutions such as Oral Roberts University, Jerry Falwell's Liberty University, or Pat Robertson's CBN University, schools that had ties with national TV programs, millions of dollars in equipment, and huge communications staffs and budgets.

What a sad misreading of the situation! The only investment in equipment a college really needs to make is in word processors or typewriters. The most critical need is for writers. That doesn't require extraordinary capital investment, and as far as the media professions go, writing provides the best background for entry and advancement in any mass medium, including television.

Right now, just about everything needed for the highest quality of Christian television and film production can be hired. But the script comes first. The program cannot be any better than its script. There is no greater need right now in the media than for a generation of Christian screen writers. And I don't mean by this, a generation of Christian screen writers who write "Christian" scripts for "Christian" films, but Christians who write genuinely creative, interesting, entertaining, and believable scripts. Many places are training Christians to write for print, but I know of no place devoting major attention to encouraging and training Christians to write for the screen.

CONTENT STUDIES

Because TV religion performs such an important role in shaping the general public's perception of the meaning of the church, the purpose of its existence, the nature of its mission, and the essence of its message, it is imperative that graduate-level research be undertaken in providing content analysis of the major ministries' programming.

This service is needed for the larger church to see exactly what religious media environment is being developed and what messages are being advanced in the name of Christ. Such studies would provide a more adequate basis for affirming those who are serving responsibly (and there are those who should be so commended) and critiquing those who are out of line and an offense to the gospel. Questions to be pursued might include the following:

What is the essential message being communicated?
What kind of gospel is being preached?
What kind of response is elicited from the audience?
To what motivations are appeals made?
How much time is spent on financial appeals?

What view of the audience is assumed in the way the content is shaped?

What presumptions are consistently set forth regarding authority, truth, respect for others, and so on?

How much content is devoted to the Person and work of Christ compared to the person and work of the celebrity?

What enticements are offered to solicit mail?

What promises are implied to viewers who will write or call to request offers?

It also would seem prudent for seminaries to offer courses on Christian faith and the media. Those being trained for roles in the church should be aware of what has been done, what is going on, and how the media can be used rather than abused in ministry. Modern Christian leaders should be equipped to take advantage of local and national TV in their work.

ENCOURAGE PUBLIC TELEVISION

Here is a simple, but meaningful, step that can be taken now. In every city many Christians are members of their local Public Broadcasting Service (PBS) station and contribute annually to support PBS programming. At the national level, and with most of the local stations, PBS has been woefully negligent in presenting religious programming as part of its required service to the public.

When the local fund-raising appeals are scheduled, it would be most appropriate for Christians who are members to renew their memberships *along with* a polite letter encouraging the station to devote meaningful air time to religious programs and concerns. PBS stations usually find budgets tight, but they can afford to televise local worship services and present studio-originated programs exploring theological perspectives on current issues.

A positive, non-threatening stream of requests from their local supporters would, in many instances, receive a welcome hearing from management. Local ministerial association support and announcements in church bulletins could create concerted efforts in this regard.

DEVELOPING TV DISCERNMENT

Every television program carries a message. It was planned by someone with some purpose. The creator may be fully aware of the message and yet, to some degree, be unconscious of how his or her background, outlook, values, are built into the approach of the program and the content delivered.

In an entertainment setting, we are usually relaxed, prepared for enjoyment rather than for critical analysis. We've had a long day, and we just want to take a break from it all. I have found, when asking people about their favorite TV shows, how often Christians—some of whom profess the most rigid, legalistic moral codes—passively absorb attitudes and outlooks of their television role models, especially when conveyed through likable characters in humorous contexts, that they would probably reject upon serious reflection.

I have always had a particular interest in television commercials and have conducted research in this area. It is telling that a survey of commercials—if, for instance, viewed by a visitor from another world—would lead to the conclusion that in our culture the "seven deadly sins" are actually virtues. In a sampling analysis I conducted, there was no room for the teaching of Jesus that "a person's life consists not in the abundance of things possessed." Quite the contrary, a person's life was seen to consist *precisely* in the *abundance* of things possessed.

For the most part, we have not faced the task of teaching our children and congregations how to discern the implicit and explicit messages being drilled into us hourly by the tube. We cannot solve the problem if we do not face the problem. We must train ourselves, at home, at the office, to analyze our environment, particularly as it is shaped by our television viewing.

For starters, I would recommend the resource material titled *Television Awareness Teaching.* It contains sound advice on how to use television intelligently and creatively, instead of being mindlessly exploited by it. (It is available for $6.00 from MARC, 475 Riverside Drive, Suite 1370, New York, NY 10015.)

SUPPORT NEW NETWORKS

Two ventures are moving forward right now that might merit the enthusiastic support of the Christian community. The ACTS network, a cable network started by the Southern Baptist Convention, is now broadening its base to represent the wider Christian community. Another network, called VISN, has started up and has the backing of the secular cable industry. This channel will be open to all denominations willing to cooperate in providing professional quality production.

These channels are distinguished by two features. First, they are nonsectarian. They are not out to build entrepreneurial empires but to represent a wide cross-section of Christian witness. They do not showcase one celebrity and would, therefore, discourage the personality cult. Second, both have a policy of not allowing any appeals for funds on the air. There is a built-in system of accountability, since the channels are run by professionals rather than by family members.

We should help these channels by watching them, promoting them, urging our denominational headquarters to become involved with them, and also by realizing that even though they are not asking for money, they will still need significant contributions from those moved to support them. They deserve our support as major efforts to reshape the face of religious television for the 1990s.

A word about giving to TV ministries in general is in order here. After the recent scandals involving TV preachers, and the damage they have caused for all of us, it is natural to wonder whether we should give to religious TV at all. But there are proper ways to go about giving to the right ministries. One pastor, John Clark, from the First Presbyterian

Church in Lansdale, Pennsylvania, made this suggestion: Designate money to television ministries *through your local church.* Instead of sending money directly, the local church should have the responsibility of scrutinizing and ensuring the credibility of a given ministry.

That is good advice. With all their recent troubles, TV ministries are going to step up high-pressure manipulation to get you to give. You are going to be encouraged to feel guilty unless you, on impulse, pick up your phone and make a donation. You will be told to use your credit card. Beware. *Thoughtfully plan your giving*—do it through your local church.

REFERRAL SERVICE

The church has many experts in various fields: education, the arts, politics. But when the media need spokespersons for the "Christian" position, they invariably call on the same few who have set themselves up as our spokespersons.

To a large extent the Reverend Jerry Falwell has become the *media-designated* unofficial pope of Protestantism. He is called upon by news organizations probably more than any other Protestant source. It is easy to understand why. Falwell has made himself readily available, and has even provided a studio and satellite transmission facilities at his headquarters so that he can be plugged in quickly, easily, and cheaply. He is a delight to news producers because he can be counted on to deliver predictable viewpoints with brevity and charm. The producer knows he or she will come away with a usable piece. So Lynchburg, Virginia, now dwarfs Wheaton, Illinois, and 475 Riverside Drive as a source of television statements from the evangelical or Protestant churches.

Yet a much broader spectrum of perspectives is needed to represent the evangelical community in this country. It would not be difficult for an appropriate agency to be created to provide a hot line to the news industry with a bank of media-savvy experts on file who could be suggested for expert comment on news items and for appearances on shows such as "Nightline," "Cross-Fire," "MacNeil-Lehrer News Hour," and "Larry King."

SCRIPT CONSULTATION SERVICE

Over the past decade, groups that have perceived themselves as maligned and distorted in television programs have taken the initiative to make their presence felt at the script creation level of the television industry. Watchdogs for women's liberation and gay rights have been particularly effective in gaining access to scripts prior to production, to critique them for stereotypes and unfavorable treatment. These groups are taken seriously.

The valid concerns of the Christian community are *not* taken seriously, although it must be admitted that religiously motivated groups threatening boycotts *have* been noticed. But the creative community needs to know that Christians care deeply about their work. While suggesting well-planned and executed boycotts, we must also seek responsible working relationships with the media industry.

The creation in Los Angeles of a Christian Consultation Coalition, consisting of qualified professionals who understand both the industry and the essentials of a Christian world and life view, would have an influence and would be well worth a foundation funding for a three-to-five-year pilot period.

DOCUMENTARY FILM SERIES

We move now to programming concerns. To date, there has not been any sustained effort from the church community to present on television an ongoing series of documentary films dealing with contemporary life and issues from a theological perspective. The documentary genre offers a dimension for exploration of any given subject area that goes far beyond the standard formats that have characterized traditional religious programming efforts such as worship services, talk shows, and panel discussions. The documentary format allows you to get out of the studio or the sanctuary and into the world at the very locations where things are happening, meeting the people who are making them happen.

The time is right for a regular, weekly, television documentary program interpreting slices of life from a Christian perspective. Such a documentary program would provide a place to show, close-up and in detail, the heroic, sacrificial, and productive work of Christian missions from many denominations.

I conducted a study for E.O. Television of Holland recently to see if we could find enough examples of missionary activity around the world where it could be demonstrated that the gospel was making a noticeable, measurable, constructive difference in the culture to sustain a regular television series. The research turned up so many compelling examples that it would be impossible to treat them all. Those are the kind of stories not covered by the secular media. Usually, they involve people and programs not interested in generating publicity or celebrity. But the stories are there just the same. They need to be shared with the larger world.

Happily, it can be reported that as of this writing, E.O. has commissioned production of four documentaries to test such a series for television in Holland, and it can only be hoped that in North America (as well as elsewhere) similar commitment may be forthcoming.

A second reason for the urgency of documentaries is to provide a forum for treating major issues or subject areas from a Christian perspective. The gospel is a historic faith, dealing with all of life, yet a biblical and theological perspective on pressing issues is no longer considered relevant in general media reporting. This weakness can be challenged by positive Christian involvement.

For example, consider how timely would be a beautifully produced documentary on the Bible and ecology, to dispel the commonly perpetrated myth that the Bible fosters a callous disregard for the environment based on the cultural mandate to subdue the earth. This misreading of Scripture could be magnificently laid to rest by a documentary depicting the biblical teaching of God's creation, man's call to stewardship over God's gifts, and responsibility for individuals and nations to stand in judgment for what we have done with God's gifts of common grace. Further, we could demonstrate the historical impact of Christian convictions on such issues and the efforts of contemporary Christians as well.

Such an ongoing documentary series might, of course, have its main appeal to a more intellectual rather than popular audience, but it does provide an ideal instrument to reach a thinking audience. Further, the documentary product would have an ongoing circulation in classroom and library utilization.

TV DRAMA

Drama for prime-time television is a critical area for future development, most feasibly through "specials" or ministries.

Drama is the most difficult format to produce and also the most expensive. It touches lives as no other vehicle, penetrating heart and mind. Drama changes the way we look at life, regard people, interpret circumstances. It provides the opportunity and permission for people to fantasize, to enter into the experiences of others, and to explore new personal territory. The viewer identifies with the screen characters. They help clarify questions and provide sought-after emotional reinforcements, healthy or unhealthy. Drama is far more than just escape and entertainment. Well-done drama gives us a safe testing ground for asking the "What would it be like if?" questions of ourselves. Drama plants time bombs in the subconscious that, over time, can mark our outlooks on life.

Because of some of these reasons, dramas draw the largest TV audiences. Consider how easily people get caught up in a TV mini-series or make sure that their VCRs are on duty to catch every episode.

Several Christian organizations have made distinguished efforts to program drama for television. "This Is the Life," "Faith for Today," and "Insight" come quickly to mind.

Yet these series were all relegated, despite their superb quality, to the "religious ghetto" time slots (early Sunday morning) by most stations.

Noteworthy attempts have also been made by Christians to minister through the dramatic format of full-length 35 mm feature films shot for theatrical release. Qualified producers such as Irvin Yeaworth, Dick Ross, James Collier, and Burt Martin have made feature films that met secular production standards with excellence. Unfortunately, the problem has always been finding a suitable marketing and distribution system. Other new attempts to break into 35 mm format by committed, and usually naive, Christian producers come along just about every year. We can only prayerfully hope that sustainable breakthroughs occur through them in the theatrical arena.

At present, producing movies made for prime-time television offers the most attractive and strategically compelling alternative. Such programs reach larger audiences than all of the other formats of religious production combined.

We have seen some encouraging developments. Ray Carlson and Nigel Cooke of International Films have placed some of their fine productions on national networks. Their film *Treasures of the Snow* was shown twenty times on Home Box Office (HBO), was sold to other cable networks, and enjoyed a long-term run over superstation WTBS.

At Gateway Films, we were totally unsuccessful, despite repeated efforts, to place *The Cross & the Switchblade* on network television in the United States. So Clair Hutchins and John Gibson of World Thrust Films licensed the film and began placing it in local television markets city-by-city. Their results have been most illuminating. In city after city, they went up against top-rated secular programs in prime time and invariably came away with excellent if not top ratings.

Our present focus of commitment at Gateway Films is in the development of dramatic production in the field of church history, an area where we have experienced a most encouraging response. Historical subjects from the saga of our Christian past represent a seemingly bottomless mine of great stories full of heroism, adventure and conflict, the stuff of which good drama is made. The stories are *made* for drama, and they communicate Christian history in a powerful, intriguing, and moving way. Many Christians, much less non-Christians, have very little understanding of church history, and this is one way to teach it in an entertaining way that appeals to Christian and non-Christian alike.

It was my privilege to co-produce a drama with the British Broadcasting Corporation (BBC) on the life of C. S. Lewis, titled *Shadowlands.* This film won two British Academy Awards and in America won an international Emmy for Best Drama and was hailed by the *New York Times* as "the best television program of the year." The world *does* notice Christian efforts in the media arts, when those efforts are marked by excellence, creativity, and craftsmanship. While the secular industry is resistant to propagandistic religious programming, these and similar efforts have demonstrated that it is not opposed to religious themes in general. If the quality (from the idea to the story, to the script, to the screen) is excellent, it will have its market.

To produce a program such as *Shadowlands* involved the cooperation of four Christian television groups: The Episcopal Radio-TV Foundation in Atlanta, EO-TV in Holland, Lella Productions of the United Kingdom, and Gateway Films, in addition to the BBC.

Another breakthrough came with Gateway's production of the historical drama *John Wycliff: The Morningstar,* which officials at Channel 4, a national network in England, accepted for transmission. Frankly, I think they accepted it without much expectation of audience response and mostly because of the management's high regard for lead actor Peter Howell. They placed it in the unattractive time slot of 4:00 P.M. Saturday afternoon.

The audience reaction was so strong that Channel 4 commissioned another historical drama, *God's Outlaw: The Story of William Tyndale.* But here again it worked only because Christian companies from different nations came together to make the production of this worthy story possible.

The openness for such dramas on the part of secular TV networks marks a great opportunity that must be seized. Curiously, the receptivity is far greater in Europe than in North America. At the time of this writing, we are working on an opportunity to produce a mini-series on the life of John Wesley. What an impact that series could have, showing how Wesley so powerfully reached a society with pressing problems in so many ways like the ones we face today. Whether this possibility is realized will largely depend on whether we can deliver significant placement in the North American market, which has yet to be confirmed. Should significant North American TV placement be found for such Christian-oriented dramatic productions, then there is solid promise for a steady stream of such programs involving international partnerships that can achieve worldwide penetration.

Thus, the opportunity for high-quality Christian drama is closer than ever before, an opportunity to reach a greater number of people in a more penetrating and profound way.

Conclusion

Television can be a marvelous gift or it can be an instrument of great harm. The church needs to take a much different approach to this medium than it has to this point. May we find the courage, insight, commitment, and *cooperation* to move ahead faithfully.

Come, all you who are thirsty,
   come to the waters;
and you who have no money,
   come, buy and eat!
Come, buy wine and milk
   without money and without cost.

—Isaiah 55:1

13

Send No Money to Martin Luther

Joel Nederhood

For Halloween, there were Jim and Tammy masks.

The newscaster reported this curious bit of information with a laugh—he thought the Bakker masks were very funny.

But this news item was not funny, nor was it an insignificant curiosity. Those masks help us bring the Reformation into focus. The Reformation? Yes, indeed. Halloween happens to fall on the same day as "Reformation Day," and because that sixteenth-century movement was a reaction to the unhealthy condition of the medieval church, it is a piece of historical irony that children should have been parading through our streets on the eve of Reformation Day sporting the masks of those whose conduct reminds us that we need a Reformation once again.

On October 31, 1517, Martin Luther, an Augustinian monk, nailed Ninety-five Theses to the door of the Castle Church in Wittenberg, Germany. Those statements took issue with church practice of his day. Though Luther expected his document merely to set off a round of discussions, it turned out that what he said was so explosive that all of Europe and the British Isles were changed by the religious revival that followed.

It is that revival of biblical religion that we call the Protestant Reformation. The upheaval not only affected the Roman Catholic church; it also caused the birth of the

Protestant denominations we know today. The term *Protestant* has become an umbrella term that covers a mixed group of people, local churches, and denominations. Many who call themselves Protestants (Unitarians, practitioners of Christian Science, Mormons, and so on) are considerably further than even the medieval church from what the Reformers would have considered biblical faith. *Protestant*, then, has become a catch-all term for a variety of denominations and sects, many of which we would not even properly call "Christian," much less "Protestant."

In many minds, *Protestant* also includes the bizarre events that have accompanied media religion. Thus, when children came to your house shouting, "Trick or treat!" wearing Jim and Tammy masks, they were masquerading as people who represent an unfortunate by-product of the Protestant Reformation.

But there is something much deeper here. The irony does not stop at descendants of Protestant religion inspiring mockery on the eve of one of that tradition's most important holidays. Such purveyors of modern spiritual quackery represent a threat to Christendom remarkably similar to that protested by the Reformers so long ago. Hence, many modern "Protestants" have become enemies of that very faith for which the Protestant Reformers lived and often died.

In Luther's day, one of the practices that made him indignant was that of using religion to raise money. As a German, he resented the papacy's raising money among his countrymen to create impressive architecture in Rome. The church received donations in exchange for forgiveness of sins. Priests sold indulgences, which, for certain sums, would spring people free of purgatory. Johann Tetzel, an especially obnoxious profiteer, worked right under Luther's nose.

Luther was a careful Bible student, a professor of theology, lecturing on such books as Galatians, Romans, and the Psalms. What he found in the Bible contradicted this mercenary religion. When he could stand it no longer, he rose in determined opposition to this corruption.

And he did not say, "From now on, you should send your money to me instead of Rome." The kind of biblical Christianity that he promoted was a "send-no-money-to-Martin-Luther" kind of Christianity. He wasn't in it for the money.

The Reformation of October 31, 1517, was a rediscovery of biblical religion, and biblical religion is about a salvation without cost. That is, it doesn't cost *us*. The reason it doesn't is not because salvation is cheap, but that it is so costly. God alone could pay the high price, and He did it when He gave His one and only Son as a sacrifice for our sin. This is the religion expressed by the Old Testament prophet Isaiah who invited, "Come, all you who are thirsty, come to the waters; and you who have no money, come, buy and eat! Come, buy wine and milk without money and without cost" (55:1). And then Isaiah assured his listeners of forgiveness of sins:

> Seek the Lord while he may be found; call on him while he is near. Let the wicked forsake his way and the evil man his thoughts. Let him turn to the Lord, and he will have mercy on him, and to our God, for he will *freely* pardon. (Isaiah 55:6-7, italics added)

Free forgiveness—in Luther's day, that kind of forgiveness was obscured. Today, it is obscured again by "bottom-line" religion—religion that puts a price tag on everything. As in Luther's day, it has become practically impossible to think of religion apart from money and fund-raising. This means that those who continue to celebrate the first Reformation must examine what is happening today and call for a second.

The fact that there were Halloween masks representing religious leaders now notorious for alleged financial mismanagement and a luxurious life-style is one sign among many that the current state of affairs in religion is seriously corrupt.

Understandably, every religious leader is earnestly distancing himself from the big-money evangelists, and there is no question that great differences exist between many of them and some of the worst examples we have seen. Attributing guilt by association is an unfortunate mistake often made. Even so, the contemporary public scandals provide an occasion for all who claim to represent Christ in churches, evangelistic organizations, and other Christian enterprises to examine their consciences and their practice.

As Martin Luther scanned the religious horizon, he saw a church that was at odds with his discoveries in Scripture. He saw that salvation was free, through faith alone. One could not come to the place where one deserved God's love or earned His favor by good works or by financial payments.

That sort of faith has been obscured in many quarters these days, not only among those who have appeared on "Nightline" and dominated headlines. Much of modern Christianity is saturated with bottom-line religion. The corruption of the gospel expressed in the selling of indulgences in the sixteenth century is an early manifestation of the marketing of religion in our more sophisticated, technological age.

It is entirely natural these days to conclude that if something religious is going to be successful, it will necessarily require a lot of money. And it is assumed that forms of religion that are not associated with "megabucks" cannot be significant. Religious leaders who feel themselves to be "anointed and appointed" expect that their status allows them to use whatever tactics will work to bring big money into their organizations.

Two years ago, I watched Jimmy Swaggart tell several of his handpicked staff who were in the studio with him that God had talked to him one morning on the street corner of a Central American city and had told him that he was going to be the one who would bring the gospel to the entire world via television. His colleagues nodded their heads in solemn agreement and made remarks that supported the evangelist with observations that proved it was certainly true: this man and this man only had to reach the world with television.

Then the evangelist and his friends bemoaned the fact that people were not obediently sending their money. Now this is a seriously flawed—I mean, *theologically* flawed—sort of religion. The fact that so many religious personalities have had revelations and convictions that forced them into a non-stop pitch for funds has resulted in a situation in which they never talk about their work without in the same breath talking about money. Whatever gospel there is, is overshadowed by money-talk, both by the organizations themselves and by the media who report their activities. The result is that religion and money are always seen together, like ham and cheese. You apparently can't have one without the other.

It was just this sort of picture that disturbed the sixteenth-century Reformers. Representatives of the church traveled up and down the country-side with their padlocked money boxes, exchanging God's forgiving grace for money. Of course, what they did had nothing whatever to do with God's forgiving grace, because the church cannot market grace that way. Grace is *God's* gift, not the church's. Furthermore, the definition of grace is *unmerited* favor.

Believers nowadays can't look back at those mishandlers of God's holy love as if they were evil and we modern Protestants are pure as newly fallen snow. We are sitting right in the middle of the same kind of confusion. Today's Christianity is just as tainted as it was then, and the people it reaches are becoming extremely cynical.

What we have to do is—well, we have to do the same thing Martin Luther, John Calvin, and others did. The world-changing events that those believers set into motion were caused by the power of the Bible. For when the Bible recedes into the background, the church loses its legitimate authority and begins promoting its own superstitions. Without the Bible's disciplines, religious leaders become religious hucksters who build their own empires and feather their own nests.

So today, as then, we must let the Bible overpower us. When we do that, we learn soon enough that if there is one thing the Bible condemns, it is religion for fun and profit. Whenever a religious leader or a church comes up with a scheme that confuses salvation with some kind of monetary payment, you have the worst kind of dishonesty. That is like trying to sell something that is not yours to sell. It is like trying to sell something again that has already been sold and paid for. It's a scam; it's trickery; it's self-serving thievery.

The Bible, therefore, speaks out strongly against those who make a business out of their religion. I should say, it *lashes out* at them! In Acts 8, the apostles Peter and John have harsh words for a faith healer who thought the gifts of the Spirit could be tied into some kind of commercial transaction: he offered to buy the Spirit's power. Peter rebuked him and said, "May your money perish with you, because you thought you could buy the gift of God with money!" He continued with this advice: "Your heart is not right before God. Repent of this wickedness and pray to the Lord. Perhaps he will forgive you for having such a thought in your heart. For I see that you are full of bitterness and captive to sin" (vv. 20-23).

The apostle Paul speaks with great disdain of those who think that "godliness is a means of financial gain." As he reacts to their fundamental misunderstanding of what the gospel is all about, he says,

> People who want to get rich fall into temptation and a trap and into many foolish and harmful desires that plunge men into ruin and destruction. For the love of money is a root of all kinds of evil. Some people, eager for money, have wandered from the faith and pierced themselves with many griefs. (1 Timothy 6:9-10)

In fact, those false teachers who "secretly introduce destructive heresies" are known by two characteristics: they "despise authority" and "are experts in greed—an accursed brood!" (2 Peter 2:1-14).

Do you see what an utterly perverse corruption of the gospel it is when people are asked to believe in the Lord Jesus Christ and then, within moments, are asked for money? The shades must be torn from our eyes so we can again see what true religion is. That was what was needed in Luther's time. The gospel costs a great deal more today than it did then. All they needed was a lavish cathedral in Rome. We need ever greater networks, ever larger churches, ever more luxury. After all, we're "children of the King"—you can't expect King's kids to go second class, can you? Money and religion—it all gets so mixed up that you can't figure out anymore where one stops and the other begins.

This is an extremely sad state of affairs. The reason it is so lamentable is not that certain religious leaders are capitalizing on this, living in lavish homes and driving around in luxury cars. The real tragedy is that in our day, as in Luther's, the gospel has been lost to big business. The people who suffer the most are those who never hear the pure gospel of God's grace.

If the Christian world was rocked at its foundations during Luther's time, it needs to be rocked in the same way again today. There may well be some who say, "We have no other choice; we have to keep finding ways to use religion to raise money because there are so many exciting, worthwhile things we can do these days." To be sure, we have a rationale for what we do, and it is convincing once you take your stand within a high-powered religious organization that has grandiose plans. Medieval Rome had good reasons, too. It was all for "a good cause." After all, they had cathedrals standing around that needed gold on their domes, and everyone thought God loved gold on cathedral domes.

Today again, Christian leaders have all sorts of ideas they think God is totally enthusiastic about, and so out go the "Tetzels"—the fund-raising wizards on their rounds. If the gospel itself must ever be obscured for "worthwhile" projects, we will simply have to drop the projects. One thing is sure, God will not be honored and His Kingdom will not ultimately be advanced if, in the process, salvation is stamped with a price tag.

It could well be that if there were to be a widespread examination of the way the gospel has become entangled with fund-raising, and if we were to experience a widespread cutting back on some of the things we do to accomplish what we think is God's work, some churches might become smaller and the size of some great evangelistic corporations might shrink somewhat. If Christian leaders cannot announce the gospel of salvation over the airwaves without obscuring and confusing that message, they had better use some other means. But surely, those who know Christ know that God is able to accomplish great things with small organizations and churches—if they commit themselves to His power and His gospel.

Because this salvation is free, the gospel can be brought to every level of society—we can go to the poor and say, with Isaiah, "You who have no money, come, buy and eat!"

So the Reformation was a time of rediscovery. As the Bible became available to more and more people, so that even common working people could read it and come to an understanding of its great doctrines, they raised their voices in jubilant praise to God for His unspeakable generosity. They were stunned by what God did for them in the Lord Jesus Christ. Now salvation has been secured. There is no further sacrifice that can improve on the sacrifice of God's own Son.

Today, if those who *want* to promote the gospel should rediscover the gospel of grace in all of its dimensions and became serious about removing every barrier obscuring its grandeur, there would again be an enormous change. There might even be some very large Christian organizations that would go out of business. Yes, even that might happen. But then, one might ask, should they have been in business in the first place?

This is what the Lord says: "I will return to Zion and dwell in Jerusalem. Then Jerusalem will be called the City of Truth, and the mountain of the Lord Almighty will be called the Holy Mountain."

—Zechariah 8:3

14

Toward a Second Reformation

Michael Horton

About noon, on October 31, 1517, a stocky Bible professor posted on the door of Wittenberg's Castle Church ninety-five propositions against the sale of indulgences. The door was the bulletin board for university events, and the professor was offering a challenge to anyone who would defend the practice of paying money in exchange for papal blessing. Evidently no one stepped forward to accept the challenge. None of the university's faculty disputed Martin Luther's propositions. It seemed, in fact, that the whole business would blow over.

But then the people read the theses. It was common for the popes to be mocked, for Rome to be the brunt of jokes ranging from ones about a highly suspect moral integrity to those about greed, self-indulgence, and hypocrisy. But no one had ever located the core of the problem. No one had ever dared to question the theological, doctrinal foundation of the medieval church. Luther did just that, and "within a fortnight," said the German monk, "it spread throughout the world."[1]

Rome invented a doctrinal system to justify the sale of indulgences. Over the centuries spiritual giants had accumu-

---

1. Ewald M. Plass, *What Luther Says* (St. Louis: Concordia, 1959), pp. 1172ff.

lated a "treasury of merit." Their Christian service was so faithful that they had an excess of merit over which the church was made trustee. After all, didn't Jesus Himself tell Peter, "You are Peter, and on this rock I will build my church"? Did He not assure Peter, "I will give you the keys of the kingdom of heaven; whatever you bind on earth will be bound in heaven, and whatever you loose on earth will be loosed in heaven"? (Matthew 16:18-19) To Peter and his successors, the popes, it was argued, Jesus had entrusted the "keys of the kingdom" to save and to damn. Therefore, the church could "bind" and "loose" whatever and whomever it chose.

If one purchased an indulgence—a letter, signed by the pope himself, guaranteeing pardoned sins—the buyer was simply paying a fee, and a comparatively *small* fee at that, for the health and blessing of what mattered to him most: his soul. Johann Tetzel, a loud and sensational Dominican preacher, was especially good at the fund-raising business. "And it's all for the building of the largest cathedral in Christendom, St. Peter's in Rome!" he assured his donors.

It would not be fair, of course to interpret the entire history and character of Roman Catholicism by this tragic fund-raising scheme any more than it would be fair to interpret modern Protestantism with the bush of "Pearlygate," but the scheme did throw into relief a particular set of doctrinal problems, problems even the very early church had been warned about. The apostle Peter severely rebuked Simon Magus, who had offered to purchase the disciples' healing power, was severely rebuked. "May your money perish with you," Peter snapped (Acts 8:20). Even the *Didache* (manual of instruction) of the early church warned of "the false prophet" who "says 'in the spirit,' 'Give me money.' " "Do not listen to him," the early church instructed.

Ever since the beginning of time, it seems, religion has been exploited by evil men and women. We will give anything for peace and salvation—even our life savings, if that's what it costs. Peter warned believers concerning the Gnostic heretics of his own day, pointing out that they "will secretly introduce destructive heresies." For "in their greed," he says, "these teachers will exploit you with stories they have made up." Peter charges, "They are experts in greed—an accursed brood!" (2 Peter 2:1, 3, 14).

Today, unofficial, nonelected Protestant popes tyrannize the masses once more. Tetzels, purveyors of saving grace, pitch their hi-tech tents under the same sky.

Huey Lewis and the News, a popular rock group, sing of a fat man who sells salvation, referring not to the plump sixteenth-century Dominican, but to the TV evangelist. And a former Christian Broadcasting Network producer has written an insider's exposé, *Salvation for Sale*. It is doubtful that Huey Lewis knows who Tetzel was, but the fact is that he—and many like him—have described Tetzel to a tee, with modern televangelists as their model. Tetzel dazzled his audience with an elaborate stage for the performance of a "judgment day" skit; today's charlatans dazzle theirs with the high-tech counterpart—lights, cameras, and lots of action.

It is interesting that when many of the modern televangelists present their justification for the modern "indulgences" they offer the public, they actually employ a doctrine similar to that used by the medieval church. Televangelist Roy Hicks criticizes the Reformers, Luther and Calvin, for insisting that the church did *not* have the "power of the keys."[2] Don't people know, he asks, that the concept is central to the enterprise? Paul Crouch writes his supporters in a similar vein in a newsletter headlined, "KEYS OF THE KINGDOM." "You give to get. Oh brother—I can hear the howls of protest already! . . . Well, partner, every believer is called into SPIRITUAL BUSINESS with God. . . . In God's kingdom you GIVE TO GET your capital"[3] (caps in original).

A further parallel between the crisis we face in our own day and the one our Protestant forebears faced is located in the tyranny of the image. Throughout what is popularly called

2. Roy Hicks, *Keys of the Kingdom* (Tulsa, Okla.: Harrison House).
3. Paul Crouch, *Praise* (Trinity Broadcasting Network newsletter), May 1987.

the Dark Ages, education was limited to a handful of persons who had wealth and station—often, church leaders. The masses were taught the basics of the Christian faith through the use of icons, paintings, statues, and other representations. Since most of the population was illiterate, the Bible's content had to be reduced to images.

Today, it seems, religious leaders are again using visual representations as a substitute for educating the laity, caving in to the basic superficiality and shallowness of the age. We reduce the great truths of the faith to a tract or a bumper sticker, or an image on a screen. Furthermore, when the images are really meaningful, they generate a million commercial trinkets. The medieval church may have had its relics and similar gimmicks, but the modern church has its own vials of water from the Jordan, handkerchiefs from a favorite evangelist, night lights, key chains, buttons, and countless other knicknacks. There is little that is authentic or genuine about this sort of religion.

The Protestants were divided initially on how to respond to images. The Roman church had insisted that the simpler (i.e., more trivial and superficial) the presentation of Christianity, the more likely it was to retain the masses. The Reformers, particularly Luther, Calvin, and Zwingli, believed Christians were, as Mohammed said.in the Koran, "people of a book," not people of an image. Instead of reducing the gospel to commercialized pablum, they insisted on raising the masses from ignorance to enlightenment. Today, with as much as one third of our population functionally illiterate and dependent on images, a second Reformation must engineer an educational revolution on the scale of the first.

That is not to say that the Reformers were united as to how much imagery should be retained in religious instruction. Zwingli, himself a lover of art, nevertheless ordered all images to be removed from the church. The walls were to be whitewashed. Calvin followed much of Zwingli's advice, but Luther was more open to the possibility of employing images for instruction and personal piety, so long as the image was subordinated to the Word. It was never to be a substitute for it.

The breadth of opinion among the Reformers regarding images is instructive. What is wrong today, as then, is not the *existence* of images but *how* the images are *used*. We need to remember that many people receive their daily bread from the television image. Their religious knowledge is limited to whatever they hear from the televangelist. They quote the same Scriptures out of context as their imaged mentor, and one seriously doubts how deeply they examine "the Scriptures every day to see if what [their leaders] said was true" (Acts 17:11). The Reformers supported the use of images where they belonged—in art and in the cultural life of the community—but not as a substitute for serious instruction. They would probably have been more excited to see a young Christian employ his or her creative gifts in the service of the general community (entertainment, cultural enrichment, and so on) than in exploitative, manipulative, and cheap religious propaganda.

So there will be differences among us concerning images, just as there were among the Reformers. Some will insist that we do away with the image altogether, that Christians refuse altogether the use of television as a means of religious instruction or personal piety. Others will accept the role of television as a supplement to sound biblical study. Where we *must* achieve consensus is on the subordination of the image, particularly in the form of televangelism, to responsible theological, as well as moral, accountability. The image must serve the Word, not vice versa.

A final parallel must be made between the medieval and contemporary church: ignorance and apathy had replaced intelligent zeal. In the medieval church, unity was the overriding concern. The church was Christendom and schismatics were simply not tolerated. Bringing scandal to Christ's name was not considered a chief sin. However, pointing out the scandal was viewed as evil. Savonarola was a case in point.

When Kenneth Copeland can make the comment, "The Bible commands ministers to be faithful, not correct,"[4] ignorance once again becomes the rule. The modern popes tell us, "Touch not the Lord's anointed," with threats of divine punishment for calling them into question. It's just easier to play the game and not rock the boat. But one wonders if it isn't better to *rock* the boat than to *miss* the boat. The issues at stake are not trivial, but basic to eternal life.

What is perhaps more discouraging to me than the televangelists themselves is the response I have heard time and time again from well-meaning brothers and sisters: "Don't cause strife. Let the Lord take care of it." What if we treated unbelievers that way? "Don't bother telling your best friend he is God's enemy and can be reconciled only through faith in Christ's substitutionary sacrifice. Let the Lord take care of it." God *takes care of it* through *our* responsible, loving, but bold confrontation.

It must cause our heavenly Father much grief that we would consider unity more important than the One in whom we are united. It must quench the Spirit to see Christians treating blasphemies, heresies, and scandalous statements as though they were no more than odd "emphases."

And what replaces intelligent zeal? What sets in when ignorance and apathy reign? A cloud of superstition is always the result of such a climate. In an earlier chapter of this book ("TV and Evangelism: Unequally Yoked?") Quentin Schultze makes the statement, "The fundraising gimmicks employed by some televangelists are incontrovertible evidence that superstition is alive and well in the modern world. It is all there for the asking: sand, dirt, twigs, and stones from the Holy Land, prayer-blessed cloths, anointed oils, sanctifying soap, and even lucky pennies. For $15 or more, the viewer can stand with the superstitious people of all ages who had their own icons to venerate and images to adore" (pp. 196-97). "Television," he concludes, "the latest mass communication technology, is now a servant of superstition, cant, rumor and hearsay" (p. 197).

4. "Praise the Lord," Trinity Broadcasting Network; tape on file with Christians United for Reformation (CURE)

In another chapter of this book ("Who Do TV Preachers Say That I Am?") Rod Rosenbladt makes a similar point, observing that Christians seem to be adopting a "theology of glory" over a "theology of the cross" (pp. 109-10). Whether the ladder of merit, the ladder of mysticism, or the ladder of speculative thought, evangelicals generally seem to have lost the biblical emphasis on the incarnation. Jacob's ladder was not a ladder men *ascended*, but one God the Son *descended*.

"Martin Luther," says Rosenbladt, "attacked medieval superstition, insisting that Jesus was *not* a magical ladder one climbed to health, wealth, and happiness—or glorification." "Could it be," he asks, "that the 'upward' tendency (that is, the desire to climb up toward or even into the divine) in some American evangelical or Pentecostal circles is similar to the 'upward' tendency Luther saw in the medieval church, with all of its superstition, mysticism, and magic?" (p. 109).

At the heart of all of this, both then and now, is a tragic misunderstanding of the gospel itself. The world is convinced that salvation, according to evangelicals, is either purchased or won by moral attainments. The perception is that if we join the right club, pay our dues (literally), and toe the line, we can coax God into accepting us. Those perceptions may be ferociously denied by evangelical leaders themselves, but they fill the newspaper editorials, "Saturday Night Live" scripts, and the lyrics of popular music.

If we are to regain this generation, it will not be enough to clean up our act. We will always have moral scandals. Even if we close in on heretical evangelists, we ourselves will still be sinners. The world doesn't mind our being sinners—they would just like to hear us admit it once or twice. Our self-righteousness and moralism has obscured the gospel, in addition to making us something of a social menace.

I have heard it said repeatedly, "The problem of the hour is not that we don't have the correct doctrine, but that we aren't living it." I disagree with that statement. Rather than failing to live up to our beliefs, I think the great tragedy is that we *are* living up to a reduced, trivialized, superficial, hedonistic, self-centered religion. We are seeing the deficiencies of our faith acted out on the stage of daily practice. To improve our public witness, we must recover our roots, the apostolic substance of Christian teaching. We must go beyond pietistic exercises and drink deeply from the well of Christian wisdom: ages of timeless insight and rich instruction. We need to find our way out of subjective, existential, "What does it mean to *me?*" religion and rediscover the objective "What does it *mean?*" faith of earlier ages.

Historically, periods of great crisis have always been opportunities for great breakthroughs, tremendous growth, and renovation. And there is no reason to believe that Jesus Christ has reneged on His promise to build His church. Winds of change are blowing. Many pastors and congregations are recognizing the state of affairs and are already making sweeping corrections. If it is true that Christ is building His church, we cannot cause division or disunity where genuine unity exists. Where Jesus is believed in as He has revealed Himself in His Word, and where the Christian faith is preached and taught with care and integrity, there is the bond of unity; there is the brotherhood of Christ.

The chief slogans of the Reformation were *sola fide* (faith alone), *sola Scriptura* (Scripture alone), *sola gratia* (grace alone), and *soli Deo gloria* (to God alone be glory). It was not that medieval Christians didn't believe in Scripture, grace, and God's glory, but that they believed that those were not sufficient. Beyond *Scripture,* the believer needed another word, another authority, additional teachings, rules, and regulations. Beyond *grace,* the believer needed free will and cooperation. Beyond *God's glory,* there was room for taking a little credit for oneself. Each of the Reformation slogans should touch a bruised nerve as we observe the popular faith and piety of modern Christianity.

A second Reformation is on the horizon. It is not Robert Schuller's *Self-Esteem: The Second Reformation;* nor is it a Prosperity Reformation. It is not a "Little God's" Reformation or a "Latter Rain" Reformation. It's not an innovation, but a renovation; not a quest for the new and improved, but of the ancient and approved. It will not spotlight a few celebrities or establish a new personality cult. It will be a movement of the common Christian, the one who has to live his or her faith in the real world under the pressures of this hour.

The contributors to this volume desperately seek a second Reformation[6] and though we would not presume to compare ourselves to the magisterial Reformers, we would like to think of this volume as the nailing of our theses to the door of the electronic church. Once again, let the cries of the people of God reach their Master's ears.

Sola Scriptura, sola gratia, et soli Deo gloria!

---

6. With the exception of John Dart, the authors are evangelicals.

Appendix A
The Ecumenical Creeds

Called "ecumenical" because they are embraced by all branches of historic Christianity, the following creeds have "set in stone" what the entire Christian family believes the Bible to set forth on matters necessary to salvation. They succinctly define orthodoxy; their affirmations (and denials) are so basic and scriptural that to deny the substance of any article is to place oneself outside the Christian family. Protestants, Roman Catholics, and Orthodox Christians have managed to embrace the creeds, even though they have diverse views on many issues; schismatics and heretics have denied them.

We have included the creeds, not because they are the highest authority for judging heresy—for Scripture jealously reserves that spot—but because they have formed the commonly, historically accepted summary of the Scripture's teaching on the most fundamental points.

Another term found in the creeds is the word *catholic*. The term should not be misunderstood to mean exclusively *Roman* Catholic; it simply refers to that substance of fundamental Christian beliefs that unite all Christians. When our forebears spoke of being "catholic" they meant that they were orthodox, Bible-believing, traditional Christians who accepted the creeds rather than being party to schismatic or heretical sects inventing their own unique theories about God, man, Christ, and salvation.

THE APOSTLES' CREED

I.   I believe in God the Father, Almighty, Maker of heaven and earth.
II. And in Jesus Christ, His only begotten Son, our Lord;
III. Who was conceived by the Holy Spirit, born of the virgin Mary;
IV. Suffered under Pontius Pilate; was crucified, dead, and buried; He descended into hell;
V.   The third day He rose again from the dead;
VI. He ascended into heaven, and sitteth at the right hand of God the Father Almighty;
VII. From thence He shall come to judge the living and the dead.
VIII. I believe in the Holy Spirit,
IX. the holy catholic church, the communion of saints;
X.   The forgiveness of sins;
XI. The resurrection of the body;
XII. And the life everlasting. AMEN.

NICENE CREED

I believe in one God, the Father Almighty, Maker of heaven and earth, and of all things visible and invisible.

And in one Lord Jesus Christ, the only-begotten Son of God, begotten of the Father before all worlds; God of God, Light of Light, very God of very God; begotten, not made, being of one substance with the Father, by whom all things were made.

Who, for us men and for our salvation, came down from heaven, and was incarnate by the Holy Spirit of the virgin Mary, and was made man; and was crucified also for us under Pontius Pilate; He suffered and was buried; and the third day He rose again, according to the Scriptures; and ascended into heaven, and sitteth on the right hand of the Father; and He shall come again, with glory, to judge the living and the dead; whose kingdom shall have no end.

And I believe in the Holy Spirit, the Lord and Giver of life; who proceedeth from the Father and the Son; who with the Father and the Son together is worshiped and glorified; who spake by the prophets.

And I believe one holy catholic and apostolic church. I acknowledge one baptism for the remission of sins; and I look for the resurrection of the dead, and the life of the world to come. AMEN.

THE CREED OF CHALCEDON
A.D. 451

We, then, following the holy Fathers, all with one consent, teach men to confess one and the same Son, our Lord Jesus Christ, the same perfect in Godhead and also perfect in manhood; truly God and truly man, of a reasonable [rational] soul and body; consubstantial [coessential] with the Father according to the Godhead, and consubstantial with us according to the Manhood; in all things like unto us, without sin; begotten before all ages of the Father according to the Godhead, and in these latter days, for us and for our salvation, born of the Virgin Mary, the Mother of God, according to the Manhood; one and the same Christ, Son, Lord, Only-begotten, to be acknowledged in two natures, inconfusedly, unchangeably, indivisibly, inseparably; the distinction of natures being by no means taken away by the union, but rather the property of each nature being preserved, and concurring in one Person and one Subsistence, not parted or divided into two persons, but one and the same Son, and only begotten, God, the Word, the Lord Jesus Christ; as the prophets from the beginning [have declared] concerning him, and the Lord Jesus Christ himself has taught us, and the Creed of the holy Fathers has handed down to us.

ATHANASIAN CREED

(1) Whosoever will be saved, before all things it is necessary that he hold the catholic faith;

(2) Which faith except every one do keep whole and unde- filed, without doubt he shall perish everlastingly.
(3) And the catholic faith is this: That we worship one God in Trinity, and Trinity in Unity;
(4) Neither confounding the persons, nor dividing the substance.
(5) For there is one person of the Father, another of the Son, and another of the Holy Spirit.
(6) But the Godhead of the Father, of the Son, and of the Holy Spirit is all one, the glory equal, the majesty co- eternal.
(7) Such as the Father is, such is the Son, and such is the Holy Spirit.
(8) The Father uncreate, the Son uncreate, and the Holy Spirit uncreate.
(9) The Father incomprehensible, the Son incomprehensi- ble, and the Holy Spirit incomprehensible.
(10) The Father eternal, the Son eternal, and the Holy Spirit eternal.
(11) And yet they are not three eternals, but one eternal.
(12) As also there are not three uncreated nor three incom- prehensibles, but one incomprehensible.
(13) So likewise the Father is almighty, the Son almighty, and the Holy Spirit almighty;
(14) And yet they are not three almighties, but one almighty.
(15) So the Father is God, the Son is God, and the Holy Spirit is God;
(16) And yet they are not three Gods, but one God.
(17) So likewise the Father is Lord, the Son Lord, and the Holy Spirit Lord;
(18) And yet they are not three Lords, but one Lord.
(19) For like as we are compelled by the Christian verity to acknowledge every person by himself to be God and Lord;
(20) So we are forbidden by the catholic religion to say: There are three Gods or three Lords.
(21) The Father is made of none, neither created nor begotten.

(22) The Son is of the father alone; not made nor created, but begotten.

(23) The Holy Spirit is of the Father and of the Son; neither made, nor created, nor begotten, but proceeding.

(24) So there is one Father, not three Fathers; one Son, not three Sons; one Holy Spirit, not three Holy Spirits.

(25) And in this Trinity none is afore, or after another; none is greater, or less than another.

(26) But the whole three persons are co-eternal, and co-equal.

(27) So that in all things, as aforesaid, the Unity in Trinity and the Trinity in Unity is to be worshiped.

(28) He therefore that will be saved must thus think of the Trinity.

(29) Furthermore it is necessary to everlasting salvation that he also believe rightly the incarnation of our Lord Jesus Christ.

(30) For the right faith is that we believe and confess that our Lord Jesus Christ, the Son of God, is God and man.

(31) God of the substance of the Father, begotten before the worlds; and man the substance of His mother, born in the world.

(32) Perfect God and perfect man, of a reasonable soul and human flesh subsisting.

(33) Equal to the Father as touching His Godhead, and inferior to the Father as touching His manhood.

(34) Who, although He is God and man, yet He is not two, but one Christ.

(35) One, not by conversion of the Godhead into flesh, but by taking of the manhood into God.

(36) One altogether, not by confusion of substance, but by unity of person.

(37) For as the reasonable soul and flesh is one man, so God and man is one Christ;

(38) Who suffered for our salvation, descended into hell, rose again the third day from the dead;

(39) He ascended into heaven, He sitteth on the right hand of the Father, God Almighty;

(40) From thence He shall come to judge the living and the dead.

(41) At whose coming all men shall rise again with their bodies;

(42) And shall give account of their own works.

(43) And they that have done good shall go into life everlasting, and they that have done evil into everlasting fire.

(44) This is the catholic faith, which except a man believe faithfully, he cannot be saved.

Appendix B
Seven Rules for Testing Prophets

Many Christians today believe the gift of prophecy, together with its office, is still in effect. Although this is not necessarily the view of the historic church, it is widely believed among many who are to be considered orthodox Christians.

One thing, however, we can all agree on is the importance of testing in the light of Scripture those who claim to be modern-day prophets. Assuming the possibility of the perpetuity of this office, how can we distinguish true from false prophets? The Bible is clear on the matter.

AUTHORITARIANISM

According to the Scripture, the false prophets "rule by their own authority" (Jeremiah 5:31). Now let's take a look at that. "Man has no right to private interpretation of the Word of God," says Earl Paulk, "apart from those whom God sets in the Church as spiritual teachers and elders."[1] Of course, one of the great accomplishments of the Protestant Reformation was the recovery of "private interpretation." Paulk wishes to return the church to the tyranny of popes, although in his case, self-appointed ones.

But this doesn't mean that Paulk wants "prophets" themselves to be accountable to authority. For "no man judges a

---

1. *That the World May Know* (Atlanta: K Dimension, 1987), p. 10.

prophet."[2] Those who support private interpretation "suggest that when a preacher finishes preaching, everyone should sit down with his Bible at home, read the scripture passages and then decide for himself whether or not the preaching he heard was truth from God."[3] Isn't that just what the early Christians did? "Now the Bereans were of more nobler than the Thessalonians, for they received the message with great eagerness *and examined the Scriptures every day to see if what Paul said was true*" (Acts 17:11, italics added). Does Earl Paulk claim an infallibility beyond that of the apostle Paul?

According to Paulk, "the greatest hindrance to the establishment of the Kingdom is our lack of submission."[4] "As long as a church determines a pastor's salary, it can set his level of service. . . . In some of the largest churches across this country, pastors have said to me, 'Earl, I can no longer sign the pledge of that denomination because it breaks my authority with God.'" "If an organization puts the reed [of authority] in someone's hand, they can take the reed out of that person's hand."[5] This sort of reasoning might account for Jimmy Swaggart's refusal to submit to his denominational authorities. Frederick K. C. Price stated on Trinity Broadcasting Network's "Praise the Lord" program (January 1, 1986) that unless a critic has as many followers as he had, he would not meet with him or her.

Larry Lea, pastor of the Church on the Rock in Rockwall, Texas, has set up a constitution for his church in which he has, for the remainder of his life, absolute control over all committees. He cannot be fired or corrected. He is the unquestioned authority of that congregation.

Jim Bakker, you might remember, was reported to have justified his activity toward Jessica Hahn on the basis that, "When you take care of the shepherd, you take care of the

2. Ibid., p. 142.
3. Ibid., p. 144.
4. Paulk, *Satan Unmasked* (Atlanta: K Dimension, 1984), p. 190.
5. Ibid. p. 187.

sheep." This deeply distorted sense of self-importance is given direct rationale by Paulk: "People cannot put the reed of God into the hand of a man called by God, nor can they take the reed out of his hand."[6] "When people begin tampering with God's anointed servants," he continues, "the road they travel is like the one that Judas traveled."[7] "If the message of spiritual authority is right," Paulk adds, "and God intends for people to be submitted to those who are over them in the Lord, some people are in danger of hell because they will not listen."[8] "God clearly warns, 'Do not touch my anointed ones; and do my prophets no harm' (1 Chronicles 16:22)." And then Paulk adds his own warning: "I intercede before God for those who attacked called ministers of the Lord today."[9]

"The prophets prophesy lies, the priests rule by their own authority," God told Jeremiah. "And my people love it this way" (Jeremiah 5:31). False prophets "use their power unjustly" (Jeremiah 23:10). Who consecrated Earl Paulk a bishop? He gathered a group of "prophets" who were equally convinced of their absolute authority and established a denomination (the International Communion of Charismatic Churches) to secure this authority. Can these new bishops be defrocked? Is there a system of checks and balances? And how about the pastor of *your* church? Can he be questioned —and even removed? If not, he is a false prophet.

The Bible is very clear about this matter. Whereas Paulk argues that "a prophet is not to be judged," God says, "A prophet who presumes to speak in my name anything I have not commanded him to say . . . must be put to death" (Deuteronomy 18:20). Capital punishment was hardly exemption from judgment! Of course, in the New Covenant, we are not bound to the Old Testament civil law. But the principle of judging prophets stands.

6. Ibid., p. 183.
7. Ibid.
8. Ibid., p. 137.
9. Paulk, *That the World May Know,* p. 125.

WHAT'S HIS TRACK RECORD?

The Bible is also very clear about unfulfilled prophecies. False prophets are "full of hot air." They prophesy events or healings that are difficult to disprove. Much like a horoscope, many "words of knowledge" are nothing but generalized predictions that might find hundreds of "fulfillments." And yet, particularly in end-time prophesy, many modern seers have made repeated predictions that have been demonstrated false. This is a serious matter as far as God is concerned. "If what a prophet proclaims in the name of the Lord does not take place or come true," God instructed Moses, "that prophet has spoken presumptuously. Do not be afraid of him" (Deuteronomy 19:22).

The true prophet, Jeremiah, recorded God's lamentation over the false prophets: "I have heard what the prophets say who prophesy lies in my name. They say, 'I had a dream! I had a dream!' How long will this continue in the hearts of these lying prophets, who prophesy the delusions of the own minds?" (Jeremiah 23:25-26). Furthermore, God even gives us instructions as to how we should respond to presumptuous prophets:

> If a prophet or priest or anyone else claims, "This is the oracle [word] of the Lord," I will punish that man and his household. This is what each of you keeps on saying to his friend or relative: "What is the Lord's answer?" or "What has the Lord spoken?" But you must not mention "the oracle [revelation] of the Lord" again, because every man's own word becomes his oracle and so you distort the words of the living God, the Lord Almighty, our God. (Jeremiah 23:34-36)

God is weary now, as He was then, of self-appointed prophets who claim to speak for God.

WHAT DO THEY PROPHESY?

This is another sure detection of a false prophet. The true prophets almost always issued declarations of judgment.

There are two types of prophecies: weal (prosperity) and woe (destruction). Notice the headings translators have placed in our texts of the prophets. Count how often "against" appears: "A Prophesy Against Tyre," and so on. True prophets are unpopular because they insist on telling people what they don't want to hear. What people *want* to hear is prosperity—that they can have whatever they want. The self-centered masses "say to the seers, 'See no more visions!' and to the prophets 'Give us no more visions of what is right! Tell us pleasant things, prophesy illusions. Leave this way, get off this path, and stop confronting us with the Holy One of Israel!" (Isaiah 30:10-11). False prophets will satisfy this appetite. They will replace a fear of God with promises of prosperity, power, and position.

This was the state of affairs in Jeremiah's day. "They have lied about the Lord; they said, 'He will do nothing! No harm will come to us; we will never see sword or famine. The prophets are but wind and the word is not in them; so let what they say be done to them'" (Jeremiah 5:12-13). The prophets "dress the wound of my people lightly," God complains. "'Peace, peace,' they say, when there is no peace" (Jeremiah 6:14). For the true prophet, the Word he proclaims brings him insult (Jeremiah 20:8), but false prophets "fill you with false hopes. They speak visions from their own minds, not from the mouth of the Lord" (Jeremiah 23:16). The "faith teachers" don't even blush to call their prophecies "the prosperity gospel."

THEY ARE MAN-CENTERED

Isaiah records that false prophets "turn things upside down, as if the potter were thought to be like the clay!" (Isaiah 29:16). Similarly, the "faith teachers" tell their followers that *they*, in effect, are the potters—decreeing health, wealth, and happiness; that *they* are gods who can tell God what to do. This teaching is tantamount to idolatry and is an affront to God's sovereignty. "They do not say to themselves, 'Let us fear the Lord our God'" (Jeremiah 5:24).

THEY ARE ANTI-HISTORICAL

The false prophets, according to Jeremiah, mock "the ancient paths" (Jeremiah 6:16). They are self-willed spirits who assure their followers that their direct insight or revelation is superior to the wisdom, orthodoxy, and knowledge of historic Christianity. The true prophet does not invent new theories—particularly theories which directly contract the plain teaching of Scripture. Again and again, the viewer of televangelism is faced with the preacher's ridicule of commonly held beliefs, "tradition," and "orthodoxy." But we should beware of ignorant prophets who give the impression that they have an "inside scoop" on things hidden from apostles, martyrs, doctors, and apologists for the last two thousand years.

THEY ARE GREEDY

"From the least to the greatest," says the Lord, "all are greedy for gain; prophets and priests alike, all practice deceit" (Jeremiah 6:13). Peter added, "But there were also false prophets among the people, just as there will be false teachers among you" (2 Peter 2:1). "*In their greed,*" he said, "these teachers will exploit you with stories they have made up. . . . They are experts in greed—an accursed brood!" (2 Peter 2:3, 14, italics added).

We remember Simon Magus who wanted to purchase the apostles' healing power. "May your money perish with you, because you thought you could buy the gift of God with money!" Peter exclaimed (Acts 8:20). Televangelist Peter Popoff was discovered to have been using fraudulent devices for his "prophetic" healing crusades. Jim Bakker was declared a fraud by a judge and jury. How many scandals will rock evangelical communications until we begin to test self-appointed "prophets"?

Greed is given a theological justification by Earl Paulk. "John Gimenez, pastor of Rock Church, was challenged about the amount of money he was making," Paulk relates.

"He told his challengers to read what the Bible says the tithe is intended to do. They studied for two weeks on the subject, and they came back to John Gimenez saying, 'Pastor, the tithe belongs to you and the ministers of this church. Offerings should take care of everything else.'" To the contrary, the Bible teaches that the tithe was for welfare relief, not for the pastor's bank account.

Nevertheless, Paul adds, "John looked at me with tears in his eyes and said, 'Earl, that was going to be over a million dollars a year.'"[10] Over a million dollars a year for pastoral salary! As you watch these megachurch ministries via television you can see crowds of 8,000 or 10,000 people. Can you imagine the enormous combined salary these men and women are making? God nowhere commands a vow of poverty of ministers. But greed is a mark of "false prophets."

THEY PRESENT THEMSELVES AS MEDIATORS BETWEEN GOD AND MAN

The Old Testament prophets were a type of the One who was to come, the ultimate Prophet, Priest, and King. The entire book of Hebrews is eager to state the case for the consummation (and, therefore, the cessation) of these offices in Christ. And yet, false prophets insist on placing themselves in the role of mediator.

Robert Tilton argues, "As a servant of God, I can only move through your accepting and acting on the words of God that come out of my mouth."[11] He adds, "I'm going to pronounce a blessing upon your life and impart God's anointing on you for your double-portion miracle blessings in 1988!"[12] A prophet "has spiritual authority with God," says Paulk. And "spiritual authority is influence with God."[13] This undermines Christ's unique and exclusive role as our Advocate, pleading our case before the Father. You don't need Earl Paulk's

10. Paulk, *Satan Unmasked,* p. 170.
11. Robert Tilton, *God's Miracle Plan,* p. 11.
12. Correspondence on file with CURE (Christians United for Reform).
13. Paulk, *Satan Unmasked,* p. 294.

prayers. He has no more influence of "spiritual authority" with God than the new Christian who has just learned to pray, "Our Father, who art in heaven, hallowed be Thy name." There is *"one* mediator between God and men" (1 Timothy 2:5, italics added). His intercession determines your eternal destiny. All other offers at prophetic or priestly mediation are engaging in sorcery, not salvation.

CONCLUSION

There could, of course, be a great many additional criteria for distinguishing true from false prophets. Nevertheless, the ones we have outlined here are sufficient for clearly detecting the wolves in our midst. It is a confusing age, and doubtless this volume will not let us ignore that. But God has not left us as orphans. He has spoken clearly, and He says, "My sheep listen to my voice" (John 10:27). The televangelists will not speak for your soul. God holds each of us responsible for what we believe. And the content of that belief can lead to salvation or to eternal loss. Do not be deceived by false prophets.

Appendix C
A Ready-Reference Guide

In no more than fifteen minutes, one may take (or be taken through) a look at the errors of those we are critiquing as they state their positions *in their own words.*

THE SOVEREIGNTY OF GOD

THE BIBLE

"All the peoples of the earth are regarded as nothing. He does as he pleases with the powers of heaven and the peoples of the earth. No one can hold back his hand or say to him: 'What have you done?' . . . And those who walk in pride he is able to humble" (Daniel 4:35, 37).

ROBERT TILTON

"We make our own promises to do our part. Then we can tell God on the authority of His word what we would like Him to do. That's right! You can actually tell God what you would like His part in the covenant to be!"[1]

---

1. Robert Tilton, *God's Miracle Plan for Man* (Dallas: Robert Tilton Ministries, 1987), p. 36.

FRED PRICE

"Man is the only creation of God that is in God's class. . . . I believe that through these scriptures we can very clearly see that God made man a god."[2]

KENNETH COPELAND

"Pray to yourself, because I'm in your self and you're in My self. We are one Spirit, saith the Lord."[3] "You need to realize that you are not a spiritual schizophrenic—half-God and half-Satan—you are all-God."[4] "Man had total authority to rule as a god over every living creature on earth, and he was to rule by speaking words."[5] "You don't have a god *in* you. You *are* one!"[6] "I say this and repeat it so it don't upset you too bad. . . . When I read in the Bible where he [Jesus] says, 'I Am,' I say, 'Yes, I Am, too!'"[7]

KENNETH HAGIN

"Physically, we are born of human parents and partake of their nature. Spiritually, we are born of God and partake of His nature."[8]

EARL PAULK

"Just as dogs have puppies and cats have kittens, so God has little gods. But we have trouble comprehending this truth. Until we comprehend that we are little gods and we begin to act like little gods, we cannot manifest the Kingdom of God."[9]

2. Fred Price, correspondence on file with Christians United for Reformation (CURE), August 25, 1982.
3. Kenneth Copeland, *Believer's Voice of Victory*, February 1987, p. 9.
4. Ibid., March 1982, p. 2.
5. Kenneth Copeland, *The Power of the Tongue* (Fort Worth, Tex.: Kenneth Copeland), p. 6.
6. Kenneth Copeland, "The Force of Love," tape BCC-56 (Fort Worth, Tex. Kenneth Copeland), on file with Christian Research Institute (CRI).
7. Kenneth Copeland, tape of crusade, July 19, 1987, on file with CURE.
8. Kenneth Hagin, *How You Can Be Led by the Spirit of God* (Tulsa, Okla., Okla.: Kenneth Hagin Ministries, 1978), p. 94.
9. Earl Paulk, *Satan Unmasked* (Atlanta: K. Dimension Publishers, 1984), p. 97.

"When I say, 'Act like a god,' I can hear people saying, 'There he goes with the theory of the "manifest sons of God."' Forget about theories! Forget about doctrine! . . . We are 'little gods' whether we admit it or not."[10]

THE INCARNATION

It is clear from the quotes above that the leaders of the "faith movement" teach that believers (or even people in general) are "little gods," and that this is not a mere metaphor. After all, they have worked out a full-blown heresy of making believers "as much the incarnation of God as Jesus Christ was."[11] The following quotations should demonstrate their position as we contrast it with the Bible's definition of Christ's unique incarnation, that is, His birth as God in the flesh.

THE BIBLE

The apostle John recorded the words of Jesus concerning salvation: "For God so loved the world that He gave His *one and only [begotten] Son*" (John 3:16, italics added). "The Word became flesh and made his dwelling among us. We have seen his glory, the glory of *the One and Only,* who came from the Father, full of grace and truth. . . . No one has ever seen God, but *God the One and Only,* who is at the Father's side, has made him known" (John 1:14, 18, italics added). In his day, this same John fought a heresy denying the uniqueness of Christ's incarnation. "Dear friends," he wrote, "do not believe every spirit, but test the spirits to see whether they are from God, because many false prophets have gone out into the world" (1 John 4:1). Consequently, any teaching that *denies* that Christ is "the only-begotten Son," "the One and Only" incarnation of God, is heresy. On that basis, judge the following claims.

10. Earl Paulk, *Held in the Heavens until..* (Atlanta: K Dimension Publishers, 1985), p. 171.
11. Kenneth Hagin, *Word of Faith,* December 1980, p. 14.

KENNETH COPELAND

Kenneth Copeland has told his followers, "Don't be disturbed when people accuse you of thinking you're God. . . . The more you get to be like Me, the more they're going to think that way of you. They crucified Me for claiming that I was God. But I didn't claim I was God; I just claimed I walked with Him and that He was in Me. Hallelujah. That's what you're doing." Jesus never claimed to be "the Most High God." Historically, Copeland says, Christians

> mistakenly believe that Jesus was able to work wonders, to perform miracles, and to live above sin because He had divine power that we don't have. Thus, they've never really aspired to live like He lived. They don't realize that when Jesus came to earth, He voluntarily gave up that advantage, living His life here not as God, but as a man. He had no innate supernatural powers. He had no ability to perform miracles until after He was anointed by the Holy Spirit as recorded in Luke 3:22. He ministered as a man anointed by the Holy Spirit."[13]

KENNETH HAGIN

Speaking to his followers, Hagin has asserted, "You are as much the incarnation of God as Jesus Christ was. Every man who has been born again is an incarnation and Christianity is a miracle. The believer is as much an incarnation as was Jesus of Nazareth."[14]

EARL PAULK

Earl Paulk has said, "We see man and woman as Adam and Eve, the two of them together in physical and spiritual oneness. God said, 'Learn from that.' This unity is God in the flesh. God in the flesh is male and female in spiritual unity.

12. Kenneth Copeland, alleged prophecy from Christ, *Believer's Voice of Victory,* February 1987, p. 9.
13. Copeland, *Believer's Voice of Victory,* August 1988, p. 8.
14. Kenneth Hagin, *Word of Faith,* December 1980, p. 14.

... When we have grown into the image of Christ we will have the same authority and power that Christ had."[15] "Because He is 'the Firstfruit,' we are also branches of that vine, an integral part of the ongoing incarnation of God in the world. ... We are ... the ongoing incarnation of God."[16] Number 13 in a list of "true seductions" of Christianity, according to Paulk, is "rejecting the incarnation of Jesus Christ and the Church as the ongoing incarnation of Christ in the earth."[17] Therefore, our being "ongoing incarnations" is not a passing theory but a chief article of faith for Paulk.

JESUS THE MORAL EXAMPLE

Once Jesus arrived, having laid aside His divinity (according to the "faith teachers"), He lived as our example. The Moral Example theory of Christ's mission has been regarded by Bible-believing Christians as a heresy and is usually associated with the modernist (liberal) attack on the biblical view of Christ. It teaches that Jesus' greatest efficacy is pointing us in the direction of happiness, morality, and perfection. But the Bible teaches that Jesus came not to *show* us the way but to *be* the Way, Truth, and Life. Before ever considering Him our example, we must see Him as the Savior who redeems us, helpless sinners, who could never follow Him well enough to be accepted by our obedience.

THE BIBLE

"It does not depend on man's will or effort, but on God's mercy" (Romans 9:16). "He was delivered over to death for our sins and was raised to life for our justification" (Romans 4:25). "It is finished" (John 19:30).

EARL PAULK

Earl Paulk has asked, "Why was the New Testament written if Jesus Christ is the end of the story? Are the gospels

15. Earl Paulk, *Satan Unmasked*, p. 280.
16. *That the World May Know* (Atlanta: K Dimension, 1987), pp. 11, 100.
17. Ibid., p. 124.

merely 'reports' or do they also offer some plan of action? If Jesus 'did it all' for us, why must we do anything? . . . Easter resurrection shows how Jesus moved from being an earthly man to being a heavenly man. Jesus stood toe to toe with the devil and overcame the principalities and powers of death, hell and the grave."[18] But notice that in Paulk's very next sentence, instead of telling us Christ defeated death, hell, and the grave *for us,* we are told that He only did it for himself; as far as *our* salvation is concerned, we just follow His example and save ourselves: "How are we doing to conquer death? We are overcomers through Jesus Christ because we are learning the tools He used. We are learning to move in authority and power. We implement the concepts of His heart and mind. Jesus, the firstfruit, teaches us the secrets of overcoming the last enemy."[19] So He is our Savior by teaching us the secrets of saving ourselves. "Understand that we must do everything Jesus Christ did. He gave us the power to complete the work that He began. . . . Jesus said, 'I cannot do it alone.'"[20]

Whereas the Bible tells us Jesus came to *be* "the way, the truth, and the life" (John 14:6), Paulk tells us, "As the firstfruit, He came to show us the way, the truth, and the life."[21] "Jesus is the perfect example of humanity living in the 'image of God' in perfect obedience and harmony with the Father. . . . We must learn how to enter into His vicariousness. . . . Jesus is our example, as One who lived in perfect harmony with God's direction for His life. . . . Now the body of Christ must complete the work which Christ began."[22]

Remember, also, Copeland's assertion that Jesus had "no innate supernatural powers." Copeland says that Christians "mistakenly believe Jesus was able . . . to live above sin because He had divine power that we don't have. Thus, they've never really aspired to live like He lived."[23] "When

---

18. Paulk, *Satan Unmasked,* p. 252.
19. Ibid., p. 253.
20. Ibid., pp. 66, 64.
21. Paulk, *That the World May Know,* p. 11.
22. Ibid., pp. 27, 132, 142, 179.
23. Kenneth Copeland, *Believer's Voice of Victory,* August 1988.

Jesus cried, 'It is finished,' He was not speaking of the plan of redemption. . . . Jesus' death on the cross was only the beginning of the complete work of redemption."[24]

THE BORN AGAIN JESUS

To further bring perfection, power, and wealth (in short, godhood) within reach, the "faith teachers" have invented a blasphemous myth about Christ's having gone to hell, submitting to the lordship of Satan, and being born again.

KENNETH HAGIN

"Spiritual death means having Satan's nature. . . . Man is now united with the devil."[25] "He is the first one who was ever born again."[26]

GLORIA COPELAND

"He [Jesus] paid the price for Adam's sin. He suffered in His own body, and more important, in His spirit. Jesus experienced the same spiritual death that entered man in the garden of Eden."[27]

KENNETH COPELAND

"God was manifested in the flesh and justified in the spirit [1 Timothy 3:16, misquoted]. Now you can't get somebody justified and made righteous in the spirit if it wasn't first unrighteous. . . . Jesus accepted the sin nature of Satan in His own spirit. . . . Why do you think Moses, obeying the instruction of God, hung the serpent upon the pole instead of a lamb? That used to bug me. I said, 'Why in the world would you want to put a snake up there—the sign of Satan? Why

24. Copeland, "Jesus Our Lord of Glory," *Believer's Voice of Victory*, April 1982, p. 3.
25. Kenneth E. Hagin, *The New Birth* (Tulsa, Okla: Hagin Ministries, 1975), p. 10.
26. Kenneth E. Hagin, *The Word of Faith*, April 1982, p. 5.
27. Gloria Copeland, *God's Will for You* (Fort Worth, Tex. Kenneth Copeland), p. 5.

didn't you put a lamb on that pole?' And the Lord said, 'Because it was the sign of Satan that was hanging on the cross.' He said, 'I accepted in my own spirit spiritual death and the light was turned off."[28] "Jesus made Himself obedient to the Lordship of Satan at the cross. . . . He [God] said, 'You are the very image and the very copy of that one [Christ].' I said, 'Goodness gracious, sakes alive!' And I began to see what had gone on in there, and I said, 'You don't mean—you couldn't dare mean, that I could have done the same thing?' He said, 'Oh, yeah, if you'd had the knowledge of the Word of God that He did you could've done the same thing, 'cause you are a re-born man, too.'"[29]

MAN AS SOVEREIGN

Once all of this is done to the nature of God, Christ, and salvation, little is left but to proclaim ourselves sovereign. After all, God is bound to laws we control by our use. Notice the following remarks by Earl Paulk and John Avanzini.

EARL PAULK

Earl Paulk has asserted, "This attack on Christians who move in the supernatural realm [he has just cited Hagin, Copeland, and others] of miracles of God is built on the critic's theological presupposition that 'God is not bound by law.' I strongly disagree with that premise. . . . God limits Himself to work within the laws He ordains. . . . Man's obedience and faith toward God allow miracles—supernatural occurrences overriding natural laws—to occur."[30] Notice that in this system, man, not God, determines whether miracles will happen. Men "decree" this or that as gods. "He has given us the name of Jesus Christ like a blank check."[31]

28. Kenneth Copeland, "What Happened from the Cross to the Throne," tape, side 2, on file with CRI.
29. Kenneth Copeland, "Substitution and Identification," tape, on file with CRI.
30. Paulk, *That the World May Know,* pp. 101-2.
31. Paulk, *Satan Unmasked,* p. 59.

JOHN AVANZINI

"God does not decide the quantity of your supply! Hold on to your hat. Don't allow traditional concepts to make the Word of no effect. You decide the quantity of your supply. That quantity of your giving decides the measure of your receiving."[32]

SALVATION BY WORKS OR MONEY

Of course, if Jesus is merely our example or prototype of what we can become, salvation is by following that example and implementing the concepts He taught us. Yet this concept of salvation is in contrast to the biblical scheme, for it teaches that salvation "does not . . . depend on man's desire or effort, but on God's mercy" (Romans 9:16). "For it is by grace you have been saved, through faith—and this is not from yourselves, it is the gift of God—not by works, so that no one can boast" (Ephesians 2:8-9).

ROBERT TILTON

Robert Tilton has said, "One day Jackie was flipping through the television channels when she heard me say, 'You can have success through Jesus Christ.' 'That's what I need,' she said. . . . Jackie began immediately to make vows [i.e., financial contributions] and God began to reward her obedience."[33] "We have learned to break every evil stronghold by making a vow of faith to the work of God and paying it."[34]

Tilton relates an alleged prophecy from God: "I reward the actions of faith. That's why Abraham was justified. He wasn't justified and didn't receive all the blessings until he had been obedient to all I had asked him to do. I asked him to give his best; and when he did, his works justified him.

32. John Avanzini, *Faith Extenders* (Tustin, Calif.: Trinity Broadcasting Network), pp. 33-34.
33. Robert Tilton, *God's Miracle Plan for Man*, p. 19.
34. Ibid., p. 28.

[You must] pay your vows unto Me. Then, in the day of trouble I will hear your prayer and deliver you."[35]

Tilton adds the story of a woman named Mary. "After Mary committed her life to Christ, she seeded a vow into the work of God for her family to get saved. . . . To date, twelve of Mary's family members have been saved and are serving Jesus Christ as Lord and Savior!"[36] Furthermore, Tilton lists "Seven Steps of Faith." Here are the first four. "Step One: Let God Know What You Need from Him. New Car. New job. Fitness. House. Finances. Salvation. Step Two: Give God Your Best Gift. Step Three: Pray The Prayer of Agreement. Take the prayer sheet I've enclosed and lay your hand on top of mine [photograph] and pray, 'Oh God, I pray in agreement right now with my Brother, Bob. By faith we decree my miracle into existence in the name of Jesus. Father, I am giving my best gift to You today; therefore, we ask that You rebuke the devil from my life according to Malachi 3. Amen. Step Four: Mail Your Prayer Request and Your Faith Gift Back To Me Today!"[37]

JIMMY SWAGGART

When a person sins, Swaggart teaches, he makes restitution and that sin

> too is washed away and cleansed and the Christian is once again justified. . . . For the Christian who fails, who falters, and is repentant, these same acts of grace are available. . . . And again, instantly, the Lord cleanses him, and justifies him. . . . A fourth teaching states that God does not actually see our sins. Instead, He sees the blood of Jesus, in which we are trusting. . . . A fifth teaching is that even though we commit sins, they are not imputed unto us. . . . Others say that all of the Christian's sins (past, present, future) are already forgiven. Of course, these statements are

35. Ibid., pp. 28-29.
36. Ibid., p. 48.
37. Robert Tilton, correspondence on file with Christians United for Reformation (CURE).

untrue. . . . Consequently, we stay free and pure in Him, but only by that continued cooperation.[38]

"So actually, a twofold work takes place here: God's redemptive work in our heart and our cooperation in that work. . . . We teach and believe that all of God's promises are conditional. Nothing, as far as God's dealings with mankind are concerned, is unconditional."[39]

PAT ROBERTSON

"Your future depends entirely on your obedience to God. . . . [Christians] should have a healthy fear of falling. . . . Why are some people closer to God than others? Some people are wiser than others, some are more learned than others, some are more diligent than others, and some work harder than others."[40]

DOCTRINE OF THE TRINITY

The final critical area of concern is the doctrine of the Trinity. It is basic to orthodox, Bible-believing Christianity. Nevertheless, the "faith teachers," borrowing from *Dake's Annotated Study Bible*, deny it. Though he is not usually classed among the "faith teachers," Jimmy Swaggart holds the unorthodox view of the Trinity espoused, for example, by Kenneth Copeland.

JIMMY SWAGGART

"I believe that in this divine Godhead there are three separate and distinct persons—each having His own personal spirit *body*, personal *soul*, and personal *spirit*. . . . Many

38. Jimmy Swaggart, *Questions and Answers* (Baton Rouge, La.: Jimmy Swaggart Ministries, 1985), pp. 183, 287-88, 291-95.
39. Swaggart, *The Evangelist*, September 1983..
40. Pat Robertson, *Answers*, Christian Broadcasting Network (CBN) Partner's Edition (Virginia Beach: Christian Broadcasting Network, 1984), pp. 14, 18, 200.

people conclude that the Father, the Son, and the Holy Spirit are all one and the same. Actually, they are not. . . . The word 'one' in this passage means one in *unity.* . . . You can think of God the Father, God the Son, and God the Holy Spirit as three different persons exactly as you would think of any three other people—their oneness pertaining strictly to their being one in purpose, design, and desire."[41]

Some of you will notice that this argument is the same one employed by the Mormons and Jehovah's Witnesses against the doctrine of the Trinity. That should not be a surprise, since Earl Paulk regards Mormons as "brothers and sisters in the faith," arguing that "for so long we have said, . . . 'Why don't the Mormons change?' Perhaps we should be the ones to change."[42]

CONCLUSION

The Bible calls us again and again to test prophets, spirits, beliefs, and revelations. You are responsible before God for what you believe. And on the day of judgment, God will separates the heretic from those who follow him. That day is prophesied by Christ Himself: "Watch out for false prophets. They come to you in sheep's clothing, but inwardly they are ferocious wolves. . . . Many will say to me on that day, 'Lord, Lord, did we not prophesy in your name, and in your name drive out demons and perform many miracles?' Then I will tell them plainly, 'I never knew you. Away from me, you evil-doers!'" (Matthew 7:15, 22-23)

41. Swaggart, *Questions and Answers*, pp. 199-200.
42. Earl Paulk, *Unity of Faith* (Decatur, Ga.: Chapel Hill Harvester Church), p. 4.

Scripture Index